GrassRoutes

San Francisco

Urban Eco Travel

Serena Bartlett

with Daniel Ling, Ilsa Bartlett,
Maria Precot, and Joy Lian Alferness

SASQUATCH BOOKS
SEATTLE

To all the individuals who are making conscientious decisions each and every day to have a positive impact on the planet. Each bike ride, each composted food scrap, each battery recycled properly, each seed planted, each volunteer effort, and each new adventure started by considering the possibilities—every singular act matters.

"Certainly, travel is more than the seeing of sights; it is a change that goes on, deep and permanent, in the ideas of living."

—*Miriam Beard*

Printed in the United States of America
Published by Sasquatch Books
Distributed by PGW/Perseus
15 14 13 12 11 10 09   9 8 7 6 5 4 3 2 1

Cover and interior design: Rosebud Eustace
Cover and interior illustrations: Daniel Ling
Interior composition: Sarah Plein
Interior maps: Map Resources / Emily Ford

Library of Congress Cataloging-in-Publication Data

Bartlett, Serena.
    Grassroutes San Francisco : urban eco travel / Serena Bartlett.
        p. cm. -- (GrassRoutes travel)
    Includes index.
    ISBN-13: 978-1-57061-605-1
    ISBN-10: 1-57061-605-1
    1. San Francisco (Calif.)--Guidebooks. 2. City and town life--California--San Francisco.
3. Ecotourism--California--San Francisco. I. Title.
    F869.S33B37 2009
    917.94'610454--dc22
                            2009016929

Sasquatch Books
119 South Main Street, Suite 400
Seattle, WA 98104
(206) 467-4300
www.sasquatchbooks.com
custserv@sasquatchbooks.com

CONTENTS

Acknowledgments

I am unendingly grateful to all the people who have helped me with this book, and to San Francisco itself for inspiring me. I'd especially like to thank Daniel Ling for his love and support throughout this process; Joy Lian Alferness, Abigail Coburn, and Maria Pecot for their contributions and help building the first edition; and small business owners who have dedicated themselves to making positive impacts on their community.

The GrassRoutes Story

Like cracking open a dusty geode, travel has revealed to me the many facets of the world, allowing me to compare my known surroundings with the previously unexplored. No other activity has had quite the same impact, offering a unique experience of both commonalities and differences in the quilt of humanity.

After each journey my reality was challenged with new ways of thinking and acting, and I found I had new interests and an altogether different perspective. The most important souvenir I brought home wasn't tangible—it was a more open mind.

I became a detective of sorts, unearthing cultures and becoming familiar with local customs by seeking out nontraditional attractions and cities off the beaten path. Wherever I was, the locals gave me the chance to have unique experiences rather than manufactured ones. When I returned home I kept up the habit, discovering a wealth of intrigue in my own country. Whether trekking across another continent or walking a few blocks to a nearby neighborhood, no matter what my pocketbook dictated, I always managed to find new cultural gems.

GrassRoutes was born out of my growing collection of ideas and inspirations drawn from my journeys. I made up my mind to promote world citizenship, but search as I might, I found no vehicle that expressed my ideas about travel, so I decided to create one.

The concept evolved from a bundle of notes collected on the road. Since I have always viewed cities as whole entities, I didn't want my guides to be divided into chapters covering specific neighborhoods. Also, chowing down on some messy barbecue doesn't equate with dining on braised rabbit, so I chose not to organize the guides simply by activity. GrassRoutes guides had to be designed around the mood of the traveler and the timing.

But organization wasn't the only thing I wanted to do differently. GrassRoutes, true to its name, champions local businesses and their corresponding contributions to the greater good of the community. Restaurants that serve sustainably grown produce share these pages with shops that showcase works by local artists. Wildlife preserves are in the mix with amusements that use energy-saving techniques. Volunteer listings give visitors the opportunity to interact with residents while giving back. Being conscientious about society and the environment is a recipe for peace: this is one message I hope to convey.

Another is that travel can fit a limited budget. GrassRoutes is more than a guide to a city's attractions—it is a reaffirmation that authentic cultural experiences are not out of reach for anyone.

As you enjoy your travels, you can be satisfied knowing that you are a conscientious consumer. With such a bounty of local businesses dedicated to the spirit of positive change, it is becoming easier to support such a philosophy. Each listing in every GrassRoutes guide meets this standard in one aspect or another. So while you are venturing out into the world and meeting real people in new places, your dollars are staying in the community.

In this spirit, I bring you GrassRoutes guides, created to benefit readers and communities. I hope you will try something new, even if you thought it was not possible. All you need to have a genuine cultural escapade is an inquiring mind, a detective's spirit, and the desire to get acquainted with the world around you. Read more about the GrassRoutes philosophy: *www. grassroutestravel.com/story*.

Urban Eco-Travel Tips

To help you prepare for your adventure, here are some tips that I have compiled over my years of world travel.

Trip Planning

Don't overplan. Pick dates that make sense, and make the fewest reservations you can get away with to take into consideration factors of time, exhaustion, and exploration.

Before embarking on a trip, tell as many people as will listen where you are going, and get their feedback and tips. Have the same talkative approach when you get to your destination so you can meet locals and learn their favorite spots.

Look at books and magazines featuring the culture and history of the area before embarking on your trip, and keep a well-organized travel guide and a clear map with you while you are exploring.

Time Allotment

When picking dates, consider what kind of trip you want to have. One game plan is to spread out your time between different sights as a good introduction to an area. Another is spending prolonged time in one or two cities to truly get to know them. Either way, in my experience it is good to slow down the tempo of travel enough to smell the proverbial roses.

Reservations

Be sure to reserve a hotel for at least the first night so you have somewhere to go when you get off the plane. Even if you prefer to travel on a whim, I recommend starting on day two—after you get your bearings.

Before you book a room, try to get an idea of your destination first, so you can place yourself in the area that most interests you. If your entire vacation will be spent in the same area, I suggest staying in the same centrally located hotel the whole time so you avoid having to carry your stuff around. After all, you probably didn't travel to see different hotels, but to see the city itself!

Whenever you do book a hotel, make sure you know its cancellation policy.

In general, don't reserve many transit engagements. That way, if you want to extend your stay in a given spot, you can do that without too many trials and tribulations. Local transit arrangements are usually easy to book without much advance notice.

Restaurants tend to have widely varying policies on reservations, so check ahead to see whether your dream meal requires one. Or forgo the reservations: when you get to your destination, look around and act on a whim, or best of all, get the locals' advice. It is hard to get a good sense of a restaurant from its web site.

Be sure to reserve tickets for any special events you'd like to attend.

Packing

Pack light, but anticipate a variety of activities. I like to have a good pair of pants that can match with different shirts. I also bring one dressier outfit and a bathing suit.

Bring more than enough underwear, but wear clothing that can keep their shape for two or three days of use, especially pants or skirts. You'll be meeting and interacting with new people every day, so no one will know you wore the same outfit two days in a row.

Buy sundry items like sunscreen after you arrive. Remember, you will have to carry what you bring, so don't weigh yourself down.

Check the climate and current weather conditions of your planned locations and pack accordingly.

Try taking your luggage for a stroll in your own neighborhood before hitting the road. Then you'll know right away if you've overpacked, with enough time to do something about it.

Read GrassRoutes' latest packing tips and gadgets: *www.grassroutestravel.com/packing_tips*.

Safety

All major cities around the world have some amount of crime. Please use your wits and stay safe. Try to avoid traveling alone to new places at night.

En Route

Travel with equipment that helps make the journey to your destination peaceful. When I travel, I bring earplugs, headphones, and a sleep mask so my voyage will be blissfully quiet. I find this is easier than asking others to tone it down.

Get enough sleep before you fly. I recommend drinking lots of water the day before traveling and the day of—more if you tend to get dehydrated easily or are prone to headaches from dry plane air. Boosting your dose of vitamin C won't hurt either.

When You Get There

Don't plan two activity-heavy days back-to-back. In general, it is good to have a combination of restful, educational, and physical experiences. Balance your time rather than trying to jam in too much activity. Ask yourself what you really want to see, and cut out the rest. Keep in mind that you can always come back, and be realistic about what you and your friends and family have the energy for.

Consider breaking into smaller groups when people in your party have different ideas of what they want to see and do.

Carbon Offsets

Despite the debate about the effectiveness of carbon offsets, they represent an important stop gap measure that can really do a lot of good. Carbon offset providers use a calculator programmed to estimate what a given trip will rack up in carbon dioxide emission. This mechanism considers factors like trip distance and the number of passengers on the vehicle so you'll only be responsible for your share. To offset the estimated carbon dioxide emission, you then pay one of these providers to plant trees or otherwise reduce carbon elsewhere.

You aren't throwing your money away if you know where to get certified offsets. For instance, some of the best carbon offset products are certified by Green-e, a consumer protection program run by the Center for Resource Solutions. Other carbon offset providers doing a stellar job, and thus endorsed by Environmental Defense Fund (*www.fightglobalwarming.com*), are Carbonfund.org and AtmosClear (*www.atmosclear.org*).

Major travel web sites are helping out by making carbon offsetting a click option when you purchase your ticket.

Green Travel

Air travel is not great in terms of being carbon neutral, but many airlines are starting to spend money investing in energy efficiency to make up for their jet fuel emissions. When you book, pressure them to do so, or buy your own credits when you fly from one of the certified carbon offset providers. Travel often necessitates flying, so try to use airlines that are more conscientious when you can, and you are sure to make a more positive contribution to the greater good. Weigh your options and do the best you can.

Public transit and biking are the greenest solutions, but other great ways exist to get around, like using vehicles that run on compressed natural gas, electricity, fuel cells, or biofuels. In these pages, I point you to the latest and greatest green transit solutions in the area you'll be visiting.

Read more about green travel: *www.grassroutestravel.com/green_travel*.

Eating

These days eating green is a tricky undertaking. Here are some tips to stay conscientious and also get your grub on whether you're away or at home.

- Lots of smaller farms operate organically but just don't have the bucks to maintain an organic certification stamp. Search these out on your next farmers market excursion.

- Organic produce that's out of season, shipped from far away, can be more taxing on the environment than buying conventional, local produce in season.

- Biodynamic farming is a wonderful philosophy of growing that takes into consideration many factors beneficial to the earth. It isn't always easy finding biodynamic produce; try farmers markets or search online for a biodynamic CSA (a group of farmers or consumers promoting community-supported agriculture). Otherwise, buy local, in season, and organic.

- For more affordable and accessible organics, buy from a local farm, join a CSA, or subscribe to an organic food box service.

- Find out which conventional produce you should avoid because it's grown unsustainably or requires soil sterility and high levels of chemicals that stay on board when you take a bite. Stone fruit and leafy veggies are two examples.

- Conventional produce that doesn't require a large amount of pesticides or to which pesticides aren't as apt to stick, such as fruits and vegetables with thick peels, are safe to eat.

- When you are ordering at one of the restaurants in this book, you may find some ingredients that aren't sustainable on the menu. Just go for the dishes that you know have ingredients that can be sustained.

- Kosher, halal, and organic, hormone-free meats are always better choices in terms of taste, quality, humaneness, and sustainability.

- Be especially careful when it comes to seafood. Shrimp, tuna, big fin fish—all no-nos. Squid, catfish, tilapia, anchovies, and mackerel, on the other hand, are all totally tasty and easy to sustain. The Monterey Bay Aquarium has an up-to-date explanation of the best seafood choices: *www.montereybayaquarium.org/cr/seafoodwatch.aspx.*

Read more about eco-friendly dining: *www.grassroutestravel.com/eating.*

Banking

Did you know that the most important factor in true sustainability is economic? Think local jobs, banks that give loans to new small businesses, and more. Business owners who live where they work care more about the longevity of their community and local environment, and when you spend your money at locally owned businesses, you support that sincere effort.

Most of the businesses in these pages have direct links to the local economy, injecting most of their revenue right back into the community. Don't consider the sustainability movement without looking into the economics of it—indeed the solution to many challenges in society today lies in the communion between green industry and economics. For more info, check out Van Jones's Green For All (*www.greenforall.org*) or Business Alliance for Local Living Economies (*www.livingeconomies.org*).

Look to this guide to find community-supporting banks in the area you'll be visiting. For specific establishments and more about keeping money circulating locally, refer to *www.grassroutestravel.com/buy_local*.

Using GrassRoutes Guides

Organization by type of venue runs the risk of muddling, say, an upscale restaurant with a drive-thru, just because both are technically restaurants. Instead, shouldn't guides be organized by what kind of experience you are looking for?

GrassRoutes guides employ a new system of organization that makes searching for activities, restaurants, and venues easy. This guide is organized by situation, with chapters such as "Stay Up Late," "Do Lunch," and "Hang Out" that pay attention to your state of being.

All phone numbers are in the 415 area code unless otherwise stated.

As authors, we want to tell our experiences from our own perspectives. The initials after each review denote the author:

SB: Serena Bartlett   IB: Ilsa Bartlett
JA: Joy Lian Alferness   DL: Daniel Ling
MP: Maria Pecot

Our Criteria

Urban Eco-Travel is defined by businesses and activities that give back to their local communities through environmental, social, or economic means. To appear in a GrassRoutes guide, a business or activity *must* have a local presence or be locally owned. In addition, if we can answer yes to at least one of the following questions, the destination passes our test:

- Does it bank locally?
- Does it hire locals?
- Does it use energy-efficient appliances?
- Does it sell fair trade merchandise?
- Does it have a positive community benefit (for example, bringing people together or providing community outreach)?
- Does it use fair trade, organic, or locally grown products?
- Is its location environmentally sound (for example, the building is not on a landfill, or the building is made with green materials)?
- Does it participate in reuse/garbage reduction?
- Does it care about the environment, community, and economy around it?
- And last, but certainly not least, do we love the place? Does something make it special? Does it blow our minds?

With these considerations in mind, we've created a series of icons to accompany our reviews. These icons (see key on opposite page) indicate which of the criteria above are particularly noteworthy at a particular business or organization.

⟋	art/cultural/historic preservation	⊘	free
⚗	banks locally	⬚	green cleaning
⚲	bikeable	⚲	green energy use
ℂⓄ	cash only	⚲	hires locals
⚱	community pillar	⚲	inspirational
⚘	composts	⊙	local organic produce/ ingredients
$	cost: cheap	⚲	locally owned
$$	cost: moderate	⛉	on public transit route
$$$	cost: pricey	⚲	recycled material use
⚲	dog friendly	♺	recycles
⛁	educational	ℝ	reservations recommended
⚲	electric vehicle use	⚲	romantic
✚	employee health care	V	vegetarian
⚲	employees reentering workforce	((ⵙ))	Wi-Fi available
⚟	fair trade		

The GrassRoutes Team

Serena Bartlett

A natural born contrarian, Serena has lived and traveled in more than 25 countries. She is an award-winning author and an active spokesperson for inspiring ways to tread more lightly on the planet. With degrees from Friends World College (now Global College) and Long Island University, she had the world as her classroom. Serena is a regular contributor to a number of national and Bay Area publications, having written stories on everything from shampoo-making with garden ingredients to green business tips to an interview with one of her role models, Riane Eisler. She has appeared on KRON4's *Bay Area Backroads* as a green travel expert as well as on other programs, and has been a featured guest on KPFA and KGO radio. Serena revels in creative solutions for becoming more self-reliant, like sewing her own sheets and quilts, designing jewelry, making wild forays in the kitchen, and growing her own edible garden. She is a ski bum at heart and a swimming junkie, equally comfortable on a pack trip with her poodle or as a city slicker. Discover more about Serena at *www.serenabartlett.com* and at *www.grassroutestravel.com.*

Daniel Ling

Born and raised in Oakland, Daniel's style of freehand line drawing continues to evolve with each new GrassRoutes guide. His art has been shown at several galleries, design studios, and cafes. Daniel studied anthropology at UC Berkeley, where he learned to see beyond the superficial by putting aside preconceived notions. He can be found zipping around the streets of Oakland and San Francisco on his speedy bike, scaling the bouldering walls at the local climbing gym, in the front row of a Sonic Youth concert, or buried in a book. See more of Daniel's designs and artwork at *www.grassroutestravel. com/illustrations.*

Joy Lian Alferness

Joy grew up in the suburbs of Boston, went even farther north when she attended college at Cornell University, and finally settled in San Francisco in 1998 when she decided she'd had enough of the snow. Working as an actor and an acting teacher, Joy began her blog, *www.restaurantwhore.com*, when she grew tired of people asking her for restaurant recommendations. She has freelanced for *Mesh Magazine*, *Chow.com*, and *Tuttifoodie.com*.

Maria Pecot

Born and raised in Oakland, Maria is continually intrigued by the cultural richness and scenic diversity that the Bay Area offers. A writer of children's stories, fiction, poetry, and reviews, she finds inspiration for her art in almost every facet of her life. She has traveled to more than 10 countries since she graduated from UC Berkeley with a degree in political science. Her knack for any social scene keeps us up to date with how workers are being treated, where to go for the best cocktails, and what is new on either side of the Bay.

Ilsa Bartlett

Ilsa has been dreaming of California since a young age, making the state her home in 1999. She has previously written on food science and spirituality, and she worked as a journalist on the East Coast. Her blog, Institute for Rewiring the System (*www.hotlux.com/angel.htm*), focuses on basic breathing meditation.

Dutsi Bap

Our cheerleader, research assistant, and referee, Dutsi boosts morale and provides support crucial to the GrassRoutes team. When he's not on the road testing out new locations, he visits local nursing homes to spread joy and fluffiness. He completed therapy dog certification and believes that the meaning of life is to eat roast chicken, run in the park, and take long naps at the feet of our writers. Dutsi also loves our freecycled leather couch!

Bay Area Overview

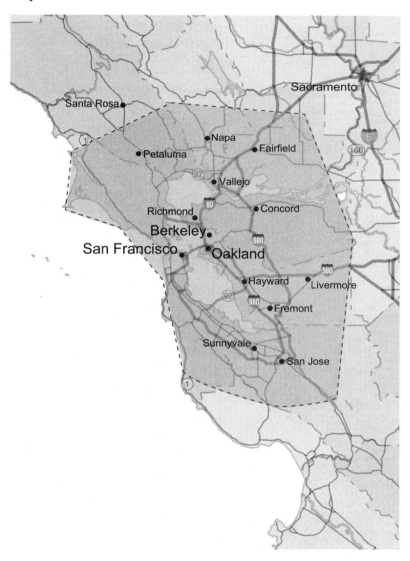

San Francisco Neighborhoods

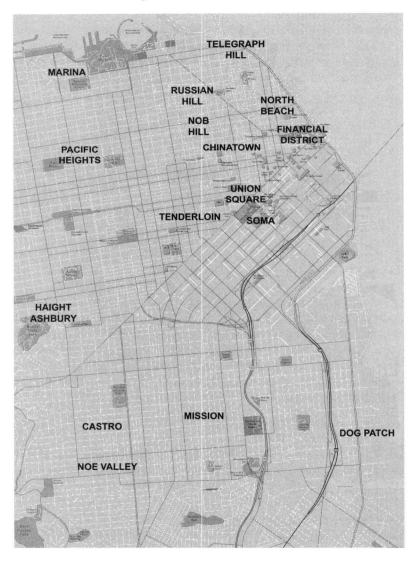

SAN FRANCISCO

About San Francisco

The land we now know as the city of San Francisco has changed hands several times in its documented history, from its indigenous people to the Spanish settlers to the Mexican government, before finally becoming part of the United States. Spanish explorer Don Gaspar de Portolà arrived in what is now San Francisco Bay in 1769 where he found several small villages of the Yelamu group of the Ohlone Indians, a mobile society of hunter-gatherers. By 1776, the Spanish had established Mission San Francisco de Asís (Mission Dolores) and their encroachment soon drove the Yelamu and their culture to extinction within two generations of European contact.

Mexico assumed control of the area following its independence from Spain in 1821, and 14 years later an Englishman by the name of William Richardson laid out a street plan for the town known as Yerba Buena. The attention of American settlers and the outbreak of the Mexican-American War would result in Yerba Buena switching owners once more. Commodore John D. Sloat claimed California for the States, Captain John B. Montgomery soon followed to take control of Yerba Buena, and thus it was renamed San Francisco. The settlement's growth was slow and would have remained so had it not been for the discovery of gold in California in the coming years.

Thousands of prospectors and treasure seekers converged on the small port town during the California Gold Rush, and the population ballooned from one thousand in 1848 to twenty-five thousand by the end of 1849. Countless ship masts in the harbors resembled a man-made forest as the crews emptied their vessels to stake a claim. The U.S. military erected Fort Point at the Golden Gate and another fort on Alcatraz Island to secure the booming city of the newly admitted state of California. The discovery of the Comstock Lode and other caches of silver in 1859 further supplied the population growth. It was at this time of greed and lawless mayhem that the Barbary Coast gained its reputation as a sordid base of prostitution and criminal activity.

Another group of people sought to take advantage of the Gold Rush phenomenon, but in a more planned and ultimately more rewarding way. Wells Fargo Bank was established in 1852, and the magnates of big industry collaborated to build the First Transcontinental Railroad. Levi Strauss, Domingo Ghirardelli, and other entrepreneurs began their respective businesses, catering to the needs and tastes of the booming population. It was at this time that San Francisco began to take on its flamboyant image; trade soared with the development of the Port of San Francisco, cable cars began scaling the hills, rows upon rows of Victorian houses were built, and plans were laid for a spacious public park. With hotels, restaurants, parks, churches, synagogues, schools, and libraries sprouting all over the city, San Francisco had become a flourishing urban center on the western frontier.

In the early morning of April 18, 1906, San Franciscans awoke to the violent shaking of their homes as a major earthquake struck the city. Buildings collapsed, and ruptured gas lines ignited blazes that would spread and persist untamed for days. Damaged water mains forced the Presidio Artillery Corps to demolish entire city blocks in an attempt to halt the advancing fires. At last, when the infernos subsided, less than a quarter of the once-thriving city remained, with a modern estimated toll of several thousand lives. Refugee camps were set up in Golden Gate Park, the Presidio, and on the beaches to house many of those who were left homeless, and the East Bay, particularly Oakland, served as a permanent haven for the rest.

Choosing to retain the old street grid, San Franciscans began a rapid rebuilding process. Rising from the ashes and rubble was a new City Hall in splendid Beaux Arts style, the mansions of Nob Hill were repaired and converted into grand hotels, and Amadeo Giannini founded the Bank of America to help finance the recovery of those attempting to restore their former livelihoods. San Francisco debuted its revival at the Panama Pacific International Exposition in 1915, along with Bernard Maybeck's grand Palace of Fine Arts (see page 137).

San Francisco continued to strengthen its standing as a financial capital in the years leading up to the stock market crash in 1929. All of the San Francisco-based banks managed to survive the trials of the Great Depression, and the simultaneous construction of the San Francisco–Oakland Bay Bridge and the Golden Gate Bridge (see page 109) provided jobs in this difficult time. Also during this era was the adaptation of the military stockade on the island of Alcatraz to begin its notorious run as an inescapable maximum-security prison.

Fort Mason became the primary port of embarkation to the Pacific theater of operations during World War II, attracting people from as far as the southern states to seek jobs in the Bay Area. Many military personnel returning from duty, as well as civilians who had come to support the war effort, decided to make San Francisco their permanent home. The United Nations Charter was drafted and signed in San Francisco in 1945 and six years later, the Treaty of San Francisco officially ended the war with Japan.

Onward into the second half of the twentieth century, the American counterculture began to blossom in the North Beach neighborhoods in the form of the Beat Generation—a term actually invented by Jack Kerouac in 1948. Beat poets and writers such as Kerouac and John Clellon Holmes, and a growing artist population, fueled the San Francisco Renaissance. One of the first public broadcasting companies in the country, the Bay Area Educational Television Association, was founded in 1952, its volunteers painstakingly forming the basis for what is now KQED (the local public broadcasting network). During the 1960s, Haight-Ashbury became a haven for the counterculture generation and the first psychedelic bands, including the Grateful Dead, Jefferson Airplane, and Big Brother & the Holding Company, began to emerge. Led by John Shen, the gay rights movement of the 1970s picked up momentum with the emergence of the Castro as a gay neighborhood, the election of Harvey Milk to the board of supervisors, and the assassinations of he and Mayor George Moscone.

The recognizable San Francisco skyline began to take shape with the completion of the Transamerica Pyramid in 1972 and the Manhattanization of the downtown sector in the 1980s. Port activity was soon transitioned to the Port of Oakland across the bay, resulting in a shift in focus to tourism as the major economic contributor. Demographics also began to resemble current statistics with the increase of immigration from Asia and Latin America.

In the late afternoon of October 17, 1989, the 6.9-magnitude Loma Prieta Earthquake struck the Bay Area. Severe damage to the Marina and South of Market districts precipitated the demolition of the Embarcadero Freeway and much of the Central Freeway. The largely unloved Embarcadero Freeway was never completed due to citizen-led opposition, and the city was happy to reclaim the historic waterfront no longer shrouded by the concrete structure. In remembrance of Pulitzer Prize–winning columnist Herb Caen's frequent lambasting of "the Dambarcadero," a small portion of the Embarcadero promenade has been named Herb Caen Way.

The dot-com boom of the late 1990s brought scores of marketing and sales professionals to San Francisco, and typically poor neighborhoods began experiencing gentrification. Despite the bursting of the dot-com bubble, small businesses and self-employed firms today make up 85 percent of city establishments, slowing the infiltration of big box retail chains and keeping a larger percentage of retail dollars in the local economy. DL

To sum up this city in a few short paragraphs would be impossible for me now, after having walked up and down the streets, the hills, and the alleyways. There's this sturdy economic center, swirled around with a generation of poets and their groupies, a world-famous LGBT scene, underground art and music movements, coffee-crazed locals, Latin American and Mexican culture, important and deep-rooted Asian living history, African-American society, and a huge French community. People create galleries and parties in empty spaces, concerts spark up on corners and in parks, impromptu adventure is what this place is all about. It is an international tourist trap to boot, and for good reason—SF offers an incredible mélange of people, food, and culture, all balanced on top of an active fault line we can thank for our plethora of steep avenues.

In many ways San Francisco represents the American Dream in Technicolor, and people still come here to reach for it. The reasons used to be gold, family ties, or job opportunities, and if you spoke to someone, either a poor art student, a suit fresh from business school, a musician, or a day laborer you'd hear some of those same motivations in chorus. San Francisco is a place where you can walk out of your door and find the whole world working toward greatness all in one place. The best chefs, the most famous artists, the most read authors, adored politicians, world-class musicians, the most unique of the eccentrics, the most savvy of businessmen—no one can walk away from this city without leaving a part of themselves here.

True also, that SF is making a serious play to contend with other towns on the way to sustainability; in fact, they are on SustainLane's top ten list for U.S. sustainable cities. With new bills up for vote and a multitude of earth-friendly policies floating in the air, SF's liable to make some pretty big moves in the next decade. The businesses and ease of public transit also contribute to the green movement, so your time spent here can be something that benefits you, the locals, and the world we all share.

Rather than spew facts about this city's greatness, and I have come to see SF as nothing short of great, I'd like to invite you to explore for yourself, search for your calling, because the so-called foggy city has a way of sounding its horn to each individual. Whether you live here and want a "new view" of your hometown, or you are just passing through, camera in hand, shed your unconscious blinders and there will be an echo of truth in your San Francisco adventure, you'll get new ideas, have inspiration for a new direction, or reverberate with your personal goals and missions. *SB*

Climate

A quotation misattributed to Mark Twain's wit goes something like, "the coldest winter I ever spent was a summer in San Francisco." Although it is an exaggeration, the quote holds some amount of truth. San Francisco's weather is best characterized as mild with little amount of change; there is almost no semblance of the seasons due to the fact that it is surrounded on three sides by water. Summertime high temperatures average 70°F and winter highs 60°F, but don't get the wrong impression because after 5pm, if you didn't bring a coat you'll wish you had. The cold ocean and high inland heat are responsible for San Francisco's reputation as the "Fog City." While the eastern side of the city is sunnier, the western neighborhoods can be covered in fog all day during the spring and early summer. The fog is not so prominent during the warmer late summer and fall months. The city's sharp topography also creates a number of microclimates throughout its neighborhoods.

Geographically, San Francisco is located at 37°47′ North, 122°26′ West, and has a total area of 47 square miles (122 kilometers square). Call 364.7974 for up-to-date weather information for the city.

Neighborhoods

Chinatown

One of the oldest and liveliest neighborhoods in San Francisco abuts North Beach and the base of Nob Hill. Follow your nose up and down the steep, crowded streets for a close encounter with life in Asia without getting on a plane. Poke your head into medicine shops with roots hanging in the windows, powders in jars, and tiny boxes lining the walls. Skip the restaurants with too many Western faces, and the over-priced souvenir shops. Head instead to the little tailor shops where some of America's most skilled seamstresses will build you an outfit, or to Eastern Bakery for some mooncakes, Sam Wo's for late-night wonton soup, or Universal Buddhist Temple for some authentic Chinese opera. I like eating fresh lychees while watching kids play in Chinatown's many playgrounds. See page 104 for a wonderful Chinatown walking tour. *SB*

Cole Valley

Just above famous Haight Street is a little pocket of San Francisco that epitomizes the city in every way. In fact, when I am in far-off lands reminiscing and I think of Cole Valley, it seems to me the most San Franciscan of all the San Francisco neighborhoods. I was introduced to the steep streets at a young age, climbing down from a family's home at Twin Peaks and winding down, past pink ladies and local florists, dog walkers and tiny sports cars toward Cole Street, where I'd eat and listen to conversations for hours at Zazie, the best French bistro (see page 32). There is no shortage of little shops and eateries; I love the murals on the auto shop and the hardware store across from Zazie, and I come back for the family-style Halloween celebration that takes place each year. Talk about costumes! *SB*

Haight-Ashbury

The main intersection of this shopping district is the stuff of legends, having been the epicenter of the "Summer of Love." Even though the neighborhood now includes a Gap and a Ben & Jerry's, you still get that feeling of time travel back to the 1960s when strolling up and down Haight Street. Brave the lines at the Pork Store (see page 36) for an enormous breakfast that is tasty to boot. The Haight is the place to buy funky used and vintage clothing at stores like Aardvark's and Buffalo Exchange. Of course, there are also smoke shops aplenty, the best of which sell gorgeous handblown glass pipes and bongs for "tobacco use only." Follow Haight Street all the way to the end (at Stanyan) making sure to stop into Amoeba Records (see page 196), where you'll find all the music you've ever wanted and more. If you continue past Amoeba, you'll end up in Golden Gate Park (see page 113), the perfect place to chill with your newly acquired possessions. *JA*

Russian Hill

One of the highest hills in the city, this famously well-to-do neighborhood is the site of that Lombard Street block that everyone seems to think is the crookedest. While it is pretty, you'll have to go to the other side of town to Vermont Street (at 20th Avenue) off Potrero for the genuine article. But back to Russian Hill, the park at the top is worth a visit for a picnic with a view down to the financial district and Alcatraz Island on the other side. Spanish tapas, the cable cars whirring by, and a neighborhood where then meets now make Russian Hill a steep but pleasant place to explore. *SB*

The Inner Richmond

If you are looking for a less tourist-oriented alternative to Chinatown, then the Inner Richmond is your spot. Focus on Clement Street between Arguello and Ninth avenues for the most concentrated shopping. A small dim sum snack from Wing Lee Bakery will give you the sustenance you need to tackle Kamei Housewares, a store selling beautiful Asian kitchenware at dirt-cheap prices. Green Apple Books requires a stop as well—be sure to check the carts outside for great literary bargains. Get Thee to a Nunnery sells corsets and the like, and is worth a trip for gawking if not buying. If you are traveling with small children, pop into Citikids, the city's biggest and best independent baby store, and follow it up with a stop at Satin Moon, where you'll find the perfect fabric for that project you've been putting off. *JA*

Embarcadero

With the Ferry Building as its hub and Aquatic Park at its far end, the Embarcadero wraps around past busy Fisherman's Wharf and a series of boisterous piers. The Embarcadero strip was freed from its shackles when the highway that once claimed it tumbled following the Loma Prieta Earthquake in 1989, perhaps the only plus side to that major quake. One of the most peopled areas of the city, here you'll find some of the most exciting experiences the city has to offer. Take a ride on a surrey, or have an impromptu trip with one of the boaters past Dock K and the sunbathing sea lions. *SB*

SoMa

SoMa, or South of Market, is what many international travelers, and "grass is always greener" subscribers imagine of San Francisco: a polished urban network of hidden art bars and undiscovered clubs where the coolest new music is pumped into fashionable people's ears. In reality, SoMa is only partially what we dream it will be, in part because it is checkered with high-end industrial lofts. It is far from undiscovered these days, but the art bars and the garage-cum-party spots are still in full force around these streets, many in the alleys between major transit routes. Skip out of the Market Street river, pass Yerba Buena Gardens, the many fabulous museums, and the solar-powered Moscone Convention Center and you'll be smack-dab in the center of this once-grungy neighborhood. A recent beautification effort on 6th St. makes it well worth a stroll, with great graffiti and decorated buildings. Brave an alleyway and you are sure to find the den of your dreams. *SB*

North Beach

North Beach is home to the most crowded streets in San Francisco. It is the only place where, if you have a camera around your neck, you have a good chance of being petitioned by a host to eat at his restaurant. I beg you, don't accept; it is safe to say that those hawks don't lead you to tasty food for reasonable prices. In the shadow of Coit Tower and bordered by Chinatown to the west, striptease shows where Lenny Bruce once did stand-up to the east, the financial district to the south, and Fisherman's Wharf to the north, North Beach is where Little Italy would be if San Francisco really had one. In all honesty, the fame of this boisterous neighborhood rests on the shoulders of the beatniks and only a few of the many pasta-rias more than anything else, but that is not to say there isn't a strong sense of history along these streets. A mélange of cultures resides here, art students are lucky to find apartments here as the bus service is ever-present in this corner of the city, and there is always pizza and fresh amaretti steps away. I bring Dutsi Bap, my poodle, and play catch on the lawn at Washington Square (see page 44) before tucking him under my coat and heading into City Lights (see page 55) to find a new Kay Ryan book. *SB*

The Sunset

Often shunned as the outskirts of San Francisco, the Sunset is where most of the city lives. Pastel row houses line the streets, not the ornate Victorian kind, but the 1960s and 1970s vertical board kind. Many gems are found in between these abodes—great bars, homey restaurants, and a number of lesser-known pockets of retail shops that beg for attention. True, it is usually a few degrees cooler here, but it is an easy trade for being that much closer to Ocean Beach. Clement and Balboa streets are my top picks of this area, featuring an authentic Russian tearoom, the only truly Egyptian restaurant in California, and one of my favorite theaters, the Balboa. *SB*

The Outer Richmond

Long ago referred to as "The Great Sand Waste," the Outer Richmond has flourished into a cultural crossroads. You just might witness a Chinese lion dance while chomping down on a goodie from a nearby Russian grocer. Geary Street is one of my favorite spots for an adventurous stroll, which one day might bring a loaf of traditional Irish soda bread, the next a sack of greasy Russian piroshkis. Clamber up the former gun monuments at Battery Chamberlain on the shores of Baker Beach or witness a spectacular 360-degree view through the Giant Camera at Point Lobos. I once slept in the bunkers at the Battery—that is, before Homeland Security prevented such things, and I still have dreams of that haunting and exciting night. *DL*

Cow Hollow

I find it hard to dwell in negativity, but my own opinion of Cow Hollow has gotten darker and darker over the years. Once a windy haven, ideally placed near Crissy Field and cluttered with neighborhood pubs and small shops and restaurants, the place where cows grazed more than a hundred years ago is now where wealthy couples come to start families, usually two or three kids at a time. Down the main drags you'll find wide strollers and many spas, plus the densest concentration of chain businesses off Market Street. Despite this, there are some precious spots to be discovered, including locally owned and low-key wine bars, a few landmark pubs still serving cheap Newcastle pints, and lots of people to watch. Wind up from the Exploratorium to see some fancy houses just off of Union Street, and find a snack to suit your window-shopping wishes. *SB*

The Castro

There's no question that gay rights, in fact civil rights altogether, are still a contested issue on many levels, most recently in the form of the conservative Christian–supported Proposition 8 writing new anti-American, unjust amendments into the state constitution. But historically, every time there has been a struggle in the LGBT community of the Castro, from Stonewall to Harvey Milk's assassination, AIDS to marriage rights, the Castro has only gotten stronger, and rallied to make change and support equality. Perhaps that's why it has become one of the most famous neighborhoods in the world. It is cohesive in the extreme, and even though it is more touristy than many residents would like, it is still home to some of the most fabulous bars and nightclubs, not to mention the Castro Theatre (see page 168) and many fashionable shops. Come for the evening and stay until the wee hours of the morning, dancing and reveling with gays and straights alike. There's always something to do, even if you just want to find a great cookbook, grab a slice of pizza, or learn a new yoga pose. If you are in town during late September or mid-October, don't miss Pride Weekend or the Castro Street Fair (see page 256). *SB*

Bernal Heights

Home to the real crookedest street in San Francisco (sorry Lombard lovers, Vermont Street at 20th Ave is a steeper grade), Bernal Heights is a haven for quaint businesses that cater to the nurtured-family vibe of the neighborhood. Follow Cortland Avenue to find tiny markets and cafes overflowing with fresh fruit and toasty paninis. Look out over the city from the vantage point of Bernal Hill, surrounded by old houses that withstood the commotion of the 1906 earthquake. In fact, the community actually expanded as a result of the quake—it is where savvy survivors trucked the wreckage from partially destroyed buildings and made new homes for themselves out of the repurposed material. *SB*

Hayes Valley

More cutesy than any other area of the city, Hayes Valley is awash with local businesses. Ideally situated near the Civic Center and the theaters and concerts that abound there, it is home to the top preshow meals: Jardiniere, Hayes Street Grill, and Absinthe Brasserie. Walk the few square blocks, making sure to wind in between the alleys with flower-covered entrances to hideaway apartments you'll dream to live in, and you'll find the best sake, a good book, some stylin' travel gear, and perhaps even a new 'do. SB

TenderNob

This is the worst name for a neighborhood ever! I don't know whose idea it was, but I'd like to write them a long letter giving them a piece of my mind. If only it weren't so useful, I could avoid the term altogether but aside from my gripes over answering the question, "Where is it?" and having to answer "TenderNob," I'll say this: the area that encapsulates Nob Hill and the Tenderloin is a true melting pot. Grace Cathedral and the high-end art deco apartment buildings around Nob Hill, the bars and eateries on Polk Street, the hole-in-the-wall finds strung throughout an ever-cleaned-up Tenderloin are all in this area, which stretches toward Civic Center. This is by far my least favorite neighborhood moniker, but also my favorite place in the city. There is more to do, more to see, and more great places to get lost than anywhere else. And if all else fails, hop on the Powell Street cable car, disembark at Washington Street, and you'll be in my old haunts—a great area with panoramic views that's rarely captured by hordes of tourists. SB

Getting Here

Tips to Get from A to B

Here are some options for travel that include everything from flying to walking. Even conscientious travelers of the globe must at times make use of transportation options beyond walking! Weigh time, cost, and energy usage to determine which transport choice best suits your needs and the needs of the planet. Though it can be more time-consuming, transit provides a smoother transition to the next spot. Choose efficient routes to avoid wasting unnecessary fuel.

The Bay Area is an international travel destination, with three international airports and other major transportation depots. Here's the vital info to get you to San Francisco.

Caltrain

Caltrain Information Line: 800.660.4287
www.caltrain.org

Caltrain is the commuter line that connects San Francisco to the South Bay. It's mainly used for getting between SF and San Jose, but runs all the way down to Gilroy should you need a garlic fix or decide to visit a peach farm. The trains, which tend to transport commuters, run on a regular schedule, making planning easy. There are two Caltrain stations in the city, at Fourth and King streets, and at 1149 22nd Street Fares vary depending on how many zones you travel between, so it's best to check current fares just before you plan to use the system.

NextBus

www.nextbus.com

When I first discovered NextBus, I wanted to find the person who started it and kiss them square on the mouth. The site allows you to enter in your location, which method of transportation and route you plan to use (Muni, AC Transit, Emery Go Round, and Water Transit Authority) and where you are going. It will then tell you how long it is until the next bus/train will arrive to whisk you off to your destination. It is an invaluable tool for calculating how much more time you have to finish your breakfast before rushing out the door to catch your ride. You can sign up for web alerts and wireless access so you can use it on the go, and the service is free. Certain bus and metro stations even have NextBus–enabled electric signs telling you when to expect the next bus or train, and having that information always makes my wait a little less stressful.

Amtrak

Amtrak Information Line: 800.USA.RAIL
www.amtrak.com

The major Bay Area terminus for nationwide, long-distance train service is Emeryville, only a few blocks away from the Oakland border. Amtrak offers trains from around the Bay Area and the country, including express service from Sacramento (*www.amtrakcapitols.com*), Los Angeles, Seattle, and Vancouver, B.C. The *Zephyr*, a rapid train from Chicago, Illinois, also terminates at Emeryville. Once you arrive in the East Bay it is an easy bus or BART ride to downtown SF.

Greyhound Bus

800.231.2222

www.greyhound.com

Greyhound operates a number of departures and arrivals out of San Francisco—call them up or check out the web site for detailed schedules.

Ferry

www.baylinkferry.com, http://goldengate.org/schedules.php

A fantastic way to beat the traffic from Marin and the outer East Bay is to take one of the ferries into San Francisco. Golden Gate Ferry operates ferries departing from both Larkspur and Sausalito, which have a regular schedule for routes to the Ferry Building. Times are best viewed on their web site for up-to-date info. A one-way fare is $7.10 for adults, $3.55 for students, youth, and seniors, and $3.80 if you have a frequent-rider ticket book of 20 tickets. An added bonus is that whenever the beloved Giants have a home game, the Larkspur Ferry also runs directly to the ballpark ($7 each way), saving you an enormous parking hassle. Baylink Ferry shuttles passengers to and from Vallejo and Solano, to both the Ferry Building and the ballpark. You can also catch the ferry back to Vallejo from Fisherman's Wharf at Pier 41. All tickets are $12.50 for adults, $6.25 for students, youth, and seniors. Children under five are free with a fare-paying adult. On a clear day, the ferry rides are nothing short of spectacular, and the view of the city from the bay is breathtaking.

Emery Go Round

www.emergoround.com

The Emery Go Round is a local, free Emeryville bus service that makes it easy for train passengers to get to hotels and nearby BART and bus stations. Emery Go Round will pick you up directly from the train station and take you as far as the Oakland Coliseum and Oakland International Airport.

AC Transit

www.actransit.org

AC Transit bus routes cover the East Bay and Transbay routes from San Francisco. Selected routes provide overnight service; these buses are identified by the addition of 800 to the normal route numbers. Take AC Transit between

Amtrak and the Oakland International Airport, or BART stations. Ask the train conductor for a Transit Transfer before disembarking and this service will be free.

Ride-Share via Craigslist

www.craigslist.org
Craigslist is the online community board for much of the United States and the world. To search your local Craigslist, choose from the city list on the right-hand side of the home page. For the carless, or those seeking to be conscientious carpoolers, Craigslist has a special section under "community" called "rideshare." Often people will post here who are looking for a ride or willing to accommodate passengers. Send a few e-mails back and forth or have a chat on the good ol' telephone to make sure that you are comfortable with the person with whom you will be traveling. Other car-sharing resources:

www.ridenow.org/carpool

www.citycarsshare.org

www.icarpool.com

www.matchandgo.com

www.spaceshare.com

www.zipcar.com

San Francisco International Airport (SFO)

www.flysfo.com
This modern airport is a hub of international travel, with many direct flights to and from Japan, Thailand, and China. Now that BART connects to SFO, it is much more convenient to reach the city, though you can still take the bus or choose from a multitude of Airporter Shuttles that will run you about $20 to downtown. If you have a long wait, head to the international terminal, where there's always an exhibit from one of SF's premier museums. There are plenty of chain food options in each terminal, which are priced higher than usual, so I opt to bring a bagged lunch or recommend waiting until you are released from the security line to get some real grub. Although you cannot bring more than three ounces of liquid with you, and may even be stopped for items like lip balm, you can still bring an empty water bottle that you

can fill at a water fountain once inside, and avoid spending extreme amounts on bottled water. Security regulations seem to change with great frequency; check with the Federal Aviation Administration, *www.faa.gov*, to see what the current restrictions are.

Oakland International Airport
www.flyoakland.com
Oakland International Airport is a less-crowded, often cheaper alternative to flying into San Francisco. When the weather is bad and the clouds cancel flights to SFO, Oakland remains open and dependable. JetBlue and Southwest are the major carriers. Private shuttles carry passengers to their hotels and final destinations for around $10. Free shuttles connect the airport with the Oakland Coliseum BART station.

Cheap Airfares
Look around for an array of cheap tickets out of Oakland, and more recently San Francisco, from airlines such as Southwest, Alaska, and JetBlue. Regular cheap routes serve destinations like Los Angeles, Denver, New York, Portland, Seattle, and more. One-way tickets can get as low as $89 if you book at least two weeks in advance. Sometimes you can get two-for-one tickets on the bigger airlines like American or United Airways. The web sites that require you to purchase the tickets they come up with during a specific search are almost always less expensive than ones that enable open searches, so if you know when you are going, use these services.

Driving
When you can't take public transit, or if a road trip is the name of the game, we all know there are times when we just have to get in the car. If you don't have an electric, hybrid, or biodiesel car, keep your tires aligned and with the right amount of air pressure to get maximum mileage, and avoid idling for too long. San Francisco is located on California's Coastal Freeway, the 101, and is also accessible by routes 80, 280, and 1. Access from Interstate 5 means a trip over the Bay Bridge. For detailed maps and driving directions look to *www.511.org*, or your local map provider.

If you find that your pocketbook is bulging, take a trip to nearby San Carlos to Tesla Motors (1050 Bing St, 650.413.4000), where you can test-drive, rent, or purchase the most fabulous of green vehicles, the high-performance Tesla, the car of choice of our favorite heartthrob, George Clooney. There's more info on green transit on page xi.

Getting Around

As soon as you set foot in this city, you'll want to start exploring. San Francisco is very hilly, and city blocks are long, so be sure to evaluate your stamina before planning a route on foot. That said, our fair city is only seven miles by seven miles and you might be surprised at how much ground you can cover on an energetic day. Take a look in the Bike About chapter for a more manageable way to take on the city using your own power. If you do go on foot, take a walking map with you—some neighborhoods are on a logical grid, but Market Street bisects the city down the center, making some of the intersections confusing. There are also parks, hills, and streets that change from two-way to one-way, so consulting a map is key. The public transportation system is excellent and covers a lot of ground; there are very few places you can't go to with a Muni pass (see below) in hand. Muni maps are essential tools for nonstressed searching, even if your aim is to get lost; after a day of following your nose, you'll know which cable car, bus, or streetcar to take home.

Transit Info

www.511.org

All relevant transit information is on this web site. On a local phone, dial 5-1-1 for exact schedules and routes for any destination in the Bay Area, including carpooling. The 5-1-1 service makes it extremely easy for anyone to use a combination of Bay Area public transit systems. Current traffic conditions and driving times are available for local highways as well.

Muni (San Francisco Municipal Railway)

www.sfmuni.com

Muni is San Francisco's public transit system that encompasses 80 different routes on buses, the metro system, streetcars, cable cars, and the recently developed light-rail. Muni has been running since 1912 and is constantly adding vehicles to its fleet. Cable car fares are $5, but the fare for all the other means of transport is $1.50 and includes a transfer good for 90 minutes. The transfer can be used to connect to any other Muni vehicle, with the exception of the cable cars (for example, underground metro to bus, or light-rail to underground). You must take your transfer, even if you don't intend to use it, as it is your proof of payment. Students and seniors (ages 65 and older or 5–17) pay $.50; monthly, weekly, and all-day passes are available for $45, $15, and $11 respectively, and include all means of transport within the system, including the cable car. (Note: A weekly pass requires paying an additional $1 whenever you ride the cable car.) Single rides require exact change, so be sure to have the correct amount handy. There are change machines in the combined BART/Muni stations for the underground piece of the metro. You can get just about anywhere in the city using the Muni system, so be sure to check the web site or pick up a map at one of the stations for a comprehensive route list. Details about each means of transport are listed below.

Buses

By far the most widespread fleet of vehicles in the Muni network, most of the buses are electric (also known as "trolley buses") or run on diesel or alternative fuels. Electric buses provide a much more efficient and clean means of transport from an ecological standpoint. A big advantage to the buses is that they have exterior bike racks that are not on the other means of transit. You could get around SF on buses alone, but it is the least expedient of Muni's vehicles, often operating on unpredictable schedules since it is subject to the city's traffic. Every bus shelter has a map of the routes just in case you forget your next connection.

Metro

This system encompasses the J, K, L, M, and N lines. All lines but the N and the J run underground between the Embarcadero station and the West Portal station from 5am to 1am (Saturdays 7am–1am, Sundays 8am–1am). There are street-level buses available (Owl service) to replace the underground once the stations close. Each metro line goes aboveground for part of its routes, with the N traveling aboveground to Caltrain after the Embarcadero on the inbound side, and out to Ocean Beach after the Church station on

the outbound side. All other lines initiate at Embarcadero, with the J splitting off at Church and heading down Church Street out to Balboa Park. The K, L, and M trains make their split once they come aground at West Portal. The K ends at Balboa Park, but goes via City College, while the M gets there via San Francisco State and Stonestown. The L train cruises through the Sunset to end up out at the zoo.

Streetcars

All part of the F-Market line, the streetcars are a fantastic way to get up and down Market street all the way to Fisherman's Wharf. On a nice day, you might find yourself on the open-topped "boat" car from England, or on the "love train," where the driver sings to you and wishes you well as you go on your way. The streetcars on this line come from all over the world, and it's easy to spot the orange cars that came from Milan (the only city that has contributed more than two cars to the current streetcar system). Several of the international cars hail from the early part of the twentieth century, while most of the U.S. cars were built just after World War II.

Cable Cars

Our famous cable cars (cars that work on an underground cable system) operate on two lines. The first runs from the base of Powell Street out to Fisherman's Wharf (Hyde or Mason street, depending on which car you hop on), while the second runs from the base of California Street out to Van Ness Avenue. During the height of tourist season, the crowds at the beginning of the Powell line can reach epic proportions. If you are just looking for a chance to ride SF's iconic vehicles, I suggest riding on the much less populated California line. If, however, where you need to get is on one of the Powell lines, then bring a companion, or a book, to help you pass the time in line, or go a few stops uphill where there is no queue. On a nice day, the views from both lines can be spectacular, and everyone is usually so giddy to be riding the cable cars that you can't help but smile the whole ride through. Tickets can be purchased at the booth on Powell Street or on board. The cars ring bells to warn pedestrians, cars, and bikers, and the sound always reminds me why I love San Francisco.

Light-Rail

The light-rail (T-Line) runs along Third Street in the Dogpatch neighborhood. This development has given residents and visitors alike access to a part of the city that could previously only be reached by car. The light-rail also provides access to the ballpark and joins up with the underground metro cars at Embarcadero station.

Bay Area Rapid Transit (BART)

www.bart.gov

Bay Area Rapid Transit is the award-winning rapid transit system serving San Francisco, the East Bay, and parts of the Peninsula. There are several stops in San Francisco, and BART can be taken to the San Francisco airport, as well as the Oakland airport (via an airport shuttle connection). BART cards, available from vending machines located in each station, can be purchased in any amount for a single trip or multiple trips; fare charts are posted. You can carry your bike on BART providing it isn't during rush hour (7:05–8:50am and 4:25–6:45pm). BART-to-Muni transfer discounts are available from white machines in Market Street Stations, so remember to pick one up before you leave the paid area of the station if you plan to connect to the subway or bus system.

Zipcar

www.zipcar.com

If a car is simply a must-have for excursions within the city limits or beyond, San Francisco has Flexcar. This is a national company with at least 10 other cities in their service area. Flexcar is a car share group that serves as an alternative to car ownership, business fleets, and car rental. They do not claim to be a cheaper alternative to renting a car, but they do promise convenience (usually there is a Flexcar to be picked up within a five-minute walk from your current location), affordability (you pay by the hour, not by the day), lower age requirements (21 years of age and older), and sustainability (they sport hybrids and ultra-low emissions vehicles). Membership is required ($35 one time fee), and the application process can take up to one week, so plan ahead.

Electric Time Car Rental

674.8800

www.etcars.com

Electric Time rents pint-sized electric vehicles for a fun, safe, and environmentally friendly way to see the city. Cars are available with two or four seats, and you can either reserve your car or walk in. All vehicles come equipped with seatbelts and have a top speed of 25 mph (the speed limit in most of the city is 20 mph). Cars can be rented by the hour, day, week, or month. GPS-based audio tours are available for the major SF attractions. The best part? The size of these adorable cars makes it a piece of cake to park in our parking-challenged city.

Green Cabs and Limo Service

EcoLimo

800.928.2566 or 310.450.7100

www.eco-limo.com

Schedule door-to-door service in biodiesel, electric, and compressed natural gas (CNG) chauffered vehicles.

Yellow Cab Co-Op

333.3333

www.yellowcabsf.com

Hybrid and CNG taxis for trips originating in San Francisco. Call ahead and ask for their green vehicles when ordering a cab.

Resources
Helpful things

Destination San Francisco
www.destinationsf.com

The one- to three-day tour itineraries on this easy-to-use web site cover many landmarks and traditional San Francisco must-sees. The Jewish History Tour is my favorite, with a healthy mix of important historical destinations plus exercise, food, architecture, and culture. These free guides are a practical way to string together many GrassRoutes picks. Peek around the web site to get an idea of an ideal SF day.

Green Citizen
591 Howard St, 4500 El Camino Real, Los Altos
877.918.8900 ext 707
www.greencitizen.com
Mon–Sat 10a–6p, Sun 11a–5p

One of the most dangerous categories in the recycling world is obsolete electronics, many of which contain caustic chemicals and acids. Green Citizen will pick up your old parts, or you can drop them off at one of their two locations, in and out of the city. Safe disposal has many incentives, which you can read about on Green Citizen web site.

Mundane Journeys
364.1465 (hotline), 978.ARTS (bus tour)
www.mundanejourneys.com
Bus Tour: info@mundanejourneys.com, departs from Yerba Buena Center for the Arts

There's a book, a weekly hotline and now a bus tour, but you won't find tourists on board. Instead it is crowded with locals seeking some out-of-the-way attractions, things that aren't attractions until you give them that title. The book has a collection of the best adventures, like Sock Monkey Dumplings and Color Theory on Geary. For the most up-do-date adventure call the number. Get on the bus; you never know where it will take you.

Sustainable Spaces

www.sustainblespaces.com

Slice and dice your energy bill and improve air quality in your home, apartment, or business with tips from these experts. Find out more on their web site and watch the transformation with their case study videos. There are always ways to be greener and save your lungs and your money.

LGBT Community Center

1800 Market St
865.5555
www.sfcenter.org
Mon–Thurs 12–10p, Fri 12–6p, Sat 9a–10p

A wonderful resource that strives for community, health, and economic and personal growth for LGBTs. There's a café and plenty of info and resources for passersby and residents alike.

Pressed Cleaners

1649 Mission St
863.3654
www.pressedcleaners.com
Mon–Fri 7a–7p, Sat 10a–3p

Pressed Cleaners is smack-dab in the center of the city and easily accessible by public transportation. This "green" dry cleaner uses no perchlorethylene, a carcinogenic chemical that damages the water supply and will be permanently banned in California by 2023. Clothes are returned smelling clean (rather than like chemicals), and rush service is available. Pressed also recycles any wire hangers you bring back, and if you are local they will give you a laundry bag to use to tote your clothes to the shop.

Grid Alternatives

www.gridalternatives.org

Get yourself out of the grid with this community group that provides renewable energy and efficiency services, equipment, volunteers, and training. Find out all the details on their easy-to-use web site. Use the sun and wind to power just about anything!

Carrot Mob

www.virgance.com/carrotmob.php

Keep your eyes and ears out for newly formed Virgance Media's next retail greening project. I was invited to go shop at a neighborhood convenience store that had promised to use a high 23 percent of profits toward making green retrofits around the store. Hundreds of people came out and bought things they'd be buying anyway—and as a result the store got everything up to par environmentally. The plan is to keep inviting people out to let their voices speak through the way they spend their money (sound familiar?). This will be one organization to keep an eye on, and something to dream of being a part of once you get to San Fran. *SB*

Walk SF

431.9255
www.walksf.org

This organization supports anyone and everyone on foot in this city. Find safety resources, strolling suggestions, and guides on their site.

SF on the Air

As with most places, the colleges and universities do the best job of getting what we want to hear on the radio waves. KALX 90.7 is my favorite, the UC Berkeley station that plays a mix of international and local tunes depending on the DJ. One day you'll tune in to hear the latest hip-hop from Japan, another day will be an emerging band from Olympia, Washington—you never know, but chances are you'll love this station immediately if not sooner. Many a musaholic comes here to get the names of the newest bands for their ever-growing collections, so they can be in the know at all times (people—you know who you are!).

KPFA 94.1 is one of the premier liberal radio stations around, airing dependable news and personal stories that make the headlines hit home. Pamela Michael's travel show (a show I've been interviewed on) is on most Wednesday mornings and always features some new and interesting travel ideas both local and abroad.

Both UC San Francisco and San Mateo Community College have great jazz stations (Jazz KCSM 91.1 and KALW 91.7) that run commercial free and play only the good stuff. KALW has progressive news and only plays jazz part- time. My favorite thing about these local stations is their propensity for giving away free tickets to upcoming shows and events. Listen on!

SF on the Tube

Every now and again we all need our fix of TV vegetation—sitting around in between the busy and exciting moments in life. I like to pack in work, play, exercise, and exploration, but for those TV-perfect times, I am glad the Bay Area has a couple local channels to watch.

KQED 9, the PBS arm of SF, has a number of great local shows in addition to my late-night stand by Charlie Rose (I love you Charlie!) and an array of great cooking shows. *Check, Please! Bay Area* brings locals together for meals around town, and the mix of reviews is always entertaining—in fact, the show won a James Beard award for their quality food programming. Josh Kornbluth, SF's resident talker, digresses in the most bubbly way, *Spark* features cutting-edge artists in all mediums, and *Quest* brings science into the mainstream by showing innovative projects and current practical applications.

KCSM 32 has an artist's showcase where classical music runs behind video, interspersed with Russian and German news programs, some of which are in English. My mother and I tune in Sundays for Croatian hour, where there's always cool music and interesting perspectives from that beautiful country.

KRON 4 has all the bells and whistles of a major network, but is locally owned and operated. KGO 7 is an ABC channel, but they have some especially notable local programs, like *Bay Area Backroads*, the long-running local travel show that I've been on to chat about free fun in Oakland and sustainable adventures. Unfortunately it was recently cancelled, though past episodes are still airing. *View from the Bay*, their daily interview, tips, and events show, often hosts authors. Channel 5, the local CBS syndicate, features *Eye on the Bay*, a lively local travel show that has lots of info on new or hard-to-find restaurants. Channel 20 is a local TV gem, with a show called *Your Green Life* (I've been featured on this show too, talking about GrassRoutes Travel and all the unexpected fun in Oakland). Skip the mainstream channels and all the propaganda and get to the goods on these local stations. *Eli Stone*, the cool show with my favorite *Trainspotting* star, Jonny Lee Miller, is filmed in SF, so check out the landmarks while you watch.

For International Visitors

Welcome—we hope you love San Francisco as much as we do!

Required Documents

Before you plan to travel to here, contact your country's nearest U.S. embassy or consulate to determine the necessary documents required for travel to the United States. You may be required to obtain a visa or passport, or to pass certain health requirements, so allow enough time before your desired departure date to obtain this information. Visit *www.usa.gov/visitors/visit. shtml* for more information.

Visitor's Information

The San Francisco Convention and Visitors Bureau (1 Hallidie Plaza, *www. sfvisitor.org*, Mon–Fri 9a–5:30p, Sat–Sun 9a–3p) provides free maps and info to visitors in a number of languages. Many of their brochures include typical tourist traps, but they have a lot of important practical information and are kind to people who are lost in SF for the first time. Their hotlines are as follows: Info Center, 391.2000; 24-Hour Hotline, English, 391.2001; French, 391.2003; German, 391.2004; Japanese, 391.2101; Spanish, 391.2122.

Customs

You must complete customs and immigrations formalities at your first point of entry into the United States, whether or not it is your final destination. At this point you will speak with a customs officer and present your forms and documentation.

Travel Insurance

The United States has no compulsory government travel insurance plan. It is advisable to purchase private travel and health insurance.

Electricity

The standard electrical current in the United States is 110 volts. Most outlets accept two- or three-pronged plugs. Laptops and other electronic devices should be equipped with a power converter.

Currency

There are a number of large banks that will exchange your foreign currency to U.S. dollars. If you are arriving in the United States via San Francisco, Oakland, or San Jose airports, you'll find exchange bureaus located inside. Here are some banks in SF that will exchange to U.S. dollars:

Wells Fargo
1 California St
396.2779

Bank of America
1 Powell St
622.4481

Thomas Cook Currency Services
75 Geary St
849.8520

American Express Travel Agency
455 Market St
536.2600

Emergencies

It is always a good idea to acquaint yourself with the emergency resources of an area you are visiting. Here is some important information in the case of an emergency:

9-1-1

Dial 9-1-1 on your phone only to stop a crime in progress, report a fire, or call for an ambulance due to a medical emergency. Like most cities, there are a limited number of emergencies that the 9-1-1 lines can attend to at a given time, so determine how urgent your situation is before making the call.

9-1-1 from Cell Phones

If you are dialing 9-1-1 from your cell phone, you will be connected to highway patrol and need to provide the dispatcher with details about the location of the emergency, your cell phone number, and, as always, the nature of the emergency. The location of cell phone calls cannot necessarily be determined like landline calls can, and sometimes calls can be cut off. If this is the case, call back. If you are in a moving vehicle, stop driving so as to not distance yourself from the location of the emergency. Check with your provider if there is a different emergency number you must dial from your phone.

Know Your Non-Emergency Number

Often incidents do not require the immediacy of a 9-1-1 call. For San Francisco, the non-emergency number is 554.6208 or 553.0123.

Emergency Updates

For updates on emergencies in the area, go online to AlertSF (*www.72hours. org*) to be texted notification of emergencies, and for details on emergency action plans and how to prepare for an emergency. San Francisco is famously vulnerable to earthquakes, though other emergencies may arise. A breeze through the info on this useful site will get you in the know about how to act, whether you're a first-time visitor or a longtime resident.

City and State Emergency Departments

Here is contact information for some important city emergency resources:

San Francisco Fire Department
698 Second St
558.3200
www.sfgov.org/fire

San Francisco Police Department
875 Stevenson St
553.0123
www.sfgov.org

San Francisco Sheriff's Department
425 Seventh St
575.4410
www.sfsheriff.com

Department of Emergency Management

www.sfgov/oes, www.72hours.org

Hospitals and Clinics

Burn Center Saint Francis Memorial Hospital

900 Hyde St
353.6230

UCSF Medical Center

505 Parnassus Ave
476.1000

San Francisco General Hospital

1001 Potrero Ave, #107
206.8000

Chinese Hospital

845 Jackson St
982.2400

San Francisco City Clinic

356 Seventh St
487.5500
www.sfcityclinic.org
Mon, Wed, Fri 8a–4p, Tues (STD patients only) 1–6p, Thurs 1–4p

Scarlet Sage Herb Company

1173 Valencia St
821.0997
www.scarletsageherb.com
Daily 11a–6:30p
Find homeopathic and naturopathic remedies here, and if they don't carry what you are looking for they will point you in the right direction.

Top Picks

If you only had one crazy, cramped day in this city

I've chosen my top eleven spots, in part because eleven is my favorite number and also as a nod to Spinal Tap fans who admire guitar amps that go the extra digit for maximum sound projection. Here are the eleven that typify this dynamic, sustainable city:

Japanese Tea Garden (see page 117)

The oldest and most established formal Japanese garden in the country is every bit as magical as you can imagine. Early on a weekday morning, climb the Moon Bridge and sit with Buddha statues on intricate shrub and moss plateaus, and you will be a little closer to enlightenment.

Mission Pie (see page 224)

Connect the dots from farm to table by sampling the best pie in the city at this worker-owned bakery brimming with passion, family flair, and mouthwatering recipes.

Exploratorium (see page 108)

Every day you can learn something new, and here at the Exploratorium they make it fun. Whether or not you're a kid, you'll be smiling ear to ear and making giant Spirographs or bubbles bigger than you are.

Amoeba Records (see page 196)

This famous record store is a San Francisco icon for good reason. With a buy, sell, or trade policy, and a finger on the pulse of the most current music sensations, Amoeba ensures you'll find what you're looking for, or what you always wanted but never knew about, all for a price that fits your budget. Rummage away, or stay late to catch a spin class (not bike spin, but DJ spin, that is).

Paxton Gate (see page 236)

Paxton Gate defies any outdated concept of what a store or museum should be. It is its own beast, quite literally. With a general message of conservation, there's a brazen collection of taxidermy, antique stamp collections, bones, succulent plants, and beetle collections, plus there's always a pot of tea on, free for guests ready to explore the natural world or Paxton's back patio, complete with orchids and a babbling brook.

Book Passage (see page 53)

I am a book lover. I am also a food lover. Coincidentally, I also enjoy a glorious view and the mist of a saltwater tide now and again. All of it comes together at my favorite bookstore, Book Passage, at its smaller, bayside location in the heart of the Ferry Building food scene. (For the whole nine yards, head to Corte Madera in Marin County.)

The Fillmore Auditorium (see page 187)

It doesn't matter who you see at the Fillmore, you are bound to have a good time reveling in the historical venue. Spend some time looking at the walls of photos showcasing past performers, and don't forget your free poster on the way out.

Mundane Journeys (see page 22)

Whenever you're looking for something interesting to do, call the Mundane Journeys hotline to find the biggest bougainvillea bush, a secret alleyway, or the best collection of Spanish fans. You never know where you'll be directed.

Palace of the Legion of Honor (see page 131)

My favorite museum sits high atop San Francisco, gazing down at its kingdom like royalty. Respect the classics, sketch Rodin sculptures, listen to the free organ concerts reverberate through the halls, and catch the latest modern art show in the basement. Don't forget to stop for an organic lunch and a quiet sit in the sculpture garden before you leave.

Land's End Park (see page 60)

Right below the Legion of Honor is the beginning of the end, Land's End, that is. Hike through wildflowers, brush, and eucalyptus toward the cliffs near the Golden Gate Bridge.

Delfina (see page 180)

I use the code word "home" for Delfina because I am so comforted by everything about it. Make your reservation early so you can be sure to enjoy the excellent Northern Italian-inspired food served by the sweet and smart staff.

Up Early

Early bird specials and morning treats

It is much easier to get up and get out knowing there are fantastic omelets, crêpes, and all manner of breakfast fare at the end of the proverbial rainbow. Whether you have to be dragged from your bed, or are the one with that annoying extra morning gusto, follow your nose on a whim and enjoy the early hours of the day. Start the day with simplicity or extravagance. I like taking it easy, stepping back for a moment from all our electronic systems and letting my feet go for a stroll. Our research-assistant poodle has helped us find some great morning walks that end with the best breakfasts in town.

Wave Organ

At the end of Yacht Road, past Golden Gate Yacht Club in Golden Gate Recreation Area
www.exploratorium.edu/visit/wave_organ

Here's one good reason to get up early, way early, that is. At 5:30am, the tide best maximizes the sounds of Pete Richard and George Gonzales' Wave Organ. Caffeine up and bring a coat, and you'll get an earful of the most incredible wave vibrations. Put your ear to the multitonal tubes, then take turns sitting in the wave booth, where tubes direct wave sounds from three angles. Before the city awakens, you can catch the natural sounds in a beautiful environment. *SB*

$$ Zazie

941 Cole St
564.5332
www.zaziesf.com
Mon–Fri 8a–2:30p and 5:30–9:30p, Sat–Sun 9a–10p

Take a tour of France from a sunny window seat in the family 'hood of Cole Valley. Sandwiched between the social buzz of Haight and the towering perch of Twin Peaks, Zazie has an air all its own. Cote Ouest is Julia Child–style scrambled eggs doused with fragrant ratatouille and perfectly roasted garlic cloves and potatoes. Order a smooth latte served in a provincial clay bowl with heaps of frothy foam. The breakfast menu is an ideal way to start the day, and one of my very first San Francisco discoveries when my aunt and uncle stowed me away for a weekend. Locals pour out the door on weekends, but it's well worth the wait, especially when it is nice out and you get your requested table in the backyard garden. *SB*

Mabel's Just For You Café

 732 22nd St
647.3033
www.justforyoucafe.com
Mon–Thurs 7:30a–3p, Wed–Fri 7:30a–9p, Sat–Sun 8a–3p

I used to go to Just For You when it was located on Potrero Hill and had half a dozen counter seats plus one three-top table. Thank the heavens that owner and New Orleans native Arienne Landry realized her southern-style breakfasts deserved some more space. Now housed in the up-and-coming Dogpatch neighborhood, Just For You serves up beignets (that's right, beignets), scrumptious omelets, crab cake benedicts, all sorts of pancakes (cornmeal, oatmeal, buttermilk), and the best corn bread this side of the Mississippi. Service is friendly and attentive, and the hilarious signs that post the rules, such as no kissing and no cell phones, always help pass the time when there is a wait. *JA*

Flower Market

548 Fifth St
371.1495
www.sfflmart.com
Mon, Wed, Fri 2–11a, Tues and Thurs 7–10a

There are times I wish I had a wholesale pass so I could buy up massive armloads of flowers at this lush marketplace. Piles of tuberoses, orchids, roses, and mums are just a few of the highlights in this huge paradise of plants. Some of the vendors will sell you single flowers or bunches, but this place is more for looking and taking photos than purchasing, unless your friend owns a local restaurant or business that warrants your flower-picking and purchasing expertise. I am an ikebana freak—I have a whole shelf of "frogs," or *kenzan* in Japanese—so I'm always on the prowl for clippings of odd lengths I can use for my creations. *SB*

Bakar Fitness & Recreation Center

 1675 Owens St
514.4545
http://mbfitness.ucsf.edu
Membership or $10–$15 drop-in fee

This state-of-the-art facility, with its brightly painted interior, features all amenities to get in shape. There are indoor and outdoor pools, a yoga room, climbing wall, weight room, squash and racquetball courts, and cardio machines equipped with LCD screens. I like to do an early-morning set in the outdoor pool, followed by some weight training, and if I'm feeling a bit impulsive, a massage treatment. DL

Aquatic Park
End of Hyde Street

One of my first cassette tapes was an Avon oldies mix. After *Up Up and Away* came *Under the Boardwalk*, which soon became worn out after I rewound it hundreds of times. San Francisco's dock doesn't have space underneath it to roll around with your sweetie, but it'll get you one of the best views of the Golden Gate and beyond. This is no Atlantic City, but a well-used dock where fishermen cast their nets and paint chips coat the short walk to the end of the municipal pier. During sunrise there's almost no one there, and of course sunset is another prime time for an Aquatic Park walk. SB

House of Bagels
5030 Geary Blvd
752.6000
www.houseofbagels.com
Daily 6a–6p

I'm on the West Coast, looking for a bagel and schmear. I'm looking, looking, still looking, until I visit my ski partner, who lives off Geary at Stanyan. At 6am, the Tahoe slopes beckon us and we roll out of bed and into the car. Around the corner she makes a stop, but an important one, and my search comes to an end. When she exits, the door behind shrouds her in early-morning steam from the hot ovens. In her hand are poppy seed, onion, and pumpernickel bagels, with a side of schmear. When you're on a bagel mission, look for the mural on Geary and your prayers will be answered. SB

$$ Mama's
1701 Stockton St
362.6421
www.mamas-sf.com
Tues–Sun 8a–3p

This is one of the city's favorite places to eat breakfast, which has its pros and cons. You know you'll love the grub and the people watching, plus Washington Square is right out front, ready to welcome post-eaters for a quick dog walk or a shady lawn laze under the shadow of the cathedral where Marilyn Monroe married. But if you are super hungry, you'll be impatiently waiting—even on weekday mornings there are enough artists, students, and tourists to pack it in. One order of French toast or the famous Monte Cristo should set you right again, but I always fend off the frustration by talking to strangers, looking at the living fashion show before me, and envisioning my day while I pace, in wait for my crab-filled omelet. *SB*

Brenda's French Soul Food

652 Polk St
345.8100
www.frenchsoulfood.com
Mon, Wed–Sun 8a–3p

If you've got at least these two syndromes, being a foodie and being a morning person, then Brenda's will satisfy. Pumpkin pancakes, watermelon ice tea, omelets stuffed with goat cheese and crawfish, and beignets in every flavor—each order is served hot with a slice of the neighborhood. In fact, if you need space in the a.m., I recommend paying your friends (in beignets, of course) to sneak into this tiny place for you and bring out the goods so you don't get a fit of claustrophobia. I like eating alone here, with a steaming bowl of the best grits in the city and a hearty mug of chickory coffee. Bring a book or a beau and you are set. *SB*

Kate's Kitchen

471 Haight St
626.3984
Mon 9a–2:45p, Tues–Fri 8a–3p, Sat–Sun 9a–4p

Lured out of their cozy lofts and shared Victorians for a morning feast, neighborhood regulars almost always take the red-and-white checkered tables. Nothing on the menu heads much above the $10 mark, even a stack of four bacon and cheddar buttermilk pancakes. Order your avocado omelet with a bowl of fresh fruit rather than the usual greasy potatoes, or opt for a homemade biscuit. French toast, served several ways depending on the day, is a consummate favorite for even the carb-haters. Even in my sleepy state I can find the black-and-white banner welcoming me and my honey; we know we'll rub shoulders with someone we know or used to know from our days romping the Lower Haight as students. *SB*

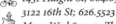 Pork Store Café

1451 Haight St; 864.6981
3122 16th St; 626.5523
Mon–Wed 8a–4p, Thurs–Fri 7a–4p, Sat–Sun 8a–4p

Once I make a decision from the seemingly unending pages of Pork Store's menu, I usually settle upon the simple Mike's Breakfast, my very first encounter with a tasty egg-white omelet. The lentil soups, made each day in a slightly different fashion with varying lentil colors and vegetable additions, will warm anyone through—a bowl is the best way I know to restore life to a wilted post-partier, or ramp up for a day of serious exploration. Grits are great (and only $1.50), cheesy omelets can be served with French toast or pancakes without having to nag the waitress, and the general sense of rejuvenation is felt throughout this early-bird cornerstone. *SB*

Bernal Hill

The big, grassy expanse rising from the far end of the Mission isn't just a patch of weed-covered soil. It is a migration stop for many birds, and one of the best early-morning walks in the city. Clamber up the hillside to check out one of the city's best views and a network of narrow dirt trails, which any four-footed friend will celebrate with you. Start at Precita Avenue and Folsom Street, heading past the Precita Park murals toward the hill. Up and over and you'll be firmly planted in the Bernal Heights neighborhood, where Good Life Grocery (448 Cortland St) serves ideal post-hike bevies. *SB*

Dottie's True Blue Café

522 Jones St
885.2767
Wed–Mon 7:30a–3p

Balance a slew of tourists against the intense flavors here and you'll still want to snag a spot just to savor the stuff. If you are a grumpy riser, you might have to exercise extra patience, but once you're in and served, the blueberry pancakes, corn bread with jalapeño jelly, and scrumptious egg variations will win you over. Take in the scene—this place is a whisper away from Union Square—and calm yourself; the breakfast goodies here are worth your while. SB

$$ Q Restaurant

225 Clement St
752.2298
www.qrestaurant.com
Mon–Fri 11a–3p, 5–11p, Sat 10a–11p, Sun 10a–10p

Finally, a brunch place that fulfills my desire for *moules frites*! OK, so Q is open for dinner, too, but the brunch, oh the brunch. Benedict with sustainable Loch Dart salmon, omelets with red onion marmalade and blue cheese, house-made granola in a huge bowl dazzled with creamy yogurt, and fresh fruit and jam . . . It isn't enough to list off my favorites, you simply have to trek over to Clement and discover this little gem for yourself. Remember too, that brunch is a morning meal where it is acceptable to order dessert, and I suggest indulgence in the grilled banana or the prize-winning chocolate chip cookies. It is easy to feel at home here, and yet the atmosphere makes you feel a little more popular, a little more special, as if to say congrats for finding Q. SB

$$ Chloe's Café

1399 Church St
648.4116
Mon–Fri 8a–3p, Sat–Sun 8a–3:30p

It is amazing that after all the French toast I've sampled across this breakfasty city I am still impressed with a newcomer. Chloe has wowed me despite my prominence as a discerning French-toast eater. Croissants are the toast used, and after being positively blessed in a bath of vanilla, whipped eggs, whole milk, and cinnamon, their distinction comes clear. Hit up Chloe's and give yourself the chance to taste something that makes you feel devilish just to think about eating. SB

$$ Toast Eatery

1748 Church St
282.4328
www.toasteatery.com
Mon–Fri 7a–9p, Sat–Sun 7a–5p

Ingredients are selected like a rich lady choosing a breed of dog for the all-star breakfasts at clean-cut Toast Eatery. Tofu scrambles are never dull, God-father omelets with spicy Italian sausage are a hit with my meat-loving honey, and Coco Loco pancakes, covered with shaved coconut and banana slices, are supremely island-licious. Fresh-squeezed orange juice is mandatory. SB

Coffee Time

Coffee beans: ground, pressed, steeped, and served

Speaking as a true coffee lover, but only a part-time coffee drinker, I can say that when I choose to have a cup, I like a good one. And San Francisco is populated with roasters as obsessed as I am with quality java. All locally owned and very much entrenched in the community, these stops are frequented by a cross section of local people who are in the know about the importance of fair trade and organic brews. Find coffee, tea, and snacks at these admirable cafés, and avoid the chains at all cost. Even an organic cup at a chain versus a regular cup at a locally owned coffee shop has a much more positive effect on the community in the long run. Each of these spots have their own vibe, like an indicator of what the spirit of the surrounding neighborhood is really like. Whether you're on a strict diet of at least two cups a day, or you like to come and go with morning bevies like I do, there's something for everyone at San Francisco's coffee Meccas.

 ## Blue Bottle Coffee

 315 Linden St

653.3394

www.bluebottlecoffee.net

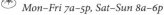 *Mon–Fri 7a–5p, Sat–Sun 8a–6p*

Few people who have tasted a cup of Blue Bottle Coffee can ever look at ordinary coffee the same way again. Blue Bottle uses a single-drip process for each divine cup, and uses only certified organic coffees roasted in small batches. While this takes a little extra time, it's worth the wait. The result is a deep, rich and flavorful brew. Since the operation is just a counter, you have the perfect excuse to take your cup on a stroll around the shops of Hayes Valley. JA

✎ People's Café

1419 Haight St

553.8842

Daily 7a, closing time varies

Take a break from your shopping frenzy on Haight and duck into People's for a chance to breathe and relax before tackling the next several blocks of retail therapy. There is a case of baked treats and café standards, like lemon poppy-seed muffins and toasted bagels to go with fair trade coffee and an altogether feel-good vibe. *SB*

🚲 Mission Beach Café

198 Guerrero St

861.0198

Daily 6a–9:30p

Pie for breakfast? It's not just for dessert anymore at the Mission Beach Café, which serves mind-altering slices of buttery goodness and steaming cups of Blue Bottle java (see page 38) from 6am on. The pastry chef/owner has honed the art of crust making so that even the salads—like the blackberry-dressed

Caesar—can be found in one of his perfectly engineered tarts. And while this turns the idea of salad with a side of bread on its head, the pairing is surprisingly delicious. If you're dining for lunch or dinner, opt for a savory treat like the rabbit pie or the grass-fed beef burger—both dishes are excellent and generous enough to share. Splitting a plate may be a good idea, because you'll definitely want to save room for strawberry rhubarb pie. *MP*

$ Café La Taza

2475 Mission St; 824.7717
470 Polk St; 392.2030
www.cafelataza.com
Mon–Fri 6a–7p, Sat 6:30a–7p, Sun 7a–4p

This is a great place to go for a strong cup of joe and a reasonably priced meal. It's also one of the few places left in the Bay Area where you can get breakfast—which is served all day—for less than $5. The portions are generous—every entrée comes with a side—and nothing on the menu, including a steak dinner, costs more than $10. Dishes range from traditional Mexican fare like the signature tortilla soup to American favorites like the tangy barbecue pulled-pork panini. Bagels, croissants, and lots of other fresh-baked café staples can also be found. The house coffee, a free-trade blend of eye-opening roast, can be purchased in bulk, so you can take a taste of the café home. *MP*

$$ Velo Rouge Café

798 Arguello Blvd
752.7799
www.velorougecafe.com
Mon–Tues 6:30a–3p, Wed–Fri 6:30a–10p, Sat–Sun 8a–5p

Cornerstone of the Lone Mountain neighborhood, Velo Rouge is one comfortable cup of coffee. Meet with neighbors ready to talk about their travels abroad over steel-cut oatmeal or a classic egg and croissant sandwich. But coffee time doesn't need to end after breakfast; come in on Thursday and Friday evenings for live music and family-style dining brought in from Radio Africa, an all-organic, nutritionally balanced kitchen. *SB*

Trouble Coffee

4033 Judah St

690.9119

Mon, Wed–Sat 7a–7p, Sun 8a–4p

There are plenty of spots around San Francisco for a good espresso, but in my opinion this place tops them all. The only exception I can think of is an after-dinner espresso at swank Jardiniere. One thing is for sure: espresso is better when it is drunk in an exciting atmosphere. Trouble Coffee is the polar opposite of Jardiniere, but being one who appreciates a multitude of ambiance, I adore this funky fresh coffee joint that surely knows its stuff when it comes to java. The beans are always fairly traded, roasted on equipment made by the tattooed and eccentric baristas, and served a supremely ideal one week after roasting. Rich and dark, there's no excuses—just full flavor, and the wacky styles present here make it more fun. Forget posh, let's focus on the beans! *SB*

Ritual Coffee Roasters

1026 Valencia St

641.1024

www.ritualroasters.com

Mon–Fri 6a–11p, Sat 7a–11p, Sun 9a–10p

On the hipster scene it is important to decipher the many shades of the style. There are single-gear hipsters, always seen wearing slim jeans in tow; the all-out DIYers, with makeshift outfits and a larger percentage of piercings; then there are the clean hipsters, who prescribe more to the fashion of the hipsters and not as much the mentality. At the risk of putting people in boxes, I will say that this supposedly hipster coffee shop, sandwiched between the vintage denizens of Valencia Street, is more chic than it should be. Fancy-pants coffee makes it worth the trip, and the smell of beans roasting over the din of Mac keyboards tapping away gives it a studious glow. Just don't expect to see as many tried-and-true hipsters, their politics and their fashion-forward factoids on their sleeve. Although the crowd may have grown up a bit since the place opened years ago, the coffee is still some of the absolute best in the city. *SB*

Coffee Bar

1890 Bryant St

551.8100

Mon–Sat 7a–10p, Sun 7a–7p

Send in the troops, I might be lost between these concrete walls and need a search party to drag me out. I am awed by the majesty of the coffee here, and come late afternoon and early evening, there's a mélange of good wines by the glass to keep me in my seat. One of the family members behind the famous Mr. Espresso brand and his two extraordinary buddies opened Coffee Bar so they could strut their knowledge on all things coffee and have a stomping ground to invite us in on the secrets. Espresso is usually made from a blend of beans for an extra rich texture and discernable honey flavor (especially in their Neapolitan version). If you are there for a single variety, expect that the competent men behind the counter will stop the shot early so it doesn't get thin or too light in color. This is the place to finish writing or reading a novel—I bring my woolly full-length sweater and hover over a private table until I am discovered. *SB*

Café Algiers

 50 Beale St, #102
512.8681
Mon–Thurs 5:45a–5p, Fri 5:45a–1p, 2:30–6p

Next door to a Starbucks and easily missable if you aren't hot on the trail of the holy grail in cappuccinos, lattes, and espressos, Café Algiers is nothing short of amazing when it comes to coffee perfection. I chatted with the man behind the bar on my last trip, while sniffing the fresh falafels being cooked in back. Zino is a wily coffee know-it-all who takes his job seriously, creating the thickest espressos and the frothiest foam in San Francisco. The family is fun too—as long as you don't show up when they are getting ready to leave after a long day (they sometimes close early). If you want to skip the Americanized versions of latte art, then ask for some magical pattern here. After all, the Mediterranean was the original place to beautify this all-important drink. *SB*

Four Barrel Coffee

 375 Valencia St
252.0800
Daily 7a–8p

After all my trips and trials in Portland and Seattle, I am ecstatic I can share a cup of caffeine-crazy Hair Bender with my coffee addict mother after mouthing off for so long but not wanting to weigh down my luggage with roasted beans. One of the owners of Ritual Roasters sprung from that ever-growing crowd pleaser to get back to something more basic. Soon they'll roast their own beans, but I am hoping they'll keep Stumptown on the menu for a bit of schmaltz. On shopping missions along Valencia, I chat at the sidewalk counter with an espresso, or have them pop my roast on ice à la Americana, and find a spot under one of the vintage animal heads hanging in the hall. At least this is one coffee stop where I am not swamped by the masses of iPod-iLife-iMac machines and can drink my coffee old school-style with the pages of a book or gab with my mother. *SB*

The Organic Coffee Company

88 Fourth St

512.7436

www.sanfranciscoorganiccoffeecompany.com/organic

Mon–Fri 6a–9p, Sat 6a–9:30p, Sun 6a–6p

It is hard to believe that the most do-gooder cup of joe in town is under the same brand (Rogers Family) as San Francisco Bay Coffee Company, the least do-gooder, but it is true. Rogers Family is the Mack truck of coffee purveyors around town—giving little consideration to recycling, energy efficiency, or fair trade beans in their major operations, but not so at their lovely Organic Coffee Company location. The social and environmental causes add up at this coffee shack, and no bean served here is from an unnamed farm in an unnamed country. I appreciate that the staff is a mix of local caffeine heads and also those new to the workforce who consistently serve yummy sammies alongside tasty coffee drinks. Grab a spot at one of the spacious wooden tables and you'll be primed for some of the best new-age people watching in the city. *SB*

Hang Out

All the best chill-out spots, from a cozy reading nook to a relaxed microbrew with your buddies

Sometimes the best way to get a sense of a place is to slow down and stop attempting to see everything and do everything. Try a pub quiz or a laid-back concert, or pop into one of SF's independent cinema houses and give new meaning to loitering. San Francisco is fast and slow at the same time, so it is very possible to chill out after getting wrapped up in the big-city rush. Bring friends or venture out alone for a moment off the treadmill of daily life.

Washington Square and Cathedral

Union Street and Powell Street
http://parks.sfgov.org
Daily, dawn to dusk

Saints Peter and Paul Church, with its twin towers, looms over this green oasis as patrons stroll around the walkways, spread out on the sunny field, and converse in Italian on the many park benches. Located at the center of the North Beach district and surrounded by cafés, Washington Square has the feel of a town square and hosts countless community events. A late-afternoon walk through the square as the sun slowly sets, followed by an early-evening dine at one of the many nearby Italian restaurants is a perfect way to end a day in North Beach. After all, this is the spot where Marilyn Monroe chose to be married. DL

$$ The Buena Vista

2765 Hyde St
474.5044
www.thebuenavista.com
Mon–Fri 9a–2a, Sat–Sun 8a–2a

On the edge of the typical weekend bustle at Fisherman's Wharf is Buena Vista, the not-so-secret place to find San Francisco's best Irish coffee. Order a one-lumper so you don't get lopped with the tourists in overly sweet coffee land (they put several sugar cubes in your drink if you just order Irish coffee). Wind through the former residence for the best seats in the room, past the turnoff for the restroom. You'll find a big table by a window away from the hubbub. SB

$ Brainwash Café

1122 Folsom St
431.9274
www.brainwash.com
Daily 7a–11p

I used to dread that day during the week when my clothes surpassed a balanced clean-to-dirty ratio. Dragging my laundry on the trolley down Hyde Street, I'd get no thrills from twiddling my thumbs while my duds sudsed and tumbled. Then my friend proclaimed dual laundry day, where we could make the trek together to the place "I just had to go." Brainwash is fun laundry. Once I was downing my second pint while transferring whites

to the industrial dryer when lo and behold, I heard a familiar voice piping up in the other room. My cousin Raina Rose was playing on the small stage by the bar! Whether I have a load of laundry on my hands or just a hankering for a good beer and some local music, Brainwash is my rainy day turned sunny. *SB*

$ Arinell Pizza

509 Valencia St
255.1303
Mon–Wed 11:30a–10p, Thurs–Sat 11:30a–12a, Sun 1:30–10p

After moving to SF from the East Coast, I spent a good year searching for the perfect slice of New York–style pizza. I had just about given up when Arinell found its way into my life. Each heavenly disc is composed of a dough that is tender and crisp, topped with just the right amount of simple sauce and shredded mozzarella. Pizza is the only thing they do, and they do it right. *JA*

Buena Vista Park

Haight Street and Buena Vista East

Every Sunday, Buena Vista Park gets taken over by small dogs. The dachshund and pug clubs of SF make regular gatherings here, so their puppies can have some fair play rather than contend with the big guys. All small breeds are welcome, and even if you don't have a pup it is a great way to spend a Sunday—for free! *SB*

Ti Couz

3108 16th St

252.7373

Mon and Fri 11a–11p, Tues and Thurs 5–10p, Sat–Sun 10a–11p

Serving organic salads and clever crêpes, this restaurant is as much a scene as it is an eatery. Ham it up with your buddies over an egg crêpe (say *"oeuf"*), or a more sophisticated coquilles—scallops seared in parsley butter with fish broth reduction. If you're not in a crêpe mood, opt for the *salad de maree* with scallops, grilled tuna, rice, egg, olives, and capers, which comes with bread and herbed butter you'll want to eat until kingdom come. There's a long list of sweet crêpes to boot, but there's only one in my mind: the honey lemon crêpe, which brings out all the happiness I've been stowing somewhere hidden until I take a bite. Drinks are a must, and get there before it gets dark so you can snag an outdoor or window seat and have your eyes on this epic block of the Mission. *SB*

Lovejoy's Tea Room

1351 Church St

648.5895

www.lovejoystearoom.com

Wed–Sun 11a–6p

Put on your Sunday best, or simply a pair of jeans, and ready your senses for a pot of tea and traditional high tea fare. Lovejoy's is a traditional tearoom tucked into a corner in Noe Valley. Patrons sit on deep couches and upholstered chairs among antique tea items while they sip 'n' snack from mismatched bone china. Food options come in "packages," like the high tea that includes two tea sandwiches of your choice, served properly with crusts cut off and sliced into little triangles, spring greens, a dreamy homemade scone served with preserves and luscious double Devon cream, and a shortbread tea biscuit. Make a reservation before heading out and you'll get the added bonus of arriving at your table to a sign reading "Reserved for Royalty." What's not to love? *JA*

Edinburgh Castle

950 Geary St
885.4074
www.castlenews.com
Daily 5p–2a, Quizzy: Tues 8:30p

The Castle is heading a revolution to bring out the next generation of underground writers. That, plus it's one of the most wonderful pubs in SF. Oh, and they host the best quiz night this side of the pond. And I forgot to mention their weekly film nights for those of us who enjoy a pint with our cinema. But wait, I know I am forgetting something . . . Oh yes, Salty Walt, the maritime musicians who liven things up over fish-and-chips once a month. Arrr! So, whatever your reason, if you head to one dingy pub while bouncing around Frisco, make that stop count at the Castle. *SB*

Dolores Park

18th and Dolores streets
www.nps.org/dopa

Dolores Park is by far the sunniest spot in San Francisco. It's perfectly situated in the cradle of the Mission, Noe Valley, and the Castro. And it's the place to be with friends on any day of the week—a proverbial (and literal) playground for families, dog owners, hippies, yuppies, queers, and everyone in between. There are tennis and basketball courts that have lights on into the night; all you have to do is search Craigslist for a tennis partner. Every weekend there's some large gathering going on, whether it be the free-trade fair, symphony in the park, a trans march, or sunbathers. Bring a picnic and some beer and enjoy the closest thing to warm summer weather as you get here. *JA*

Feel Real Organic Café

4001 Judah St
504.7325
Tues–Fri 11a–3p and 5–9p, Sat–Sun 9a–3p and 5–9p

There's nothing like the feeling you get when preparing a unique and delicious meal made from vegetables and herbs in your own garden. After watering my garden each morning, I assess the bounty: a zucchini here, a tomato there, a sprig of rosemary or thyme . . . Feel Real re-creates the experience of serving up a truly homemade meal without the preparation. Vegan delights fill the menu, such as the steamed greens over potato hash, but the Homegrown veggie burger is especially enticing and comes with almost anything. Feel Real is the perfect place to shed the anxiety of living in the fast lane, so bring that novel or knitting project you've been putting aside and relax as your meal is carefully prepared. DL

Charlie's Deli Café

3202 Folsom St
641.5051
Daily 7a–10p

Even though I don't hail from the neighborhood, this locals-only spot has greeted me with open arms. Nadim is as friendly as any coffee shop owner could be, and together with generous Charlie, who opens the space for fund-raisers and art openings at the request of regulars, the duo is really what makes Charlie's a mandatory hang spot in this city. All the beans are fairly traded, the art on the walls is always fresh, and the lox slices are thick and plentiful—just how my East Coast soul needs them to be. SB

Baker Beach

Lincoln Boulevard and Bowley Street
www.nps.gov/archive/prsf/places/bakerbch.htm
Daily, dawn to dusk

Because of its exposure, this beach is not well suited for swimming, but when the weather is nice the beach is packed with kite fliers and sunbathers. Watch the tides crisscross and wash ashore as you explore the old barracks off the beach. This is also considered the main nude beach of San Francisco, but I rarely find it overtaken by nudists. When the weather turns windy, gray, and cold, many still go to take in the sunset and amazing views of the Golden Gate Bridge. There is also a cypress grove with picnic tables and grills, so bring the whole gang. JA

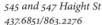

Rosamunde Sausage Grill and The Toronado Pub

545 and 547 Haight St
437.6851/863.2276
www.toronado.com
Rosamunde: daily 11:30a–10p, Toronado: daily 11:30a–2a

Seldom does one find a relationship as symbiotic as the one between Rosamunde and the Toronado. After all, what, aside from chocolate and peanut butter, goes together better than sausages and beer? Although Rosamunde has only a few seats, the best plan of attack is as follows: Order one (or more) of their beautifully crafted sausages, such as spicy lamb and beef-stuffed merguez, the refined duck and fig sausage, or an incredible version of the spicy Italian. There is even an organic vegan sausage for meat-free folks. Once you've ordered, head next door to the Toronado to choose from more than a hundred beers. This is no easy task as the Toronado offers premium selections that hail from near (several from within 100 miles) and far (Belgium is represented quite nicely), and offers both draught and bottle options. By the time you've made your choice, you can trot on back to Rosamunde to grab your sausage. You'll be given the choice of two free toppings on your dog: sauerkraut, hot or sweet peppers, grilled onions, or spicy beef chili. Before you depart, slather on some condiments—Rosamunde offers options like a prickly wasabi mustard and curry ketchup. Once you've created the perfect combo, saunter back into the Toronado to enjoy it. The bar allows food from Rosamunde to be brought in, sagely knowing that a well-crafted sausage deserves a well-crafted beer. Repeat the cycle at will. *JA*

The District

216 Townsend St
896.2120
www.districtsf.com
Mon–Fri 4p–close, Sat 5p–close

Baseball used to go with a stadium frank and a freezy lemon water ice. Now I dress up weekend afternoon games with a sip of wine at the District on nearby Townsend Street. They pour more than 30 wines by the glass, and serve house-brined olives like the Greek gods used to munch on. If you are hungry, because you didn't down enough stadium dogs previously, order mussels with cream and sausage or roasted tomatoes and calamari with aioli. This ultra-ritzy lounge takes baseball fare to new heights. *SB*

Tadich Grill

240 California St

391.1849

Mon–Fri 11a–9:30p, Sat 11:30a–9:30p

Ever since I traveled in London's tube during rush hour, I got in the habit of finding places to hang out while a flood of men in ties swayed back and forth to the movement of the train. Although this isn't a train, it satisfies my desire to see a rainbow of ties while I savor local oysters or a beef brisket luncheon. Tadich Grill is the choice of the lawyers and businessmen in San Francisco's financial district, and has been for more than one hundred years. Hearty lunches are served in booths and at the marble counter, where I like to sit with an ice tea and read while taking in the atmosphere. *SB*

$$ Presidio Bowl

93 Presidio Blvd

561.2695

Sun–Thurs 9a–12a, Fri–Sat 9a–2a

Stringy mozzarella sticks, heaping burgers, and more hot dog choices than I care to mention, Presidio Bowl is the most fun you'll have bowling, especially if you take advantage of the huge selection of bottled beers behind the bar. Take a seat, don your dorky lace-up shoes, and go for a strike! *SB*

Samovar Tea Lounge

498 Sanchez St

626.4700

www.samovartea.com

Daily 10a–10p

After gazing at inspiring art all afternoon, even the most cynical of us will want to calm our minds in new-age fashion, and there's no better place for that than Samovar. This neutral-colored, peaceful-spirited tea lounge is where I turn over my understanding of tea to the waiter, who will tell me what is fresh and prepare it like it is done where the tea itself is grown. Simple vegan fare is served alongside; the Moorish Platter with veggie kebabs and the Egg Bowl with grilled duck are your best bets. Last trip, my mother and I met a young Spanish musician and have been going to hear his performances ever since. You never know who you'll find sitting on the cushions next to you. *SB*

Bookish

Reading retreats in every flavor

Technology can come and go, but as far as I'm concerned, the beauty of a bound book will never fade. Not only a comical, moving, challenging, or inspiring experience, a volume of words impacts every aspect of life, from early learning to individual solace. I think about where I've been with a good book—in a new city, at a favorite café, sitting in my grandfather's rocking chair, on the top of Mount Whistler giving my legs a little break from the steep slopes. Search for a book, and watch as it, in turn, takes you on a journey. Make your own book, share the experience of reading, take your books on your world travels. San Francisco is home to a great many writers and readers, showcased at the popular annual event LitQuake (see page 256), and is known for several major literary movements. Create your own tales and get to the business of reading in the many nooks around town. My favorite spots for reading are under the shadow of the cathedral at Washington Square, at the park across from Grace Cathedral, and at Trouble Coffee or one of the other great coffee shops around town. Find your own spots after gleaning a new title from one of these San Francisco bookstores.

Omnivore Books on Food

3885A Cesar Chavez St
282.4712
www.omnivorebooks.com
Tues–Sat 11a–6p, Sun 12–5p

The newest addition to San Francisco's lit scene is focused more on the foodies in town, not the bookish types. Find every kind of cookbook—Escoffier and Bastinaich are both well represented—but also books about, and inspired by, food. If you enter with questions about the distinctions between eating local, eating seasonal, and eating organic, you won't be confused after a perusal around these shelves. Eat up this plethora of pages suited for any one of the many cuisine persuasions. If you dream of a first edition of *Mastering the Art of French Cooking*, or the first book to identify San Francisco's now-famous food scene, *Bohemian San Francisco: Its Restaurants and Their Most Famous*

Recipes—The Elegant Art of Dining, from 1914, amazingly, you can find these antiquarian titles here. *SB*

The Booksmith

1644 Haight St
863.8688
www.booksmith.com
Mon–Sat 10a–10p, Sun 10a–8p

An impressive collection and a knowledgeable staff of dedicated book buffs distinguish this store from run-of-the-mill chains; yet it lacks the chaos that typically characterizes independent booksellers. *SF Weekly* once named Booksmith the best store for new books in the city, and *Time* magazine noted them as the best independent bookstore to shop online. Don't be surprised if your sales rep is armed with a master's degree and literary knowledge that would put your high school English teacher to shame. Booksmith is probably the smartest bookstore around. A calendar full of events includes several book signings a week with noted authors and the occasional celebrity or politician. Signed books are among the store's specialties and can also be purchased online. *MP*

San Francisco Center for the Book

300 De Haro St
565.0545
www.sfcb.org
Daily 10a–5p, plus various workshop hours

Books, books, and more books. But what is a book? This wonderful hands-on learning and exhibit space brings many forms of "books" into consideration. Structure a unique design, build a book like you would a house, or learn how to print one with their Steamroller press. Whether traditional or experimental, Center for the Book brings back the art and craft of fine bookmaking for those who appreciate the written word. *SB*

Aardvark Books

227 Church St
552.6733
Tues–Sun 11a–7p

A paradise of used books awaits your discovery at Aardvark, right across from everyone's favorite diner, Sparky's. We've found some of our best cookbooks, a poodle grooming book for our beloved research assistant poodle Dutsi Bap, and some philosophy to read on long Muni bus rides. *sb*

Alexander Book Co.

50 Second St
495.2992
www.alexanderbook.booksense.com
Mon–Fri 9a–6p

Taking after Powell's in Portland, Alexander Book Co. has expanded its independent business to online sales, but these guys plant a tree for each order you place through their web site! Three floors stocked with more than fifty thousand new books—including extensive African-American, children's, and graphic design departments—are waiting to be explored. So grab that new best-seller or diamond in the rough and be satisfied knowing that 45 percent of your money spent here (as opposed to 13 percent at the nearest chain) will go back into the community. *DL*

Book Passage

1 Ferry Building
835.1020
www.bookpassage.com
Mon–Fri 9a–7p, Sat 8a–7p, Sun 9a–7p

Another Ferry Building asset, Book Passage's second location has an ideal selection of travel books, food and recipe volumes, and local fiction and poetry. The knowledgeable staff members are my favorite book people in town. After a ferry ride, or a gourmet taco at Mijita across the hall, few things top a conversation with one of Book Passage's worker bees on the upcoming titles and breakout authors. The original Corte Madera store is a well-spent afternoon with triple the books and author events almost every day of the year. It's also home to a most excellent annual travel-writers gathering! *sb*

Bibliohead Bookstore

334 Gough St
621.6772
www.bibliohead.com
Sun–Tues 12–8p, Wed–Sat 11a–9p

When I was a kid my closet was like a world in itself and I could disappear inside for what seemed like hours. A small window was the perfect vantage from which to spy on unsuspecting visitors to our front porch, and a shelf covered the entire wall with books. Stepping into Bibliohead conjured up memories of my childhood hideaway—cozy and lined wall to wall and floor to ceiling with new, used, rare, and even oddball books. *DL*

McDonald's Book Shop

48 Turk St
673.2235
Daily 10a–7p

Despite the dingy façade and the neighborhood that's far from posh, this well-stocked bookstore has an incredible selection and even more incredible prices. Head to the comic section for a historical journey down superhero lane, or to the foreign language area for novels in French, Chinese, Spanish, Thai—the list goes on . . . The complete collection of *Life* and *National Geographic* magazines are perfect for school projects or collages, whatever your fancy. Make a point to include this shop in your San Francisco tour; it is quite possibly the oldest bookstore in the city, and a world of discovery no matter what your interest. *SB*

Get Lost Books

1825 Market St
437.0529
www.getlostbooks.com
Mon–Fri 10a–7p, Sat 10a–6p, Sun 11a–5p

Traveling is our passion. Wait, books are our passion. Get Lost combines our two favorites. Plan your trip by flipping the pages of this inclusive travel bookstore. *SB*

European Book Company

925 Larkin St
474.0626
www.europeanbook.com
Mon 11a–4p, Thurs–Sat 11a–5p

San Franciscans have a love affair with Europe. Some of us want to learn the languages, eat the food, and travel there, some want to live a European

lifestyle, others are the genuine article. Head to European Book for language tools, comic books, dictionaries, philosophies, and the most incredible selection of French and German magazines. I never go before an appointment 'cause I can never make this a short trip. The French fashion mags and German design mags draw me in, plus I am working on a French comic book collection—it is the most fun way to keep up with my studies! *SB*

City Lights Books

261 Columbus Ave
362.8193
www.citylights.com
Daily 10a–12a

The most famous bookstore in San Francisco was actually started as a small press for the San Francisco Renaissance and Beat poets (see page 57) to publish their writings. History is alive here, and the store continues to live up to its famous roots, hosting poets and writers often and keeping a local feel in the midst of touristy North Beach. Titles laid over large wooden tables urge you to pick up this one and that. Book snobs run the joint, in my view a good thing, so ask your questions and be prepared for the long answers. *SB*

Dog Eared Books

900 Valencia St
282.1901
www.dogearedbooks.com
Mon–Sat 10a–10p, Sun 10a–8p

The mother hen of three cross-city book dens, Dog Eared sells many books that are true to the name of the shop. Find new editions sprinkled among fanciful tales of intrigue. I always stop by the free bin in front of the door for a few new pieces for a collage. Don't be surprised if you find writers reading here; it is a popular spot, even in a string of Valencia Street bookstores, for the last remaining poor poets in the Mission. *SB*

 Different Light Bookstore

489 Castro St
431.0891
www.adlbooks.com
Sun–Thurs 10a–10p, Fri–Sat 10a–11p

Specializing in books on queer subjects by queer authors, this shop is everything I've ever asked for when it comes to celebrating the LGBT culture, something I've learned much more about since getting under the skin of this city. LGBT lit is much more than Ginsberg, trust me! *SB*

 Green Apple Books and Music

506 Clement St
387.2272
www.greenapplebooks.com
Mon–Thurs 10a–10:30p, Fri–Sat 10a–11:30p

Set aside your preconceived notions that all the best San Francisco bookstores are near Market or Mission. Tried-and-true music geeks and bibliophiles have sought solace on Clement Street for more than four decades. Picky booksellers chew through title after title, ensuring that only good reads make it to their shelves. They even exhaust the annals of publisher overstocks to give you great deals. Zooming through Green Apple is near impossible— you are sure to be stopped in your tracks by the next book that will change your life. After all, green apples are the best kind anyway. *SB*

Stacey's Books

581 Market St
421.4687
www.staceys.com
Mon–Fri 9:30a–7p, Sat 11a–6:30p

Geeks, dorks, nerds, and dweebs unite! I've found the spot for us! Stacey's has enough events to keep things socially buoyant, but enough nitty-gritty books to satisfy us knowledge mongers. Look through the medical book section and you'll see what I mean—the best medical illustrations and the newest scientific discoveries are at a fingertip's reach. Look for the little slices of paper wrapped around some books—that means they have been signed by the author! *SB*

Read the City

Any trip to San Francisco should include a little poetry, if not writing some yourself, then at least reading some. The San Francisco Renaissance involved many local writers—why not look one up and tote a nice thin book of poetry in your back pocket for coffee breaks and bus rides?

William Rexroth: Buddies with my faves William Carlos Williams and Ezra Pound, Rexroth's first collection, *In What Hour,* came out in 1940, the same year that the Renaissance really kicked off. This guy was a proactive poet, emceeing on KPFA Radio and organizing some of the most pivotal and famous salons and lit events in the city. A consummate pacifist, he also helped Japanese Americans escape encampment in one of this country's darkest moves to unjustly capture and imprison people based on race.

William Everson: Brother Antonius, as he was better known, wrote with the best of the California poets, adding his own peaceful slant and lending his more traditional spiritual views (and fuzzy beard) to a movement where most clung to Eastern beliefs. His time as a conscientious objector brought about the most important of his collections, *The Residual Years.*

Jack Spicer: This talented guy was one of the first to write beautiful poems about language itself, and had a slew of bookish jobs in every

corner of the country, including Berkeley and San Francisco. He always thought for himself, and his ideals came before anything else. The movement he was a part of gave him new life, and his poems gave the movement new life in return.

Robin Blaser: Lifelong friends with Jack Spicer and editor of Spicer's posthumous collected works, at 85-plus he is still writing and teaching in Vancouver, B.C., at Simon Fraser University. His writings on nature are an important part of American literature. *Harp Trees*, *Pell Mel,* and *Nomad* are all fantastic, and his latest, *The Holy Forest*, won the Griffin Poetry Prize.

Robert Duncan: Part of the Renaissance, he was also at the core of the Black Mountain Poets and the New American Poetry movement. He took many future great poets under his wing and taught at San Francisco State College. His just beliefs and incredible fearlessness in a pre-Stonewall era contributed to many young men being more free and able to come to terms with themselves and with the discrimination of gays. After the famous club in New York City gave more voice to the movement, people realized the importance of Duncan's essay "The Homosexual in Society."

Beat poets, which came a few years later, produced some of the more popular names: Allen Ginsberg, Gary Snyder, Philip Whalen, Michael McClure, and Philip Lamantia, all worth reading as long as you have a healthy sense of rule-breaking.

Get Active

Hikes, runs, rides, bikes, boats—anything and everything to get you moving

Whether you are simply getting from A to B, or seeking some good sweaty fun, getting active always has a refreshing result. I started on swim team at a young age and have been known to go through various ski bum phases now and again. I've also been challenged by Pilates and yoga, and bouldering walls and rocks, indoors and out. Whatever thrill level you're seeking, from kayaking the bay to jogging the Presidio, San Francisco is the kind of place that offers all manner of sport and non-sport ways to jam.

   ## Lombardi Sports

1600 Jackson St

771.0600

www.lombardisports.com

Mon–Wed 10a–7p, Thurs–Fri 10a–8p, Sat 10a–6p, Sun 11a–6p

Lombardi Sports is an adventure in and of itself. Nothing gets me more excited about an outdoor excursion than exploring this multilevel sports Mecca and consulting its knowledgeable staff. The store hosts informative and hands-on clinics to ensure that you are mentally and physically prepared to tackle the outdoors—whether on bike, board, or foot. Lombardi's sports-movie night (held every Thursday at 7pm) will get you psyched for your next bout. DL

Steps

Lyon and Green streets
16th Avenue and Moraga Street
Sansome Street at Montgomery and Greenwich streets
Various other locations: www.sisterbetty.org/stairways, www.tiledsteps.org

OK, so walking up and down the stairs of our house may not be my favorite thing, but taking the stairs is great for fitness and, in this city, it is easy and fun to make stepping up your passion. Look at Sister Betty's web site for a complete description of all the stairways. I like Filbert Steps and the tiled 16th Street Steps the most, both because of their design and their location. Lyon Steps are perhaps the most famous, flanked by formal gardens and fancy houses. Filbert Steps take you up above North Beach and Embarcadero via three terraced sections, planted gardens, and a flock of gaggling green parrots. Take the Greenwich Steps back down. Sixteenth Avenue's steps are mosaicked and wind up to a great little neighborhood. Look from the base of the steps to see a swirling mural of life and the solar system. *SB*

Seward Street Slides

Seward Street down to Douglas Street
Daily 9a–7p

The best part of the Seward Street Slides is the park signs that state: "All adults must be accompanied by children." But these long slides are fun for even the most cynical and hardened adults. This park is a hidden gem tucked away in the Castro. Make sure to wear jeans and bring some cardboard to sit on as these slides are made entirely of concrete. You are going to want to keep your hands in close or up in the air so that you don't hit or rub them on the concrete sides. If you can get enough speed going, you'll definitely get launched out of the bottom. Have fun! *JA*

Land's End Park

898 El Camino Del Mar, below Palace of the Legion of Honor

A sharp bend down the road from the Palace of the Legion of Honor is the entrance to Land's End, one of the most beautiful recreation areas in the country. With sharp cliff views, trails hedged by the fuchsia flowers of ice plants, and a network of trails leading to beaches and viewpoints, this is one walk to remember. It is a great spot to clear your head, get ready to make a decision, or grapple with life changes. The vastness of the natural beauty of the edge of our continent has a way of putting a perspective on things. Go alone or share the experience with a puppy, loved one, or family member. Bring jogging shoes if that would help you with the insights. *SB*

Helen Wills Park

Broadway and Larkin streets
www.sfnpc.org/helenwillspghistory
Daily, dawn to dusk

When I lived around the corner from this playground, I went there whenever I was down. Even though I, how should I say, suck at basketball, it was always nice clearing my head by trying to shoot a few hoops and when I gave up on that, climb around on the colorful play structures. The regulars who come to this little park are friendly Nob Hill residents—anything but the "Snob Hill" joke that's been circulating the city. Take your mind off the "big questions" and just play for a bit, or bring your crew and duke it out on the b-ball court. *SB*

Garfield Pool

1271 Treat St
695.5001
www.parks.sfgov.org
Hours vary, call ahead

Swimming is the perfect exercise. It uses all your muscle groups without putting strain on your joints because of buoyancy. I am a swimmer, always have been, always will be—my mom says I learned how to swim before I could walk. (I was born 12 pounds, 1 ounce, so I could pass for the 6-month-old swim class at under two months.) Whether you're new to the sport or a regular pro, make time to get wet at Garfield Pool, where there are lap and rec swims each day and you can even arrange for beginner or advance lessons. I always meet a new and interesting person in my lane when I do laps here—it is a perfect opportunity to chat it up with the locals. *SB*

Lake Merced

Skyline Boulevard
831.2700
Dawn to dusk

Lake Merced is nature for city lovers. The peaceful lake is surrounded by a 4.5-mile paved path for walking, biking, stroller-pushing, running, and skating. Bring a picnic basket or cooler with some snacks so you can stop at one of the picnic tables and enjoy the scenery. *JA*

Iyengar and Vipassana Yoga

Yoga studios cover the city like a New Age blanket. Even though I am not a regular, I do go from time to time for an exercise/meditation/fashion show. I am not meaning to be disrespectful, but every time I go for yoga, everyone is dressed to the nines in the newest, coolest yoga gear, well, except me, of course. Besides that, there are a number of truly amazing studios; here's the info for a few favorites. Get there early, especially for Rusty Wells' classes; they fill up quickly! *SB*

Rusty Wells Yoga

97 Collingwood St
206.0650
www.rustywells.com
Class times vary

Mission Yoga

2390 Mission St, second and third floors
401.9642
www.missionyoga.com
Class times vary

Yoga Tree

519 Hayes St
626.9707
www.yogatreesf.com
Class times vary

Yoga Garden

286 Divisadero St
552.9644
http://yogagardensf.com

Bocce Ball Courts

Aquatic Park
Beach Street near the Maritime Museum
Seasonal hours vary

What better way to spend a day than tossing boulder-size rocks at smaller, brightly colored rocks, in a manicured court while sipping a glass of store-bought vino. Enter the world of bocce ball, where the whole scenario is slightly absurd but oddly elite. Think of it as an antiquated version of horseshoes, first practiced by early Romans more than two millennia ago. If you're curious about the sport, it's still very much alive in San Francisco. In a quaint and sheltered spot, atop a hill with breathtaking views of Alcatraz and Angel Island, most afternoons, a small group of mostly older Italian men can be found enjoying a game. It's not as trendy as the bocce ball scene at some of the wineries and clubs in the greater Bay Area—there's one in San Rafael—the Aquatic Park club is gaining popularity. Newcomers are welcome, to watch or play! *MP*

Margaret Hayward Playground

1016 Laguna St
Daily, dawn to dusk

The central point of the Western Addition neighborhood is historic Margaret Hayward Playground, a park where kids of all ages can revel in a four-square game, basketball, or the monkey bars. A collection of wood and metal play structures have been built on this same spot since "the golden age of recreation" in the early part of the 1900s. Women's clubs met here and kids have grown up to see their kids play here, so commence the horsing around! *SB*

ODC Dance School/Rhythm and Motion

351 Shotwell St
863.9830
www.rhythmandmotion.com
Times and locations vary, check online schedule

If you're like me, then putting on your sweats and heading to the gym sounds just about as thrilling as scrubbing the toilet or organizing your closet. You know you'll feel great about yourself afterwards, but getting there couldn't be more of a nag. That's why I love Rhythm and Motion Dance Studio—their classes will work you like a trip to the treadmill, but you'll have so much fun you'll hardly realize it. Take a class and let your inner diva shine—and yes, men are welcome too. The Fusion Rhythm series, which is my favorite class, is a type of cardio hip-hop, designed for people who want a fun way to get in shape. In it, they teach a sequence of short routines, which alternate every few weeks so you really get a chance to learn the choreography. Classes for more serious dancers are also available, with choices that range from classic jazz to samba and belly dancing. *MP*

California Coastal Trail

www.californiacoastaltrail.info

The trail that dreams of forming a complete lemniscate around the whole of the Bay Area is very much finished and well trodden in its San Francisco County section. Begin at Fort Funston and hike up toward beautiful Lake Merced (see page 61), then continue on to the zoo (see page 104) and along the beach all the way north to the Presidio before reaching the Golden Gate Bridge (see page 109). There's a detailed map on the web site, and plenty of markers to tell you that you're on the right route (unlike the same trail in other Bay Area counties, ahem . . .). Bike the section along the Pacific from the zoo to the Geary Street terminus on a smooth, paved path. When I'm on foot I take the opportunity to walk on the sand when I can; it makes me feel so free and so alive! *SB*

Dance Mission Theater

3316 24th St

826.4441

www.dancemission.com

Once you see a performance here you'll most likely think to yourself, "How'd they do that?" Answer the question for yourself at a one-day workshop or a longer class that leads to getting on stage for a performance. The teachers are a fabulous mix of talented, patient, and strict. After a little tutelage you'll be skilled and have had one fabulous workout. *SB*

The Jewish Community Center of San Francisco

3200 California St

292.1200

www.jccsf.com

Mon–Fri 5:30a–10p, Sat–Sun 7a–8p

Admission: $20 for a day pass, $10 if joined by a member

This beautiful facility is a perfect getaway for a prolonged day of activity. Start with a dip in the pool, walk a few laps with watery resistance, then swim some laps. Hop out and chill in the sauna or hot tub, then change and get ready for a relaxing class in stretching and breathing. Zoom up imaginary hills in a spin class and make your way to the weights, then if you've got any juice left, walk up an imaginary hill while watching the BBC news—you can plug in at many of the cardio machines. I'm not suggesting you should go this crazy in one fell swoop, but the options seem limitless at the brand-new, glass-enclosed JCC. *SB*

Bike About

Two human-powered wheels

Getting around on a self-powered, two-wheeled contraption is indeed a part of American history, in fact, California history. Some of the most important biking innovations were developed back in the day in this very state. Nowadays there are a myriad of biker types: the spandex-covered weekend peddlers, the laid-back beach bikers, the hipsters with their single gears, practical commuter bikers, and the odd bike historian, rolling around on an antique cycle. San Francisco continues to push for increased bike lanes and has "sharrows," arrows that bike and car lanes share on major routes to make turns easier. BART and Muni both make it easy for bikers to bring their ride en route for longer journeys. I recommend getting city biking training before heading out onto these busy streets, and making sure your bike is in tip-top shape before taking to the roads. Have fun and get there at a slower, more intimate pace by biking San Francisco—after all, there are loads of resources and great bike shops to help make your ride all the more merry.

  American Cyclery

510 Frederick St
664.4545
www.americancyclery.com
Mon–Fri 11a–7p, Sat 10a–6p, Sun 10a–5p

As you would expect from the oldest independent bike shop in San Francisco, American Cyclery strives for individualized service and offers all the standard fare of road, mountain, and hybrid bikes, parts, accessories, and repair services. Going beyond expectations, this shop is nationally recognized for its participation in many cycling legacies, earning its staff the honor to curate a show on the history of bicycle culture at the Yerba Buena Center for the Arts. American Cyclery is the premier spot for the fixed-gear enthusiast. (Why there are so many of you in San Francisco, with all the hills, perplexes me, but you'll know why I didn't follow that trend when I blow past you up a steep grade.) Take a look at the web site for a slideshow of vintage track-cycling mishaps, if you're into that sort of thing. *DL*

The Bike Kitchen
650H Florida, between 18th and 19th
www.bikekitchen.org
Tues–Thurs 6–9p, Sat 12–5p

The 1979 film *Breaking Away* inspired my passion for bikes, and the Bike Kitchen has taken it to the next level. Bicycles have the power to bring people together like nothing else, and this cooperative DIY repair shop honors that spirit by encouraging participation every step of the way. The shop is open to all, regardless of financial status; memberships and parts can be earned through volunteering. Innovative events and classes are offered, such as On-the-Road Repair, a ride with frequent stops to demonstrate the correction of typical problems experienced while on the road. *DL*

Biking the Basins: A Bike Tour of San Francisco's Planned Blue Greenway

Hop on a bike to see the eco-city highlights from Embarcadero out to Hunter's Point. Admire the sea lions, bite into an organic peach, catch a fly ball, and watch birdlife on the Bay from the vantage of a rebuilt wetland. Ride the well-defined streets of the city's center all the way to San Francisco's new vision. There might be no better way to see the eco-highlights of San Francisco than by bicycle.

Despite its famous hills, San Francisco is a city full of bicyclists. You'll find them commuting, taking relaxed weekend rides, or weaving in and out of traffic as bicycle messengers. With the Blue Greenway project already under way, the city's bikers are looking forward to a new 13-mile path from Fisherman's Wharf to Hunter's Point. The path features many wide-open spaces with some great Bay views, including several areas of sweeping waterfront destined to become city parks. This tour will give you a glimpse of what that project has envisioned for "the city's last frontier," an area with a close-knit community at the center of San Francisco's energy and land-use debates.

The Blue Greenway will represent the compromise and solution agreed upon by residents, government, and several key organizations. A major player in the creation of the Blue Greenway project has been the San Francisco Bike Coalition (SFBC), an organization that looks beyond day-to-day bike concerns to envision the greater implications of urban biking, ". . . creating safer streets and more livable communities for all San Franciscans," as their mission statement describes. The SFBC can provide reliable bike maps, lists of favorite rides, tips, safe city biking classes, and a full schedule of guided bicycle tours—it is a resource for anyone about to embark on two (nonmotorized) wheels around this city.

To follow this tour on the future Blue Greenway, start by heading down to Fisherman's Wharf (if you're on Market Street, the F-Market Streetcar or Muni bus lines 10, 20, or 27 will get you there). Locals will tell you that Fisherman's Wharf is nothing but a tourist trap, but if you need to rent a bike, it's an ideal spot to start. Look for a locally owned bike shop, like Bay City Bikes, where you can rent anything from a high-performance bike to a kid's bike or tandem for $20 to $45 per day. Once you're saddled up, bike slowly through the tourists hovering around the fish-and-chip shops and postcard stands, using your imagination to recall the vibrant past of this international port. Try tuning out the attractions that have little local connection and think instead about the history of this neighborhood. Here in the 1930s, the air was rich with the aroma of coffee roasting in the roasteries and San Francisco's longshoremen were unionizing to secure workers' rights. When the strikes turned violent, Fisherman's Wharf made front-page headlines around the world, but the courage of these workers helped change America's workforce forever.

Head east on Beach or North Point streets until you reach the Embarcadero, a series of piers that rims the northeastern tip of San Francisco. If you have time, head along Pier 39 to greet the sea lions at Dock K, where the

playful sea mammals pile themselves up to bathe in the fog and bask under the adoration of gawking humans.

Back on the Embarcadero, you'll be breezing by a bustling section of waterfront offering everything from office space and public transit to restaurants and a dinner theater. Cyclists will appreciate the outdoor attractions such as the appealing green oasis at Levi's Plaza Park, views of the Bay and of Telegraph Hill, monumental sculptures, and several renovated piers that are open for public enjoyment. The public spaces came about under the Waterfront Land Use Plan enacted in 1990.

The next stop is a treasure trove of the Bay Area's gastronomic bounty. Inside the historic and beautifully renovated Ferry Building, circa 1898, is a veritable feast of local comestibles. It's nearly impossible to make a quick run through this incredible space, which houses one of the city's best local bookshops, and food stalls with names made famous by the slow food movement. It shouldn't be too hard to convince your traveling companions to lock the bikes and take a stroll through the main corridor before getting back on the road, even if it is just for a melty handmade caramel from Miette Confiserie. You'll also want to stop for samples and supplies from Marin County's Cowgirl Creamery (try the triple crème) and Frog Hollow Farm (if it's not peach season, try Farmer Al's delectable dried peaches). Choose a few favorites to stash in your bike bag for a picnic at India Basin, near the end of your ride.

On Saturdays the Ferry Plaza Farmers Market pours out of the hall and into the streets, but on other days of the week, you can easily walk your bike behind the building, past Taylor's Automatic Refresher and The Slanted Door to watch the ferries roll in. Heading to the Ferry Terminal from points around the Bay, disembarking passengers are welcomed by the likes of Boulette's Larder and Mijita, two highly recommended restaurants that are both locally owned and dedicated to using organic, sustainable ingredients.

Before leaving the Ferry Building, stop to check the time on the Ferry Building's handsome tower. The Ferry Building's clock has been keeping reliable time for most of the 110 years that it's been looking out over the Embarcadero. Herb Caen, San Francisco's most beloved journalist, called the clock tower "a famous city's most famous landmark." This area of the Embarcadero has been fittingly named Herb Caen Way.

With your wheels turning again, cross the Muni tracks and head south toward the Bay Bridge. You can't miss the monumental piece of public art by Claes Oldenburg and Choosje van Bruggen called "Cupid's Span." It echoes the shapes of the bridge above and the boats out on the water, but it also hints at the lyric "I left my heart in San Francisco." The reconstruction and redevelopment of historic piers 1½, 3, and 5 in this section have called for a large percentage of public space. What you see here is an example of the public access planned for the shoreline you are approaching to the south.

Duck under the Bay Bridge, still following along the Embarcadero. You will round a slight bend toward Pier 38, and then reach the soon-to-be Brannan Street Wharf Park. The scene here contrasts new high-density construction and colorful old container shipyards against the backdrop of the glistening Bay. At Pier 40, where Embarcadero changes its name to 24 Willie Mays Plaza, you'll start to see rows of boats bobbing behind the Giants' ballpark. On game days, you can lock your bike by the waters of China Basin and head up the stairs to the public standing area (always free of charge) and look out over the water to see people wearing catcher's mitts while sitting in day trip boats or kayaks, hoping to catch that historic fly ball. The preferred launch for the various watercraft here is likely to be nearby Pier 52, the only major public boat launch in the city, though the water path feeding from China Basin offers several launches and stopover points.

After passing the ballpark, turn left onto Third Avenue and cross over Lefty O'Doul Bridge to China Basin. This charming drawbridge was designed by Joseph Strauss, the same engineer responsible for the Golden Gate Bridge. Once across, jog another left and you'll be on Terry A. Francois Street, also known as China Basin Street. As a bicyclist, you'll be relieved that you're not hoping to park your car, since the Giants' parking lot prices are astronomical.

As you continue south, you'll pass a number of shipping piers and Mission Bay Boulevard. The waterfront area at the terminus of Terry Francois Street is the site of the planned Mission Bay Park. The site surrounds The Ramp restaurant, known for its fabulous live Latin music, which is now approaching "classic" status in the Foggy City. Turn left onto Illinois Street and continue along to historic Pier 70, where you can visualize the future Crane Cove Park. Located adjacent to the oldest operating civilian shipyard in the United States, this park, if it is constructed, would offer more than 1,200 feet of bayfront access, a historic slip with two cranes, and a small boat/aquatic center.

A little farther along is Warmwater Cove, which has begun to receive heightened attention as a part of the Blue Greenway. The nonpermanent renovations have been controversial and present a notable contrast to the well-funded cleanup projects on the city's National Park lands. At this place previously nicknamed "Toxic Tire Park," wood chips now covering the mucky waterfront are but a band-aid over the toxic debris. Re-creation of the natural environment seems like a faraway dream. The area has experienced only minor improvements, and controversial ones at that. Many longtime residents and local artists have seen the park as a canvas for creative expression. (It has been the scene of independent outdoor art and music shows over the years.) Some of the best graffiti in the Bay Area was painted over in an effort to make a cleaner, safer park, but many community members feel they have lost a cultural asset and don't agree that the taggers present a danger. It remains to be seen whether a compromise can be reached that will allow the informal artwork to retain a place in the midst of the changes. Plans for in-depth restoration and park development have been put before the community and government in hopes of bringing together what some see as gentrification and others see as community building. Spend any time talking to one of the area's talented graffiti artists, neighborhood pillars, or new residents who have helped erase graffiti, and you may be surprised to find that most everyone is happy that the land has been reserved for open space, regardless of how it winds up looking. It will be interesting to return to find what compromise has evolved. One proposal for a skate park at the site of some abandoned sugar factories would include a café in addition to the waterfront park, and dog walking space.

Perhaps the greatest point of debate has been over the power plants operating in this area. A PG&E plant is currently being dismantled, and another has signed terms that could mean a closure 10 years down the road. Replacement energy might come via an "extension chord" (as it's been called by the *SF Chronicle*) from across the Bay, and a natural gas "peaker" plant that would only run at peak energy times.

Continuing on, make a right onto 25th Street and a left at the first intersection onto Third Street and you'll be going through the historic Dogpatch neighborhood, a part of San Francisco that survived the post-1906 earthquake fires. The area contains architecturally and historically significant workers' cottages, factories, warehouses, and public buildings that date back to the time of the California Gold Rush.

After passing Cesar Chavez Street and tipping your helmet to the champion of farmworkers' rights, cross the Third Street Bridge or the newly completed Illinois Street Bridge that runs parallel. Take the first left onto Cargo Way and follow it to Jennings Street, where you'll find Heron's Head Park. Formerly Pier 98, the park is now a thriving marsh built on landfill, which extends out into the Bay, providing great views of water all around. The project is exemplary in the way it has served as a living classroom. Thousands of students have learned to maintain the site while studying the local ecosystems and participating in the upkeep of their community.

Literacy for Environmental Justice, the youth-based environmental advocacy organization, is now building the "greenest" classroom in San Francisco on this site, a self-sustaining education center and demonstration greenhouse that will be the first off-grid building in the city. Topics featured will center on sustainability, such as renewable energy, wastewater treatment and reclamation, and green building techniques, and the structure itself will utilize a solar energy system, an ecological wastewater system, a living roof, and Structural Insulated Panel (SIP) construction. The center will operate not only for the students but also for visitors and the surrounding community.

What used to be a polluted wasteland is now home to 78 species of resident and migrating birds and thousands of native plants. Revel with the butterflies at the scent of the Palmer's penstemon as you get back in the saddle for the last short jog over to India Basin.

A left onto Evans Avenue and another bend left to Innes Avenue will bring you into a vibrant southern San Francisco neighborhood where the sense of community comes on strong. India Basin's bayside park is well established, and has been maintained as a healthy habitat for wildlife for many years—long before the Blue Greenway was conceived. This is the time to unload that picnic you packed at the Ferry Building. Find a bench, relax, and watch the hikers, bikers, and boaters gliding by.

If you're ready for more biking you can retrace your steps, enjoying all the sights that always look utterly different when you're going the opposite direction. If it's siesta time, or if you are ready for a change of pace, bike straight up Hunter's Point Boulevard, which turns into Evans Avenue. After crossing Mendell and Newhall streets you'll reach Muni's light-rail T line, where you can rack your bike on the train and fly back to the city's center. On your next San Francisco adventure you may find the new bike path complete and ready for you to test out and compare the befores and afters.

Fresh Air Bicycles

1943 Divisadero St
563.4824
www.fabsf.com
Mon–Sat 10a–7p

In the movie *Breaking Away*, Dave Stoller transformed a piece of junk into a racing machine that carried him across the finish line of the Little 500, and Fresh Air Bicycles takes the same pride in turning throwaway bikes into reliable transportation. A range of repair and maintenance options are offered, such as your basic tune-up and all-encompassing overhaul; they also offer custom wheel builds to give your bike a unique flair. DL

Freewheel Bike Shop

1920 Hayes St; 792.9195
914 Valencia St; 643.9213
www.thefreewheel.com
Tues–Sat 11a–7p

If you still need a costume for this Halloween, consider going for a bike ride in heavy rain without fenders—you'll look like a skunk with a black muddy stripe down your back in no time. Riding around the Panhandle in a downpour, I came upon the quaint Freewheel Bike Shop and decided I'd rather be a pirate. As the friendly and knowledgeable staff helped me select a fender, I took advantage of the public tools and with a few adjustments I was back on the road feeling dry and contemplating new costume ideas. Bicycle repair classes are offered and a full workshop space is available to members. DL

BikeNut

2221 Filbert St

931.0666
www.bikenut.us
Mon–Sat 11a–7p, Sun 12–5p and by appointment

Before I bought my bike, I had a very specific idea of what I wanted, and I soon realized that most shops didn't have it. As luck would have it, I found exactly what I was looking for, but the feeling of settling on something that's not quite what you wanted is one I know all too well. With two words, BikeNut has the solution to buyer's remorse: custom builds. These master mechanics will select the best parts and components and perform biomechanical adjustments to produce a bike that fits you in every way. Ride with confidence. DL

Box Dog Bikes

494 14th St
431.9627
www.boxdogbikes.com
Mon–Fri 11a–7p, Sat 10a–5p, Sun 12–5p

When a bunch of yuppie college kids—or chain sporting-goods stores—move in and transform your hometown, what do you do? You beat them at their own game (yet another *Breaking Away* reference, I can't help it). Box Dog is a worker-owned and -operated collective offering affordable repair rates, common and high-end used parts, and even locally made products. The community bench allows you to rent tools and get advice so you can do your own repairs. *DL*

San Francisco Bicycle Coalition

995 Market St, Ste 1550
431.2453
www.sfbike.org
Workshop hours vary, check web site

One of the oldest bicycle advocacy organizations in the country, the SFBC has created a citywide network to promote bikes for everyday transportation. The coalition offers an extensive calendar of events and tons of resources to build confidence in riders young and old, experienced and novice. Perhaps the most beneficial for bicycle commuters is the Urban Bike Training, taught by expert riders who know the city well. You'll also find a comprehensive guide to bicycle laws, and tips to prevent accidents and theft. Discounts at local bike shops and other services are available to members, as well as an opportunity to participate in the quest to reduce automobile dependency. (For more info, see our ecopedal trip around the proposed Blue Greenway, page 66.) *DL*

Bike and Roll Bike Rentals

899 Columbus Ave
229.2000
www.bikeandroll.com
Rates and distances vary

Cars may rule the roads in San Francisco, but on a bike you can choose not to be caught in the exhaust fumes of an old VW Bug. When I'm presented with the decision to drive or bike, I think, "Hmm . . . get stuck in traffic and maybe find parking or cruise around the coast and witness some spectacular views . . . that's a tough one." Bike and Roll gives you plenty of incentive, with rides showcasing the majesty of the Bay Area, such as the popular Golden Gate Bridge to Sausalito or, for those challenge seekers, the climb up Mt. Tamalpais. A variety of bikes are offered depending on the nature of the ride. *DL*

📖 Bay City Bike Rentals

🏠 *1325 Columbus Ave (second location on Taylor Street)*
📞 *346.2453*
🚲 *www.baycitybike.com*
Daily 8a–8p

Make sure to keep your helmet on while biking around San Francisco, and don't forget to stretch after a pedal up and down this city's many hills. Biking here is a great way to get around if you follow these simple rules. Pick up a day-rental at Bay City near Fisherman's Wharf and start by whizzing through the crowds around the Embarcadero. There are dorky little lunch boxes attached to the front of these bikes, but they come in handy so often that I got one for my own bike after trying out theirs. *SB*

Daniel's Cross-City Bike Ride

To avoid the worst of the hectic downtown traffic, I like to take the BART to Civic Center where I begin my ride. I cruise westward down McAllister Street past City Hall and the Herbst Theatre, where I once saw Norman Mailer give a talk about the past and present realities of the publishing world. Next I hang a left on Gough to get over to Fulton and prepare to ascend a four-block hill to reach Alamo Square. Occasionally, I like to take a detour through the square to admire the elegant architecture of the Painted Ladies—some will recognize the view as it was featured prominently in a 1980s sitcom that will remain nameless.

Continuing west down Fulton, I coast past my aunt and uncle's house to the intersection at Divisadero. Café Abir is a great place to pick up an energizing drink or snack before heading south toward Fell Street. I follow the one-way street to the tip of the Panhandle where a winding trail guides me past some of the oldest trees in San Francisco County. Just north of the Panhandle on Hayes Street past Ashbury is Freewheel Bike Shop, in case I need to make some adjustments. I soon enter Golden Gate Park by way of John F. Kennedy Drive, passing by first the Conservatory of Flowers and then the de Young with its twisting observation tower. I press on through the park past Spreckels Lake until the road funnels out to the Great Highway and a spectacular view of the Pacific horizon from Ocean Beach. Now is a perfect time to sit and enjoy the scenery while munching on your preferred brand of energy bar.

For the return trip I reenter the park at the southwest corner via Martin Luther King Jr. Drive then follow Kezar Drive to Waller Street. Exiting the park, I head a block north to Haight Street for a ride through the historic epicenter of the San Francisco counterculture movement. I can never resist the urge to check out Amoeba Records or one of the countless thrift stores before heading back to Market Street and the home stretch toward the nearest BART station. *DL*

Pacific Bicycles

345 Fourth St
928.8466
http://pacbikes.com
Mon–Fri 10a–7p, Sat–Sun 10a–6p

Admittedly, I am no pro cycler. But I do love to ride, especially when it means the wind in my hair and a basket of farmers market goodies in my bike carrier. For San Francisco peddlers like me, the $500–$600 commuter cycles, by Bainchi and Giant, have lower bars for easy mounting, gears for San Francisco's hills, and comfort in cute colors. For the men and women who are prepping for a triathlon rather than a relaxing ride, Pacific Bicycle is aimed and ready to individually serve you. Find handy replacement or upgrade parts here and get tips from the helpful bike techs on their favorite routes around town. *SB*

Do Lunch

Outstanding midday eating of every sort

Lunch is my favorite meal of the day. When I lived in Switzerland, it was an event, with several courses and mandatory attendance by the entire family. In fact, some parts of the world consider this the largest meal of the day, accompanied by a siesta. There are many types of lunches—savoring something from the Ferry Building, a fabulous burger, or a chile relleno burrito in the Mission. Even though I've avoided the "eat" or "restaurant" sections typical of other guide-books and incorporated food into various chapters, I had to dedicate a spot for lunch. From business power lunches to lazy afternoon munching, it's a state of mind. Let's do lunch!

$$ Liberty Café

410 Cortland Ave

695.1223

www.thelibertycafe.com

Tues–Thurs 11:30a–3p and 5:30–9:30p, Fri 11:30a–3p and 5:30–10p, Sat 10a–2p and 5:30–10p, Sun 10a–2p and 5:30–9:30p

Bernal Heights is one of those neighborhoods that feels like a true community, with adorable shops and neighbors waving to each other on the sidewalk. While the inviting Liberty Café is open for dinner, I tend to visit during their weekend brunches so I can partake of their delicious baked breakfast goods. The challah French toast is filling without being heavy and is served with a delicious fruit compote. If eggs are your style, the Eggs Florentine are positively divine. Just be sure to order the assortment of fresh baked breads if you go the egg route, since anything from the café's ovens is not to be missed. A cup of coffee or some fresh-squeezed juice rounds out a leisurely Sunday morning meal and makes me want to do nothing for the rest of the day but stroll up and down the friendly streets just outside Liberty Café's doorstep. *JA*

$$ Slow Club

2501 Mariposa St

241.9390

www.slowclub.com

Mon–Thurs 11:30a–2:30p and 6:30–10p, Fri 11:30a–2:30p and 6:30–11p, Sat 10a–2:30p and 6–11p, Sun 10a–2:30p

Flat bread and burgers have found a home at Slow Club, where they are both elevated by the cute cooks behind the small square grill. The toppings for scrumptious flat breads change frequently—the ultimate way to savor the season. Throw your idea of a burger and fries by the wayside; this burger, made from nearby Prather Ranch dry aged beef, is cooked to perfection and smothered with balsamic onions and housemade aioli; fries are crispy and soft at the same time. St. George whiskey is behind the super stylish bar—I order a cool and tangy Joe Rickey with a squeeze of lime if I am having a lunchtime celebration, and come back later in the evening for a proper fete, complete with a delicately balanced plate of antipasto. I bite into zingy caper berries and Zoe's spicy coppa in the same mouthful—the smoothness of the thin-sliced pork brings out the freshness of the bright green briney treats. Nothing compares . . .*SB*

$$ Pizzeria Delfina

3611 18th St
437.6800
www.pizzeriadelfina.com
Mon 5:30–10p, Tues–Thurs 11:30a–10p, Fri 11:30a–11p, Sat 12–11p, Sun 12–10p

The little sister restaurant of the acclaimed Delfina, Pizzeria Delfina is a star in its own right. Featuring mozzarella that is hand pulled daily, luscious pies with a crispy-chewy crust, and cannolis made with Bellwether ricotta, this pizzeria will satisfy even the most hardened purists. Daily specials can include deep-fried baby fava beans and house-cured anchovies that melt in your mouth. The *salsiccia* pizza, covered in housemade fennel sausage, onions, and peppers, is a taste of home if you are from the East Coast. To quench your thirst, look to the excellent wine list featuring exceptional Italian wines between only $15 (you heard right) and $44 a bottle. Try going for a late lunch to avoid the crowds—the restaurant is open straight through from lunch until dinner. *JA*

Noontime Concerts

660 California St
www.noontimeconcerts.org
Tues 12:30p

Muscle up five bucks and you'll have enough for a ticket to St. Mary's to hear the best classical performances in bite-sized pieces. Relax for a midday moment, snacking on sounds that have moved people for hundreds of years. This is one place where the rich European cultural lifestyle is resurrected in the City by the Bay. *SB*

$$ Ton Kiang

5821 Geary Blvd
752.4440
www.tonkiang.net
Mon–Thurs 10a–10p, Fri 10a–10:30p, Sat 9:30a–10:30p, Sun 9a–10p

While there is plenty of good dim sum to be had in SF, Ton Kiang is the place to go if you want excellence. Stacks of dumplings, are made fresh each day by a brigade of chefs. The gossamer rice noodles stuffed with crab, pork, beef, or vegetables should not be missed, nor should the garlic-laced snow pea tips or the crispy roast duck. Round out the meal with some silky mango pudding or chewy sesame balls. I love going with large groups of friends so we can try as many dishes as possible. The restaurant can accommodate parties of just about any size, but be prepared for a wait if you show up after noon on a Sunday. *JA*

Lit and Lunch

111 Minna St
www.catranslation.org
Second Tuesday of each month, 12:30–1:30p

Skip out of the office, stray from a day inside world-class museums, and head for 111 Minna (see page 164), where lunch comes with words. Tasty boxed lunches, made for vegetarians and omnivores alike, are served up alongside readings from some of California's most revered writers. Listening to Robert Pinsky, Yoko Tawada, or Robert Hass read in between business meetings or retail shifts sure has a way of making time pass. Hold on to the verses and let them circulate in your head for hours to come. *SB*

$ Café du Soleil

200 Fillmore St
934.8637
Daily 7a–10p

There are several ways to do Café du Soleil and all of them are right. You could eat a flaky croissant with their delicious coffee while rehashing the previous evening's adventures. You could meet a friend for gossip over some Lillet and the oh-so-divine hand-cut potato chips dusted with Parmesan and herbs. Or you could snack on one of the open-faced sandwiches while sipping a beer or lemonade, and review the presentation you have due at work tomorrow. You can spend as long as you like enjoying any of these activities at one of the long, rustic communal tables or outside in one of the sidewalk seats. Be careful of lingering too long as you might just end up sampling every irresistible thing on the menu before the day is through. *JA*

$ Pancho Villa

3071 16th St
864.8840
Daily 10a–12p

While there are a million taquerias to choose from in San Francisco, few are as beloved as Pancho Villa. There are other locations at both the Ferry Building and down in San Mateo, but the original in the Mission is the best place to sample what PV has to offer. Housed in a space almost as large as the diverse menu, Pancho Villa dishes up burritos (including four different vegetarian options), quesadillas, nachos, tortas, and a whole host of other slamdunks. My favorite of the several bean choices are the pintos, prepared without lard, or you could go Tex-Mex with black beans. The *agua frescas*, particularly the strawberry, will help soothe your mouth after you've sampled their award-winning and mouthwatering salsas. *JA*

$$ Fog City Diner

1300 Battery St
982.2000
www.fogcitydiner.com
Mon–Thurs 11:30a–10p, Fri 11:30a–11p, Sat 10:30a–11p, Sun 10:30a–10p

To call it a diner is a misnomer—what diner do you know of where the typical meal consists of local oysters on the half shell and toasted brioche? Some may say that any restaurant with shiny metal siding, neon, and jukeboxes at every table is a diner, but the white tablecloths, extensive wine list, and haute cuisine don't match my vision of classic Americana. Some weekend mornings I am ready to order before I even make it to the Embarcadero—cinnamon vanilla French toast and the veggie frittata are perfect for two to share. After a meal, head out the back entrance (facing away from the Embarcadero) and walk over to Levi Park or up the steps of Telegraph Hill. *SB*

Roxie Food Center

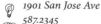

1901 San Jose Ave
587.2345
Mon–Sat 7:30a–8p, Sun 8a–8p

Crowds come in droves to experience the subs at one of the two locations of Roxie Food Center. All the sandwiches are served hot and come with lettuce, tomato, onions, jalepeños, mayo, mustard, salt, pepper, oil, and vinegar. You can customize your sub however you like; bacon and avocado are available for an extra cost. Even the most hardened carnivores concede that Roxie's veggie sub is worth ordering. The store also sells groceries, including a very impressive European candy selection, but the sweetest thing is that Roxie's has also been a longtime sponsor of local youth sports teams. *JA*

Boxed Foods Company

245 Kearny St
981.9376
New location, in Yerba Buena Gardens
www.boxedfoodscompany.com
Mon–Fri 8a–3p

The owners of Boxed Foods look as good as their lunches, always hovering around the small cafés (and their newer restaurant B in Oakland) in chic outfits with their eye on the details. There is one dish that reigns supreme at this popular lunch stop: chicken salad. There's simply none better in the city. Every ingredient is chosen for quality—there's triple bottom line employed here. Order a sandwich, either the famous chicken salad or a delectable pear and Brie pressed sammie, and the grilled vegetable salads—asparagus is in season in the spring, heirloom tomatoes in summer, and tempeh with roasted peppers for a warming winter bite. *SB*

Lucca Delicatessen

2120 Chestnut St
921.7873
www.luccadeli.com

At this deli that is absolutely cluttered with tasty Italian grocery items, standing in line for hot lemon chicken breast or fluffy frittata slices is a joy. I eye the selection of cheeses and pastas, but usually can't leave without an armload of Lucca's handmade ravioli, which was the cornerstone of this family business, which sold it exclusively to the Fairmont Hotel back in the 1920s. Mortadella is made in-house, FraMani meats—the highest quality organic, hormone-free sausages—are trucked over from Berkeley where they are made, and hard-to-find sweet Sicilian sausage makes a taste splash for those who aren't familiar. Either create your own dream sandwich or choose an organic roasted chicken from nearby Rosie Farms, cooked to perfection. If you're nearby and don't want to come in for lunch, call ahead and they'll deliver with a minimum order! They even oblige me a discount on the fatty bottom prosciutto I use for sauce bases . . . fettuccine à la romana . . . yum . . . SB

El Tepa

2198 Folsom St
255.8372
Mon–Fri 10a–8p, Sat 10a–6p

I like to think of El Tepa as the Clark Kent of taquerias. Underneath it all, there is a superhero. The inside of the restaurant looks like any other taqueria, and so does the large menu, but El Tepa's little secret is that it caters to heat junkies like me. Even if spice is not your thing, you can be very happy at El Tepa, choosing from their vast menu that includes four types of tortillas, eight meats (plus tofu), three types of beans, four salsas, and even two types of rice (one being completely vegetarian) to mix and match in a burrito as you choose. JA

Frjtz Gourmet Belgian Fries

590 Valencia St
864.7654
www.frjtzfries.com
Mon–Thurs 9a–10p, Fri–Sat 9a–12a, Sun 10a–9p

There are fries, and then there are fries. I'll let you in on the secret: for a perfect fry, you have to soak the whole peeled potatoes in a bowl of water in the fridge overnight, then resoak after the potatoes are chopped to your preferred thickness. The excess starch will be pulled out and the potatoes will fry with just the right amount of mush inside and golden crispness outside. I am guessing that is what they do here, because the result is glorious. Even though there aren't other types of fries, the sauces make things interesting. Try curried mayonnaise or a Dutch mustard mayo rather than the typical ketchup. It is a wonderful thing to walk up to the counter and get fries to go while window shopping the rest of Hayes Valley's interesting storefronts. SB

Jay's Deli

501 Connecticut St
824.5297
www.jaysdelisf.com
Mon–Fri 7a–7p, Sat–Sun 8a–5p

It seems too good to be true, but this Jay's has everything I could possibly want in a deli and more. I go here when I'm fixing to build the ultimate sandwich with artisan bread and cheeses, natural meat, and organic veggies and condiments, but it doesn't stop there. Join the Wine & Chocolate Club and you'll be invited to stay after hours for the Thursday-night tasting—a pairing of exquisite wines from New Zealand and California, and delicious gourmet chocolates. And for the proverbial cherry on top, Jay's is a member of the San Francisco Green Business Program, with goals to compost and recycle 100 percent of their waste and convert the entire building to solar energy. *DL*

Park at Front and Jackson

Daily, dawn to dusk

My first discovery of this beautiful inner-city spot of green was right before my first radio experience. I was devastatingly early for an interview at the nearby ABC building and, bag lunch in hand, found myself in a park where there were actually knolls, several of them. The rolling grass mounds on this central square are the vibrant surprise between a network of low-rise and high-rise office complexes. This is where people working in the area come to eat, but the atmosphere at lunch isn't the same as the rest of the financial district. Since there are many artistic companies, media, and architecture firms nearby, there is a more colorful crowd of worker bees. Bring a bite to eat and sit amid the daily community congregating on this sculpture-sprinkled lawn. *SB*

Underdog Hot Dogs

1634 Irving St
665.8881
www.myspace.com/underdogorganic
Mon–Fri 11:30a–9p

This brightly colored eatery represents the unlikely matrimony of "green" living and the classic, not-so-healthy but oh-so-yummy frank. The end result is a concept and a product that will have you hooked. Everything from the juicy pork bratwurst to the spicy mustard is organic and delicious. For non-meat eaters, they offer vegan choices like the Veggie Italian with sweet sun-dried tomatoes and the Beer Bratwurst. A side of crispy golden "potater tots" will bring back schoolyard memories, and they complement any dog on the menu. If you're disciplined enough to save room for dessert, top off your meal with a slice of pie, baked locally at the Mission Pie Company (see Sweet Tooth chapter). The food here is so good it's hard to believe it's also good for you. And the prices are reasonable as well, with nothing sans a salad over $5. And now Nick, as in Nick's Crispy Tacos (1824 Irving St; see page 152), has invaded the dive next door, serving tacos "his way" in the Richmond. Nothing like $1 (on Tuesday only) for a taco after an Underdog! Yippie! *MP*

Heavens Dog
1148 Mission St
863.6008

If you are in the mood for Slanted Door (see page 181), but it is lunch time and you aren't up for the attitude or the price tags, then head to the Mission instead, to sample Charles Phan's Heaven's Dog. It not a hot dog place, but if you order the Niman Ranch pork belly in a clamshell bun, you can pretend. Order sustainable versions of your favorite Chinese delights, and try to get used to the how posh the place looks. I recommend starting with a Small Hands (a San Francisco quality spirit producer) grenadine and absinthe to get you in the mood, who cares if it's too early? *SB*

$$$ Medicine Eat Station
161 Sutter St, in the Crocker Galleria
677.4405
www.medicinerestaurant.com
Mon–Fri 11a–6p

If I didn't have such an intimate relationship with San Francisco, I'd have a vision of a Fog City eatery as this über-cool scene with art served on every plate and foamed glass somewhere in the decor. Medicine Eat Station, at the corner of the materialist paradise of Crocker Galleria, is every inch my dream. After a fresh renovation, this popular lunch spot piles in businessmen, dieting office workers, and shoppers alike. Forget your image of veganism as a sibling of dreadlocks and Birkenstocks; Eat Station is trendy vegan. Locally grown ingredients combine with rare international fare, making up the most color-coordinated menu. If I wasn't afraid of looking foolish in front of all these chic people, I'd order three of their white salads and make it a meal, well a snack, anyway—I have a hard time really filling up here. *SB*

$$$ Perbacco

230 California St
955.0663
www.perbaccosf.com
Mon–Thurs 11:30a–10p, Fri 11:30a–11p, Sat 5:30–11p

My sister and I were exploring the financial district when our stomachs began to rumble. Now I have to admit, we did have our hearts set on dining at San Francisco's oldest restaurant, but Tadich Grill was packed. We hung our heads in disappointment and continued down the block when the reflection from large steel block letters glimmered in our eyes. "Perbacco," the letters spelled. "Wow," we exclaimed (which happens to be the loose translation of the name). Inside, Perbacco makes excellent use of the historic warehouse space where sharp angles complement the retained 1912 brick wall. We sat down at the marble-topped bar and noticed mirrors above the liquor shelves, allowing us to sneak a peek at the dishes on the table behind us. The Berkshire Pork Shoulder al Latte immediately jumped at me from the menu and came with savoy cabbage and a delicious, creamy polenta. My sister chose the organic watercress with shaved fennel, and radishes with a perfect lemon herb vinaigrette. This may sound odd, but the restrooms are a cut above the rest; the "stalls" are more like separate rooms, each with its own speakers playing soft jazz. Suffice it to say, our earlier setback was soon forgotten. *DL*

$$ Mijita Cocina Mexicana

1 Ferry Building, #44
399.0814
www.mijitasf.com
Mon–Thurs 10a–7p, Fri 10a–8p, Sat 9a–8p, Sun 10a–4p

The craving can hit at any time in any place without warning and it must be quenched; I'm talking about Mexican food here. Not a day goes by that I don't thank my lucky stars I'm living in the Bay Area. Here's a scenario: My friends and I are weaving through the bustling Ferry Building crowd when suddenly the craving hits us (did I forget to mention it's contagious?). My innate hunter-gatherer senses pull us toward the scent of fresh lime and tortillas emanating from Mijita Cocina Mexicana. Traci Des Jardins, the nationally known chef/owner of Jardiniere (see Dress Up chapter), serves up a mixture of regional dishes, such as Oaxacan chicken tamales, and street food classics, such as carne asada and ceviche. Aside from using organic ingredients, Jardins has furnished the space with environmentally friendly building materials. The big reclaimed leather basket-like benches are surprisingly comfortable, and the soft tacos with crispy battered and fried fish, cabbage, and avocado-cilantro cream are enough to fulfill my desire. *DL*

$$ The Sentinel

37 New Montgomery St
284.9960
Mon–Fri 7:30a–2:30p
www.thesentinelsf.com

Look for the vintage cigar adverts and follow your nose to the best lunch in the South of Market area, if not the city. Belly up to the counter and pick between the BLT (basil, lettuce, avocado, and tomato), the smoked salmon sammie with horseradish crème, the marinated scallop and tomato salad, the corned beef with Gruyère and Russian dressing, or the smoked trout with fennel and apples. I can't imagine a visit to San Francisco without a stop at this ideal eatery; each dish is made with love and the kind of attention to detail you'd expect to find at a jewelry store, not a lunch counter. Prepare to be wowed. Look ahead online to find the daily specials and start planning your midday meal early. *SB*

$ Soup Freaks

200 Pine St
90 New Montgomery St
433.SOUP (7687)
www.soupfreaks.com
Mon–Fri, 9a–3p

It looks a bit corporate and bland, but the soups are anything but. All ingredients are organic, and they'll even deliver to nearby San Francisco locations.

When the fog rolls in and you get a chill up your spine, order the chili (made with Scharffen Berger chocolate), other vegan moody soup with pumpkins, or the rich white cheddar ale soup with bacon bits. Yummo! *SB*

$ Mehfil Indian

600 Folsom St

974.5510

Hours vary

I can never get my fill of Indian takeout, and after a survey of the San Francisco options, which wasn't always pretty, I am convinced this is the best option. The tandoor grill must have special powers at Mehfil, where never-tough chicken and lamb tikka are served smothered in homemade cumin masala or with little plastic (reusable for picnics or to store beads!) dishes of green and red dips. Lunch boxes to go are a mere $5—try that on for size! Take your mango-based *amm ka murga* or the cauliflower and eggplant *tarkari haryala* to a nearby park and you'll be one with the universe. As the family says each time they prepare an order, "Namaste, America!" *SB*

$ El Tonayense Taco Truck

Usually parked at 22nd and Harrison streets

Line up after a long BART ride for a $1.25 invitation back into the above ground world. These tacos are just what the doctor ordered when you are on the run and wouldn't think of typical fast food as an option. Why would you when you're smack-dab in the middle of the Mission? *SB*

$$ Swan Oyster Depot

1517 Polk St

673.1101

Mon–Sat 8a–5:30p

Part of a proper San Francisco initiation is a raw oyster, even if you've been diametrically opposed to taking on a snotty air by sipping down a grayish, wiggly creature. Set aside your fears, Swan's is here! Digress over a rainbow of fresh fish, many from the Pacific proximity, but don't stray from your mission! Oysters are waiting for you, and if you want a beer to go along, no worries, Anchor Steam is waiting for your attention. Mission accomplished. Really. *SB*

$$ Bocadillos

710 Montgomery St
982.2622
www.bocasf.com
Mon–Fri 7a–11p, Sat 5–11p

Spanish cuisine gets gussied up at Bocadillos. Be prepared for a smattering of tapas choices that you used to be hard-pressed to find on other menus around town: stewed mussels with lemongrass, warm octopus with confit potatoes, roasted beets with harissa . . . There are so many choices you'll be, like me, always ordering something new. A fresh take on the underdog of western European cuisine, you'll be cashing in your frequent-flier miles for a trip to the real places where this extrovert menu was thought up. Dress to impress and you'll be more comfortable in this über-cool scene. *SB*

$$ Burma Superstar

309 Clement St
387.2147
www.burmasuperstar.com
Sun–Thurs 11a–3:30p and 5–9:30p, Fri–Sat 11a–3:30p and 5–10p

I've never encountered a restaurant as unanimously adored as Burma Superstar. Fresh, creative, and unique, Burmese food is a splash of flavorful combinations; rainbow salad has a full 22 ingredients, like noodles, tofu, and tamarind. It is satisfying to bring picky eaters here and get them hooked on something they'd never before imagined. There's always a crowd, at least all the times I've lined up in anticipation of the *on noh kauser,* coconut chicken soup topped with crunchy pea shoots, or *see jyet kauswer*, garlic noodles with duck. *SB*

$ Ananda Fuara

1298 Market St
621.1994
www.anandafuara.com
Mon–Tues 11a–8p, Wed 11a–3p, Thurs–Sat 11a–8p

Cheap spirituality? Inexpensive enlightenment? Ananda Fuara serves up tasty vegetarian delicacies with a side of goodwill and good karma. Samosa or curry dinners are my top picks—order right and you may just find your soul skipping out on the bardo! *SB*

Banh Mi in the Foggy City

These fresh Vietnamese sandwiches aren't usually made with organic or local ingredients, but I still consider patronizing these small, family-run businesses part of a strict urban ecotravel regimen. Banh mi shops are often the center of the community, a family-friendly spot where generations of the same gaggle cook, serve, and run the show behind the scenes. Many bank locally at Bank of the Orient, a San Francisco banking tradition. Plus there's nary a cheaper, more delicious lunchtime option—spiced and roasted pork coupled with cilantro and sliced cucumbers is divine. Try these shops and you'll see why. *SB*

Saigon Sandwich

 560 Larkin St
474.4698
Mon–Sat 6:30a–5p, Sun 7a–4:30p

Crusty bread envelops tender chicken or roasted pork (or a combo of both) with housemade pickled carrots that really make Saigon's banh mi stand out. The family is über friendly, but this is one of the most popular sammie shops so don't be surprised if there's a line.

Hoang Dat Coffee Shop

930 Geary St
923.5254
Mon–Sat 6a–4:30p

Although you can definitely find banh mi here, complete with flaky buttered rolls, the highlight here are the soups and stews. Meatball soup is meaty and fabulous, plus it comes with the aforementioned buttered roll, just without the sammie fillings. Pâté is served in the banh mi or on its own—it is creamy and better than the other spots on this banh mi tour. Skip the poker machines in the back and learn a few words in Vietnamese and you'll be welcomed here; after just a few visits I was remembered, and they always know to leave off the spicy jalapeños on my order.

Irving Street Café and Deli

1919 and 2146 Irving St
681.2326
Daily 8a–6:30p

The banh mi and the green jelly desserts have been so popular that there's now a second Irving Street location. Barbecue chicken is the clear favorite filling choice, but the spring rolls are better than other spots; I don't leave without at least one for the road or for my honey back home. There aren't as many smiles around, which surprises me because the classic Vietnamese desserts here are some of the best in the city—I love the coconut milk and mung bean dessert soups, and I'd think they'd be enough to sweeten these folks up! Oh, and did I mention the addictive condensed-milk coffee?

Baguette Express

 668 Larkin St
345.8999
Mon–Fri 7a–6p, Sat 10a–7p

At the only spot that serves tasty banh mi and offers an outdoor table, I am set! Plus you can take home extra rolls for your own creations. This place is the cheapest, at just $2.50, compared to the $4 to $5 at other places mentioned. I get the sardine sandwich here, *ca moi*, or the barbecue chicken, unique compared to the usual roasted or pulled versions elsewhere. Vegetarians are covered too—*bi chay* is stuffed with veggies and a tangy sauce with zero meat, a rarity in the Vietnamese diet.

$ Sing Sing Sandwich Shop

 309 Hyde St
 885.5159
 Daily 7a–4:30p

Rather than catering to your every need in Vietnamese delights, Sing Sing dials in on the best banh mi, serving these sandwiches exclusively—in fact, the only other thing on the menu is coffee. And it's paid off—there are a growing number of loyal lunchers who seek the tangier, soy-infused version served here, rather than the sweeter sauce dabbed on at other establishments. It's small and a bit sketchy, but even my tender stomach has never gurgled the wrong way after their perfect banh mi.

Explore

Places where the wide world is explained, nature abounds, or adventure is to be had

Curiosity can lead down many a path; we've all seen our friend Curious George getting in over his head. But fostering a healthy curiosity about the world is as important as taking our very first steps. If we fill our imagination with programmed images and digital friends, we miss out on all there is to explore for ourselves in the big wide world. History and science, nature and adventure are waiting around the bend to expand your knowledge of the world around you. Seek out the big questions, ask your own, and most of all, enjoy the ride!

Grace Cathedral

 1100 California St
749.6300
www.gracecathedral.org
One of the most beautiful structures in the city is certainly Grace Cathedral, but I am more taken with the outside than the interior. The maze that

replicates the one at Chartres, the spiritual center outside Paris, has a centering effect like a walking meditation. I used to live a few blocks away and would come here at night to walk in silence, the only sound being the chapel fountain bubbling nearby. Concerts and beautiful classical performances of faith-based music are regular standouts at this already magnificent cathedral. Take a swing on the play structure across the street, where you can dream of life as a wealthy businessman in the early 1900s as you gaze at the Railroad Baron building adjacent to Grace Cathedral. Sometimes there are free concerts on the weekends, so cruise their web site before heading over. *SB*

49ers

490 Jamestown Ave, off of Hwy 101
464.9377
www.sf49ers.com
Game times vary August–December

San Francisco's football team is a favorite up and down the West Coast, albeit not the greenest adventure to be had. Share smiles with the crowd as the Niners catch some passes, and maybe take a walk around South San Francisco for post-game relaxation. Some of the concession food is locally sourced, and I've heard rumors about possibly using renewable energy to fuel the stadium. *SB*

Anchor Steam Brewing Co. Tour

1705 Mariposa St
863.8350
www.anchorbrewing.com
One public tour each weekday afternoon by reservation only

One of SF's breweries opens its doors to the public nearly every weekday of the year. Get on a tour and you'll get a behind-the-scenes glimpse at what goes in to these classic suds, and afterwards, get free tastes at the in-house pub. *SB*

Free Standing Room

Giants Stadium
24 Willie Mays Plaza
To purchase tickets go to www.giants.mlb.com

Giants games aren't cheap. Much to my chagrin, "the game of the people" is becoming the game of the wealthy as prices skyrocket and stadiums shrink in size. Thank goodness for the A's stadium across the Bay, where you can still get a ticket for $5 (Wednesdays are $2!). To make up for their base ticket price of $30, the Giants have made a concession: the in-room deck is free for all games, so you can stand by the food carts and look at the Bay behind you or the outfield in front of you. Not a bad idea to stop by and have a bit of a cheer on your way to a Mission Bay gallery or the Ferry Building in the other direction. *SB*

Ferry Plaza Farmers Market

291.3276

www.ferrybuildingmarketplace.com/farmers_market.php, www.cuesa.org

Tues 10a–2p, Sat 8a–2p

The Ferry Plaza Farmers Market is the best reason for getting your tush out of bed early on a Saturday. Going early helps beat the crowds (ten thousand to fifteen thousand people on an average Saturday) and gets you the best selection of what the market has to offer. This market brings the Range Rover, well-dressed posh set out of the woodwork, so get ready to race against the gourmands for armloads of produce and lavish ingredients. The market is operated by the Center for Urban Education about Sustainable Agriculture (CUESA) and is filled with vendors selling local and sustainable produce, nuts, honey, jam, flowers, cheese, bread, herbs, meat, eggs, and more. Much of what you'll find is organic, and I like to take a spin around the market before I buy to find who has what I'm looking for at the best prices. You can spend hours at the market itself, but there are many other attractions to witness once your bags and coolers are full. Blue Bottle operates two kiosks to get your morning caffeine fix (Note: The one in front is much less crowded than the one on the eastern side of the building), and across the Embarcadero local artisans sell photography, crafts, jewelry, and more. While it can be busy, this is also a great time to explore the inside of the Ferry Building. The Imperial Tea Court serves carefully selected teas with a small selection of dim sum, and the Ferry Plaza Wine Merchant will allow you to sit and sip while enjoying your purchases from the market. Brave the lines at Cowgirl Creamery for expert advice and tasty samples of excellent cheeses. Once you pick a few, hop to the next shop, Acme Bread, for the best loaves in the Bay Area. Keep your eye out for many of the other places mentioned in the book (Recchiuti Chocolates, Oak Hill Farm Stand, The Slanted Door, Mijita, Hog Island Oyster Company, and more). *JA*

San Francisco for Free

Just as the saying goes, "the best things in life are free," so are many of my favorites in San Francisco—or they can be free if you know when to go. Even those without many financial choices can be a part of our rich cultural web. Music and art are the stuff of the soul. Nature abounds in San Francisco's many parks, and breathtaking views of the Bay inspire the photographer in everyone. There are many adventures to be had without reaching for your wallet. I encourage everyone to try one day for free, bring a picnic and enjoy museums, open-air markets, parks, and summer concerts. My favorite free activity is museum hopping on first Tuesdays. Many locals are out and about, and though the museums can get packed, it makes for great people-watching so bring your sketchbook! When I lived in London I got used to having museums at my reach—the museums are free or pay-what-you-can. This "high art" should be accessible to all. It is more than just beautiful objects, but expressions of humanity's ups and downs that can speak to all our senses. So even though the United States has put many of these places of art and culture on the pedestal of luxury, these are the days and times when you can see it all for free. Remember that there is more to life than machines and mass media; art is as necessary to life as these tools. The arts community is under constant financial threat due to our skewed priorities, so if you can make a donation to art and music it will make life more livable for those who cannot, and for future generations. Watch for the free icon throughout this guide and free times on museum reviews!

Crissy Field

The Golden Gate National Recreation Area is at the forefront of a national movement toward urban ecological restoration and stewardship. Stretching 60 miles along the coastlines of three California counties, the GGNRA harbors 33 federally listed threatened and endangered species and dozens of different ecological communities. The GGNRA is part of the Golden Gate Biosphere Reserve, a unit of UNESCO's Man and the Biosphere Program. The Nature Conservancy considers the San Francisco Bay Area one of six biological diversity hot spots in the United States, and Conservation International calls the California Floristic Province a global biological diversity hot spot.

Crissy Field is the flagship ecological restoration project of the GGNRA, not only for its spectacular setting and ambitious conservation goals, but also for its cost: $34 million, the majority of which was raised from private sources. The site is 100 acres, of which only about one-third harbors an ecological restoration of the park's natural resources. The salt marsh and lagoon are the central features of the restoration, but the area also harbors sensitive coastal dunes as well as a freshwater dune swale. The federally threatened snowy plover visits the west end of the site each year; the bird and aquatic wildlife diversity are a striking example of "build it and they will come."

Across Marina Street from the Exploratorium and Palace of Fine Arts is the diagonal cypress-tree grove that marks the Marina Gate entrance of Crissy Field.

Take a moment to survey the scenery from the grassy overlook. It is hard to believe that before the restoration, Crissy Field was just the Presidio's backyard, ignored and covered with debris. With support from the Evelyn and Walter Haas Jr. Fund, the Presidio Trust has constructed a stone observation plaza above Crissy Field with benches and interpretive panels. The scenic overlook, to be opened this spring, will offer impressive views of the tidal marsh and airfield, as well as the Golden Gate Bridge, Alcatraz and Angel Islands, and the iconic San Francisco skyline.

Continuing down the trail brings you to the Golden Gate Promenade and East Beach. The Promenade, extending along the shore all the way to the Golden Gate Bridge where the Civil War–era Fort Point rests beneath, is ideal for bikers, joggers, rollerbladers, and amblers. The East Beach is a popular location for sea kayakers and sailboarders due to the frequent winds and lack of wave break.

Back on Marina Street across from the tidal marsh is the Crissy Field Center, an urban environmental education laboratory working to bring the park to the people and playing a significant role in the environmental justice movement. The center offers classes, as well as an interactive sand dune exhibit and multimedia computer lab where visitors can track changes in the nearby ecosystems. Monitor the lagoon and dune swale from the observation deck, then head down to the café for refreshments before moving on down the promenade. The programs and retail operations found at the center are all certified green businesses.

Halfway along the lagoon you can witness the progress of the salt marsh restoration. The salt marsh once extended as far as Chestnut Street and into the Marina District. Looking for more useable land, the planners of the 1915 Panama-Pacific International Exposition filled in the marsh and covered much of the sand dunes. Until restoration efforts began in 1999, the desolate strip was covered with asphalt and debris. Since 1999, more than one hundred thousand native pants have been planted or seeded and biologists have identified 17 fish and 135 bird species in the area, including herons, egrets, ducks, and gulls.

At the west end of the lagoon, the marsh soils serve as an ideal substrate for restoration of rare native plant species. The National Park Service has overseen the planting of native grass, beach strawberries, seaside daisies, and pink sand verbena. The sand dunes between the beach and promenade are among the few places on the park's bay-front locations where native dune grass still grows.

The dune swale is a bonanza of biodiversity, able to sustain a community of rare plants. Many of these dunes are a prime example of restoration success and native plant diversity. These protected habitats are roped off to prevent the intrusion of human visitors (and their pets), save those who wish to volunteer in the plant-life revitalization efforts.

Crissy Field is named in honor of Major Dana Crissy, who perished in 1919 while testing the limits of airpower. The Historic Airfield was the location of many early feats in airpower; flying records were set and many aviators stationed here went on to fame in the world of aviation. The field was closed to fixed-wing craft in 1974, and more recently to helicopter activity.

The region along the shore between the dune swale and Torpedo Wharf has been designated as the Wildlife Protection Area. This area serves as a peaceful habitat for the western snowy plover, which has been listed as a threatened species since 1993. The small shorebirds do not nest at Crissy field, but spend up to 10 months of the year here resting in shallow depressions in the sand where they feed on small invertebrates to build up their fat reserves for the breeding season.

Stop in at the Marine Sanctuary Visitors Center where you can learn more about the protection and restoration of the many native plant and animal species found at Crissy Field.

Architecture

San Francisco has many notable architectural landmarks, among them:

Hotaling Building

451 Jackson St

Built in 1866 by Anson Parson Hotaling, this Italianate structure features cast-iron shutters and fire-resistant construction that's contributed to it making it through SF's fires and earthquakes. Hotaling had a whiskey business that made the church figures of the city loathe him.

Fugazi Bank Building

4 Columbus Ave

Built in 1909 by A. P. Giannini, founder of the Bank of Italy that became TransAmerica Corporation. Bring paper and a pastel or Conté crayon to do a rubbing on the terra-cotta facing.

Hallidie Building

130–150 Sutter St

Named after the inventor of the cable car, Andrew S. Hallidie, this 1918 architectural landmark features curtain wall construction with a cast-iron and glass façade that gives it a modern look, and a sturdy structure that made waves when it was first erected.

Queen Anne Victorians, Whittier, and Bourne Mansions

2090 Jackson St and 2550 Webster St

These four-story houses that date back to the late 1800s housed the richest families in San Francisco at the time. Built of a unique combination of brick, sandstone, and wood, they each have more than 30 rooms.

Gough Street Victorians

2019, 2021, 2023, and 2645 Gough St

These impressive, brightly painted homes are also of the Queen Anne Victorian style and include intricate design elements and hand carving. Number 2645 is the Octagon House that was constructed earlier than the others, during a time when it was thought that health and longevity would be had by living in an eight-sided house.

Sidney Kahn House

66 Calhoun Terrace

This Neutra house, dating from the 1930s, is the best example in SF of this influential movement in modern architecture.

Yerba Buena Lofts

Stanley Sailowitz' ultra-modern take on city living is worth checking out—you'll want to pack your bags and move in ASAP.

The Plaza Apartments

Sixth and Howard streets

The brilliant yellow and orange stack of apartments brings sunshine to this block 24 hours a day.

Haas Lilienthal House

2007 Franklin St

With its turrets, rounded windows, brocade layers of wood carving, and coordinated, vibrant colors, this is my favorite of all the SF Victorians.

Pacific Avenue Victorians

3200 and 2600 blocks of Pacific Avenue

When Victorians are all lined up, they're really something. Take a walk along these upper Pacific Avenue blocks and you'll be happily surprised. The homes on the 3200 block are all from 1900, designed by famous architects Ernest Coxhead, Bernard Maybeck, Willis Polk, and William Knowles. I wonder what it would be like to live in a neon pink house . . .

TransAmerica Pyramid

600 Montgomery St

Since the early 1970s, this pointy financial tower has been what people remember on the SF skyline.

California Historical Society

678 Mission St
www.californiahistoricalsociety.org

Visit this resource and museum to find out more about historic structures and other cultural events around the city.

⑤ Walking Tours

Even with the crazy steeps, steps, and valleys, San Francisco is a great city to walk, though it might be more like a hike if you take some routes. Get out on your feet with a tour guide, whether you're a local or a visitor. Many of these tours are free, and others include enough food and juicy stories to make them worth your while.

Cruisin' the Castro

255.1821

A historical tour of SF's most stylin' neighborhood and famous gay Mecca.

Wok Wiz Tour

981.8989
www.wokwiz.com

Imagine a tour about food led by a chef! A perfect combination, you're guaranteed to fall in love with Chinatown's many food varieties on this perennial favorite, a tour loved by locals and visitors.

Vampire Tour

650.279.1840
www.sfvampiretour.com

Find all the haunting spots around SF, and come in costume to make it even more freaky.

Victorian Home Walk

252.9485

All the most amazing Victorians for which SF is known are revealed on this inside and outside tour.

Russell's San Francisco True Crime Tour

387.1549

Follow in the steps of the Zodiac Killer, hatchet man Jim Jones, and other ne'er-do-wells along the San Francisco streets.

My Taste of the Mission

333.4457

A most delicious culinary tour of the many flavors of the Mission.

San Francisco City Guides

557.4266

These great tours are always free and feature various neighborhoods and themes depending on the time of year.

Javawalk

673.9255

Comb the entire city for the best coffees, espressos, and cappuccinos in town, many from local roasters.

HobNob Tours

851.1123

The railroad barons and big money men that pumped up SF in the early years left behind some interesting tales and glorious edifices of their supreme power.

Flower Power

863.1621

The music, free love, and mind-bending experiences are all revealed and remembered on the Haight-Ashbury walking tour.

Mural Art Tour, Precita Eyes Mural Arts

285.2287

Find out the hidden meanings behind SF's many murals, with these knowledgeable guides.

Barbary Coast Tour

775.1111
www.sfhistory.com

A self-guided tour along what used to be the coast of SF will give you the secrets behind this city's evolution and murky past, including an active shanghai trade. Get the map online and head out whenever you want to get the dirt on Fog City.

Cable Car Barn, Mason Street

1201 Mason St
474.1887

Stop by this warehouse full of SF's classic cable cars. Climb all over them, and stick around for daily demonstrations of what it takes to drive one of these suckers—no easy task. When I lived on Hyde Street, my favorite driver let me try my hand on an unbusy morning on California Street and I had to sit down, using all my strength and body weight to stop the car from rolling past Leavenworth Street. Totally memorable and amazingly difficult! *SB*

Alcatraz Island Tours

Blue and Gold Fleet, and private reservations
Fisherman's Wharf
705.5555

When the first inmates came to Alcatraz Prison in 1934—among them infamous gangster Al Capone—the island had just been built up from its previous incarnation as an army facility. As the years went on, "the worst of the worst" were transferred here from other prisons, and Alcatraz became known as the last resting spot for the most heinous criminals. Visit "Broadway," the main thoroughfare of prison cells, and explore the wickedness and escape attempts by taking a ferryboat tour from the wharf. I recommend the "night" tour, departing at 3pm, a little colder but full of frightful excitement that the tamer tours don't offer. *SB*

Pet Cemetery, Yoda Fountain, and Presidio

Above Crissy Field
www.nps.gov/prsf, www.presidio.gov

The expansive groves of nonnative eucalyptus and rows of historic army homes take up a big chunk of the most beautiful hills near San Francisco's Golden Gate Bridge. Follow along a network of hiking, running, and biking trails and you'll find the Yoda Fountain and the Pet Cemetery. The Pet Cemetery, at the corner of McDowell and Cowles streets includes everything from dogs to pigeons to rabbits, with gravestones like "Here lies Trouble, he was no trouble," and the most ridiculous pet names. Lucasfilm has an office in the Presidio, and out front you'll see Yoda, the all-knowing, all-seeing character. Here he sits atop a goblet with four falls heading to a glistening blue pool of knowledge, I like to think. There are plenty more little perks and discoveries to be had in the Presidio, so do a little jog around the site when you get there to pick you own favorite attractions as you smell the eucalyptus on the breeze. *SB*

Zeum

221 Fourth St
820.3320
www.zeum.org
Tues–Sun 11a–5p
Admission: $6–$8

When I first moved to San Francisco, my family friend and her two wonderful sons took me to Zeum to make music videos and ride the carousel. A swirled museum that finishes with a little sound studio at the top is a fun way to share educationally influenced smiles with your mini-pals. Making a Van Morrison video of my own wasn't too bad either. There's a great padded playground out front and bowling next door. *SB*

Levi's Plaza Park

1270 Battery St

In between your North Beach and Embarcadero adventures, peep through the hedges and be transported to a little gem of a park in the middle of all the hustle and bustle. Levi's is like the eye of the storm—everything seems to slow down, and you can sit under a weeping cherry tree and lunch on a sandwich while a babbling brook flows by from a little waterfall up the knoll. You'd never expect such a mini-paradise to appear just off of an SF thoroughfare, but sure enough, this park does exist—it isn't Narnia's magic or a figment of my imagination. Named after our famous dungaree maker (my mother still calls them that), Levi's is the best SF oasis. *SB*

Herbst Theatre

401 Van Ness Ave
392.4400
www.cityarts.net, www.performances.org
Concert times vary

Herbst is where I met Norman Mailer and his dashing son. It is where I heard Maria Schnieder's SF debut. It's where I listened to lectures on the life of Mahler, and where I was when Richard Stolzman mystified me with his clarinet solos. Home of the City Art and Lecture Series, and SF Performances, there is always something happenin' here. The Herbst Theatre has a small stage, but big personality. Frescoes cover the walls, giving the place a fresh yet historic personality all its own. Herbst is the location of some of my fondest San Francisco experiences, and if you check the calendar, it might be yours too. *SB*

Butler's Uniforms

345 Ninth St
863.8119
Daily 11a–5p

A trip into the lives of SF's laborers can be had at Butler's, where cutesy nurse uniforms, Carharts, work boots, and waiter's penguinlike attire share the racks. Peruse the uniforms worn in this city for a behind-the-scenes look into the lives and jobs of the people who make it go 'round. An ounce of appreciation and a smidgen of respectful curiosity—I've found some of my best lounge-around scrubs here. *SB*

Murals

 www.precitaeyes.org, www.riveramural.com, www.transistor6.com

The many murals around San Francisco give me reason to always have my eyes peeled for strokes of paint when I'm out and about. Precita Eyes Mural Arts is responsible for some of the most incredible life-sized paintings around, all with mystic and meaningful subject matter. Perhaps the most famous collection of murals is on Balmy Street (between 24th and 25th streets), but I can't get enough of Diego Rivera's work at the San Francisco Art Institute (800 Chestnut St) and at SF City College (Ocean Avenue Campus), where a peek into the theater rewards with his Pan American Unity mural of grand proportions. For graffiti art around the Bay Area, check the Transistor 6 web site (above). Other murals around town to check out: Clarion Alley (between 17th Street, Valencia, and Mission) of 17th and Mission, Vallejo and Stockton, Rincon Center Mural, Leavenworth and Bay, Gough and Grove, 15th and Moraga (near the tiled steps, see Get Active chapter), Duboce Underpass, Folsom and 21st streets, Castro Playground, Victory Hall, Coit Tower at Telegraph Hill Boulevard, Women's Building (3543 18th Street), and WPA Murals. Keep your eyes open and you're sure to find some great public art. *SB*

San Francisco Zoo

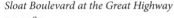

Sloat Boulevard at the Great Highway

753.7080

www.sfzoo.org

Daily 10a–5p

Admission: $9–$15

One of this country's premier educational zoos, with special exhibits, bird and primate houses, and snow leopards—my favorites! Enjoy the wild side of the world while learning the importance of natural habitats and how to protect endangered species. This zoo has had some negative press lately with a tiger incident a while ago, but the zoo has some of the highest animal care and safety standards now that *meshugas* has passed. Come support this key institution in protecting endangered species and fostering a love for all wildlife. *SB*

Fort Mason Center

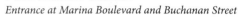

Entrance at Marina Boulevard and Buchanan Street

441.3400

www.fortmason.org

Located in the historic piers and buildings of Lower Fort Mason is a plethora of educational and recreational activities. On this bustling campus you'll find theaters, museums, a music school, a maritime library, a radio station, a gourmet vegetarian restaurant, and much more. Take a foreign language course, learn tai chi, or participate in a number of other classes and workshops offered here; my favorite would have to be the Improv Comedy Traffic School. As part of the Golden Gate National Recreation Area, Fort Mason is the setting for more than fifteen thousand meetings, conferences, performances, and special events each year. The Cowell Theater at Fort Mason brings some of San Francisco's finest performing artists to its stage. Returning annual events include the San Francisco Tribal, Folk & Textile Arts Show, the Fall Antiques Show, and the Pacific Orchid Exposition, to name a few. *DL*

Chinatown: Compact, Sustainable Living Derived from a Painful Past

San Francisco is home to America's largest Chinatown. This central area of the city grew as immigrants gathered to build the new city and the Transcontinental Railroad in the 1850s at the time of California's Gold Rush. As time went on, the community responsible for many projects crucial to the development of the growing city had less and less access to real estate, and their neighborhood shrank. One example of this was when racist city planners restoring the city after the devastating 1906 earthquake and resulting fires made plans to relocate Chinatown altogether to the Hunter's Point area to the far south of the city. Thankfully, a combination of commercial and government agencies blocked this idea, and the 24-block area we know of today as Chinatown was preserved. Even after the geography was worked out, unjust immigration policies relating to the rounding up of Chinese-American citizens on Angel Island made this a dark spot on American history.

Although the formation of this area represents a painful history of racism, the resulting neighborhood is representative not only of one of San Francisco's biggest tourist draws—Chinatown attracts more visitors each year than the Golden Gate Bridge—but also of compact and sustainable eco-city design. Residents work, live, and play in a neighborhood that offers many amenities and a great cultural and community base. The busy, colorful atmosphere endears visitors and begs for stories to be told and repeated, like those of the famous native author Amy Tan. Cantonese is the primary language spoken on these streets, but as new primarily Asian communities spring up in the Richmond and Sunset neighborhoods, and Oakland's Chinatown grows, there is a growing mix of Asian populations on the streets of San Francisco's main Chinatown blocks. Vietnamese, Taishanese, and Fujian are in the mix on these bustling streets and alleyways, where an authentic communal feel gives locals and travelers alike a real sense of place.

Begin your tour on the steps of Grace Cathedral. Head down the steps, past the famous labyrinth to the cable car stop at California and Taylor streets. If you're up for it, head downhill for a steep hike to Grant Avenue. Once you arrive at the intersection of California Street and Grant Avenue, head one block south, to the right, down the most touristy block of Chinatown toward the Dragon's Gate at Bush Street. This gate was given as a gift by the Chinese government in the late '60s and echoes the furling dragon-mouthed lampposts on either side of the street.

Jog right at Pine Street and follow a tree-lined pathway to the contrasting quietude of Old St. Mary's Square.

Walk through to the far end of the square toward California Street, where you'll see San Francisco's first cathedral. Considering the area of Chinatown is compact for reasons of discrimination, it is interesting to read the inscription on the clock tower on Mary's Cathedral, for which the square is named: "Son: Observe the time and fly from evil." This church was constructed of nonlocal materials in 1854: the brick was brought "round the horn" (Chinese Cultural Center, *www.c-c-c.org*) and the granite cut in China's quarries. On the corner of the intersection is the oldest telephone booth in Chinatown, significant because this neighborhood was the first in the city to have telephone service.

Follow along Grant Avenue past Sacramento Street to narrow Commercial Street and take a right. Walk down past Kearny Street to the Pacific Heritage Museum, long known as the best place in San Francisco to view art and historical treasures from the Pacific Rim. The building itself is a landmark; what used to be the United States Subtreasury is now listed as a California Historical Landmark (*www.noehill.com/sf/landmarks/default.aspx*).

Come back out Commercial Street to Kearny Street and turn right, walking half a block to Clay Street. Turn left and go half a block to Portsmouth Square. This small courtyard is the birthplace of San Francisco, and each morning welcomes the quiet movements of tai chi exercise groups.

Retrace your steps back to Kearny Street and take a left onto Merchant Street, one of Chinatown's alleys. On the corner you'll see The Hilton, which houses the Chinese Cultural Center. Go to the third floor to see the theater, museum, gift shop, and amazing exhibits of modern Chinese art on display.

Continue down Kearny to Washington Street and turn left. On the right side of the street you'll see Buddha's Universal Church. In addition to being one of the biggest Buddhist temples in America, this church is also home to authentic Chinese opera performances throughout the year.

Continue on Washington Street up to Grant Avenue to see the oldest pagoda structure in San Francisco, now a branch of Canton Bank. Before this multinational, Asian business-oriented bank took over and refurbished the historic structure, it was the first telephone exchange in the city, where members of the exchange were known by name by the switchboard operators.

Turn left onto Grant Avenue. Between Washington and Jackson streets, explore the Ten Ren Tea Company, which sources its high-quality teas from near and far.

Continue on Grant Avenue to Jackson Street, turn right, and walk up to Wentworth Alley, where you'll find the first spot for a taste of Chinatown on the tour at Great Eastern. This old-school eatery is the best place to get adventurous if you aren't accustomed to Cantonese delicacies. Try steamed frog legs flavored with smoked ham, their famous duck renditions, or a quick bite of local Dungeness crab cooked in Chinese wine when these tasty crustaceans are in season.

Cross back over to Jackson Street to Beckett Alley. Follow along, looking out for interesting Chinese temples.

At the end of Beckett Alley, turn left onto Pacific Avenue and make a quick right back onto Grant Avenue. Follow along to the next block, Broadway, and stop for handmade lychee or durian gelato (the latter an acquired taste to be sure) at Yoogo Gelato.

Head left on Broadway, making a midblock stop at the Chinese Historical Society, where you can get a real sense of the role of Chinese muscle and mind in the Old West.

If you passed over Great Eastern, you'll have another, very different style cuisine to savor. Yuet Lee, on Stockton Street at Broadway, offers some of the best seafood dishes in Chinatown. If you can't make sense of the menu, ask for salt and pepper squid, clams in black bean sauce, or any of their wide noodle dishes. The steamed Chinese greens will lighten up your smorgasbord, covering tables that keep diners happy until the wee hours of the morning.

Turn left onto Stockon Street at the corner of Broadway and follow down to the next block, Pacific Avenue. If you managed to turn away the treats of the aforementioned restaurants, or you've been smart and shared a dish at each spot with your touring partners, get ready for an inexpensive and authentic dim sum feast at Y Ben House. Try classic *har gao*, shrimp dumplings, and pork taro balls that are real crowd-pleasers. Suck the nutritious marrow from chicken feet, or whatever the whirring carts bring to your table.

Walk another block on Stockton Street to Jackson Street and turn left, walking less than half a block to Ross Alley. Make a right and, midway down the block, find Golden Gate Fortune Cookie Company, where you can buy cookies with your own message inside. Watch the cookies being mixed, rolled, and folded, and take the opportunity to buy some while they're still hot!

At the end of Ross Alley, make a right on Washington Street toward Stockton Street. On the corner, find Sam Wo's, several generations' favorite late-night hangout and the most affordable and delicious handmade wontons around.

Backtrack down Washington Street to Waverly Place and make a right. Midway down the alley, known as the "street of painted balconies," you'll find three temples: Jeng Sen at 146, Tin How at 125, and Norras at 109.

At Clay Street make a left to the corner of Clay and Grant streets. Pop your head in the Chinatown Kite Store, where you'll be surrounded by every type of kite, from single lines to top-of-the-line quad-line parafoils. Take mental pictures of the vibrant ceiling, covered with a rainbow of kites in all shapes and sizes.

Retrace your way down Clay Street to Stockton Street and turn left for a brief look at the Kon Chow Temple, America's oldest family association, now housed above a bank in a modern building.

Back at Sacramento Street, turn right and look for the Donaldina Cameron House, which began as a Presbyterian Mission Home for Girls to intervene on behalf of young Asian immigrant females who had become disenfranchised upon arrival to the United States (*www.sanfranciscochinatown.com*).

Take the clean-running Muni trolleybus line 1 up Stockton, or hike back up Sacramento Street to Taylor Street, turn left and you'll be back at Grace Cathedral.

Exploratorium

3601 Lyon St
561.0360
www.exploratorium.edu
Tues–Sun 10a–5p
Admission: $9–$14, free the first Wednesday of each month

An excellent playground for the sciences, this place is crawling with hands-on exhibits that illustrate various physical principles. There's a living exhibit showing how things decompose and who helps in that process. Draw a loop picture using an ink-filled pendulum. Blow the biggest bubbles while learning about the properties of reflection and vision. Regular community events, science programs, and art showcases fill this award-winning, lively museum with students, locals, and visitors of all ages. The Exploratorium is the most fun you'll have at a museum, a place where science is made fun. The Palace of Fine Arts, a wonderful outdoor pantheon and park, is right next door. *SB*

Ghirardelli Square

900 North Point St
775.5500
www.ghirardellisq.com
Mon–Sat 10a–9p, Sun 10a–6p

In 1893, Domingo Ghirardelli's sons purchased an entire block of property to serve as the headquarters for their father's business. More than 60 years later, the company was bought and relocated, prompting two prominent San Franciscans to save the Ghirardelli block from the threat of modern development. The old chocolate factory was restored and evolved into the brick-terraced courtyard of shops and restaurants we now know, and has since achieved National Historic Register status. Despite it being a major tourist attraction, I still enjoy perusing the many shops and restaurants as the large distinguishable Ghirardelli sign looms overhead, and I can't say no to chocolate either. Visit the square during Fleet Week to watch some amazing aerial acrobatics performed by the legendary Blue Angels. *DL*

Golden Gate Bridge

http://goldengatebridge.org

Everyone remembers this city for its famous bridge, the rusty-colored Golden Gate. Spanning from the shores of the Marin Headlands to San Francisco, it is a magnificent monument to human evolution. It has as shady a past as many projects of its day; in fact, it was set to be opened before the Bay Bridge, on the other side of San Francisco, but due to unforeseen design flaws and safety issues it wasn't traveled across until months after the Bay Bridge was in use. I find it funny that as soon as crews finish painting it they have to start all over again at the other side—after all, it isn't naturally red! Don't miss the long and leisurely walk across, which is especially luxurious on a sunny day when the fog lifts, but bring a coat no matter what—the wind loves gliding through this gap in the Bay. If you aren't scared of heights, take a look down and you'll see some strong currents that, thanks to Mayor Newsom, have been harnessed to power parts of the city without harming wildlife. If you want to gawk with tourists, find yourself a post at the launch point on the south side of the bridge right above where *Vertigo* was filmed—there will be plenty of smiling picture takers to commiserate with. *SB*

Asian Art Museum

200 Larkin St
581.3500
www.asainart.org
Tues–Wed, Fri–Sun 10a–5p, Thurs 10a–9p
Admission: $6–$12, free the first Tuesday of each month

One of the best collections of Asian art in the United States is housed in this modern San Francisco museum. Organized by geographic region, the jade carvings, Tibetan Thangkas, Japanese baskets, and Indonesian puppets are special highlights. Bring the entire family on Sundays—there is likely to be a craft project in the main veranda, free for all museumgoers. *SB*

Mexican Museum

202.9700
www.mexicanmuseum.org
This museum is moving to the Yerba Buena Cultural District at Third and Howard; check web site for current info.

The intermingling of cultures in California has been backed by Mexicans and Mexican Americans, so their history and traditions have become part of California life. Hear the voices and understand how hope, faith, beauty, and family have inspired and strengthened our community. Viewing the collection of crafts and listening to first-person stories of immigration will shed a new light on our roots. It's an outstanding collection, awaiting its permanent structure at Howard and Third streets in Yerba Buena Gardens. *SB*

Contemporary Jewish Museum

736 Mission St
344.8800
www.thecjm.org
Mon–Tues 11a–5:30p, Fri–Sun 11a–5:30p

The Jewish diaspora represents a rich quilt of humor, artistic dynamism, cutting-edge design, and historic significance. The exhibits at the new Daniel Libeskind building are elegantly organized, housed in an obtuse-angled structure imbued with fine style. Free cell phone tours make the dorky headsets a thing of the past, while offering a behind-the-scenes take on each exhibit, including info on the building itself. Download the tour to your iPod to get it right through your headphones (415.294.3605, *www.thecjm.org*, search podcast under "connect"). *SB*

San Francisco Public Library, Main Branch

100 Larkin St
557.4400
http://sfpl.lib.ca.us/index.htm
Mon 10a–6p, Tue–Thu 9a–8p, Fri 12–6p, Sat 10a–6p, Sun 12–5p

My favorite library in the entire Bay Area—I feel like we are best friends. The first travel guide I ever purchased, in fact, the first guide I looked at with any seriousness, was from the used volunteer-run shop near the south entrance. It's safe to say this library even got me through mono. When I was sick and feeling more depressed and lifeless than ever, I scooped up the books on tape and got through all of Henry James, which effectively made me want to get better and go out into the world again. Find your own savior at this massive library—it's the answer to all my prayers. *SB*

Museum of Craft and Folk Art

51 Yerba Buena Ln
227.4888
www.mocfa.org
Tues–Fri 11a–6p, Sat–Sun 11a–5p
Admission: $5–$7

Ever heard of synesthesia? It is the Technicolor neurological condition that brings colors to each number and letter to the beholder's eyes. For Jeremy Chase Sanders, each character is associated with a vibrant hue, which he matches to thread dyes in his amazing handwoven plaid textiles. Part of a recent Museum of Craft and Folk Art (MOCFA) exhibit, Sanders' fine handwork mingles with other recent California College of the Arts (CCA) students like Scott Oliver's "The Valley" and the spongy cardboard eclipse by Yvonne Mouser entitled "Tubes." Across from the new Contemporary Jewish Museum, this museum shouldn't be skipped over, but rather, sought after. *SB*

Twin Peaks

Top of Market Street to the far side of Sutro Tower

"The Fork," as my late grandmother used to call Sutro Tower, looks over SF with a constant blink of red light, making it the north star of this fine city. Look up to see it and you'll be better able to comprehend your bearings, since it marks the tippy-top of Market Street from the east and the heights above Cole Valley from the north. Surprisingly, it is not too touristy, considering the lot below it offers a sweeping view of the cityscape. If you turned on your imagination, or took it to the next setting on your internal dial, you could think of Sutro as one monster, born to outdo the other "monsters" in the bay—Bay Bridge and Golden Gate—like Herb Caen did in his writings on the city. Looking over from my late grandparents' Berkeley Hills apartment, I'd always see the big fork. Then when we'd go visit my uncle's parents, who lived it its shadow, I'd see it was much more than just a fork, and that the view from the opposite direction was as fascinating as from the East Bay. Watch the river of traffic down Market Street, lit up at night in a flow of colorful glimmers. I like hiking up from the top of Market Street (where there's a bus stop) and giving the tour buses a good girth, sitting just below the paved viewing area to take in the view. What amazing stories are being told right at that moment? Who is being born? Is someone being scolded for breaking a crystal goblet? Or is one of the people in the humming mass below discovering something, creating something that I'll use soon in my life? Ah the questions—it's hard not to ask them when you see what humanity has created from the perch of Twin Peaks under the big fork. *SB*

City Hall

1 Dr. Carlton B. Goodlett Pl, in Civic Center
www.sfgov.org/site/cityhall_index.asp
Mon–Fri 8a–8p

This is one City Hall that deserves a visit even if you aren't here to elope. Standing under the gilded dome—the fifth largest dome in the world—is a site to behold. Wander freely inside the building, a living masterpiece of current affairs and Renaissance architecture. The same designer, Arthur Brown, was responsible for the Opera House behind City Hall and Coit Tower, the pinnacle of North Beach. Stand on the stairs where Harvey Milk spoke and where countless protests have proven the might of democracy. *SB*

Golden Gate Park

The ups, downs, and all-arounds of one of America's greatest parks

Nothing is missing from Golden Gate Park, what is clearly, in my opinion, the best inner-city park in the United States. Perfect layers of gardens and lawns, native plants and overhanging trees, expertly designed English gardens, lakes, swamps, rivulets, a herd of bison, and an impressive AIDS memorial garden set the stage for the cultural and community place this park has become. Inside you'll find weekend concerts aplenty, the majestic mini-landscapes at the Japanese Garden, the de Young Museum, the natural history museum and aquarium, the Conservatory of Flowers, and more intertwined walking paths than you can shake a stick at. Whatever your mission, whether to play on your guitar for hours in the sun, to learn about native plant species at the botanical garden, to hear some reggae at a concert, or to go for a long run, you'll have the space and landscape for the activity of your choosing. I say forget the map and just get lost walking around the park for a day—you'll never be too far from a bus or knowledgeable stranger.

Conservatory of Flowers

John F. Kennedy Drive, Golden Gate Park
666.7001
www.conservatoryofflowers.org
Tues–Sun 9a–4:30p

Walk in to this glass palace of steam and old-fashioned elegance and you walk into a garden that has been tended by conservationists for generations. After a complete renovation, the plants having been salvaged from fire and earthquakes, this place is better than ever, with a tropical entryway, a room of potted plants including rare Japanese varieties, and an Amazonian lily pond with the largest lily pads on the planet. Free tours are held a few times a day, and circulating exhibits fill an adjunct room throughout the year. Free days are first Tuesdays. *SB*

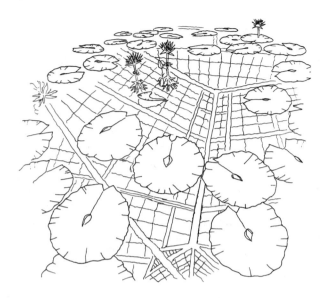

🏮 Succulent Garden in San Francisco Botanical Garden
💲 *Lincoln Way at Ninth Avenue*

💡 Now, I'm not one to argue with a beautiful garden, or to pick favorites, but the succulent garden in Golden Gate Park is by far the wildest assortment of plants I've ever seen. The whole botanical garden is a gem (and free!), but if you take the time to walk deeper into the garden, you'll come across a succulent paradise that looks to be from another planet. You'll get lost wandering among sections devoted to South Africa, Australia, and the Mediterranean. There are endless nooks and crannies to stumble upon or benches to smooch your loved one on—yet another reason that Golden Gate Park is the place to be when the raindrops are at bay. *JA*

California Academy of Sciences

Our tour begins at Golden Gate Park, 1,017 acres of green that represent the third most visited park in the country and hold a special place in American history. The park we see today was first planted by Scottish-trained landscape designers William Hammond Hall and John McLaren in the late 1870s, in such a way that the original landscape, unruly sand dunes, were hemmed in. By the 1880s there had been more than one hundred fifty thousand native and nonnative trees planted in the park, a number that steadily rose with the park's many conservation and recreation projects. By the World's Fair in 1894, Hagiwara Makoto, a master gardener and inventor of the fortune cookie, designed and kept up the first authentic Japanese garden in the United States. The first version of the de Young Museum was also finished for this occasion. Winding promenades connected attractions like Kezar Stadium, Stowe and Spreckels Lakes, the Conservatory of Flowers, the Strybing Aquarium, and a 55-acre botanical garden and arboretum, many constructed with WPA funds in the 1930s.

Today Golden Gate Park is where San Franciscans come for a meandering weekend walk or to hear a free concert at one of the many annual music festivals. At any given time there is a mix of locals and tourists, dog walkers and nature lovers, art appreciators and people who are happy to get lost for a couple hours in the many wonders the park offers. The park is always a hotbed for new ideas in the city, from the restoration of the Conservatory of Flowers, to the new de Young Museum, to the constant enhancements being made to the Botanical Gardens. The excitement is building for the opening of the new Platinum LEED California Academy of Sciences Building, a revolutionary project that represents San Francisco's forward-thinking values and the ability to see many entities working together for sustainability.

As you begin your tour, take the chance to connect the dots around you. With Herzog and de Meuron's de Young Museum behind you, the Japanese Tea Garden is around the bend to your right, and in front of you is the courtyard facing the Academy. Beyond the Academy is the Shakespeare Garden, blooming with flowers named for various Shakespeare characters. The east end of the park hosts handball and tennis courts, several baseball diamonds, historic Kezar Stadium, and McLaren Lodge, named for the park designer who lived there until his death at 90 in the 1940s. Lincoln Way, and behind it Irving Street, bound the park to the south and form a close-knit community of mostly locally owned businesses, including some of the city's best sushi and traditional high tea. Stowe Lake sits to the west, with the San Francisco Botanical Gardens wrapping most of the lake's southern edge.

Now that you have your bearings, it is impossible to ignore the location's significance. Golden Gate Park is a place where education, culture, conservation, and recreation are all accessible. The new Academy building will be a monument that attests to San Francisco's dedication to sustainability while promoting education in the sciences, conservation of both regional and global environments while meshing with the other diverse facilities in the park. This is a true example of the "world as your classroom" philosophy.

As you enter the Academy, notice the open feel that synchs the indoor space with the surrounding natural environment. Before you set out on your tour, SFEnvironment's Mark Palmer offers an introduction to the successes of the Academy:

SFEnvironment (SFE) supported the California Academy of Sciences project as a part of their goal to promote sustainable city design. The organization's range covers energy efficiency, green building, toxics reduction, environmental justice, clean air, zero waste, urban forestry, public outreach, and school education. The SFE has been a part of many LEED-certified buildings around San Francisco, a map of which can be found on the web site (see the information page of this chapter), and have brought ordinances to the private sector, such as incentives and requirements.

The new Academy of Sciences embodies many of the principles SFE wishes to promote, from the integrated design process to the solar photovoltaics on the roof of the museum. Zoning was pushed through bureaucracy, and rapid permitting is one of the incentives for green building that made the timing of this project possible. During the construction and demolition of the old structure, a full 90 percent of the nontoxic waste was reused, recycled, or otherwise diverted from landfill. The inner workings of the structure were designed to be more than 30 percent more efficient than California Energy Code, and the naturally ventilated spaces marginalize the use of electric heating and cooling devices. The roof of the museum, described by the architect as lifting the ground and placing a museum under it, is covered with 2.5 acres of native plants that thrive without irrigation. Photovoltaic cells generate onsite renewable energy. Water reduction is 30 percent more efficient than mandated by building codes, and 93 percent reduction in wastewater conveyance gives the museum a smaller impact on the already overworked water treatment facilities in the Bay Area. The materials selected are all nontoxic, and either recycled or rapidly renewable, qualifying the new Academy for LEED Platinum certification, the highest recognition. The motive of the museum is to educate visitors of all ages about the environment, not only the many species but also the need for environmental protection and sustainable living, making it a leading force for a much-needed turnaround in our way of life.

On the ground level, a 90-foot-diameter dome houses three rainforest galleries with living animals native to Borneo, Madagascar, and Costa Rica. Next door, the Climate Change exhibit inspires activism by immersing visitors in the biodiversity of California and the impact of climate change on its natural habitats. At the rear of the building is the Academy's most popular exhibit—the swamp returns with turtles, a rare alligator, and subtropical fish. Read up on the latest scientific discoveries in the newsroom or learn about the findings from the Academy scientists' field expeditions. On the lower level, the Philippine Coral Reef exhibit boasts the world's deepest interior coral reef ecosystem, with three thousand exotic fish. At the floor's center is a showcase of aquarium habitats supporting seahorses, snakes, turtles, frogs, fish, and more. Continuing to the other end of the floor is the Amazon Flooded Forest, where visitors descend by elevator beneath the rainforest dome exhibit to witness the Amazonian rainy season. The upper level features an interactive resource center with space for lectures and the open-air observation terrace, allowing access to the Living Roof and spectacular views of surrounding Golden Gate Park.

Garden of Shakespeare's Flowers

Martin Luther King Drive

www.sfgov.org/site/recpark_page.asp?id=17796

This is one of the smaller attractions of Golden Gate Park, but if you're a fan of the Bard then it can't be missed. It's filled with flowers and plants that are mentioned in Shakespeare's works, and is the perfect spot for organizing a "match the play to the plant" scavenger hunt. *JA*

Japanese Tea Garden

Tea Garden Drive, Golden Gate Park

752.4227

Daily 8:30a–6p, but hours vary slightly by season

Around the bend from the de Young Museum, the tea garden has a history much earlier than any of the other buildings in the vicinity. The first shrubs and water elements were placed in the late 1800s, designed specifically to surround the wonderful authentic Japanese Tea House. To this day you can visit for a brimming pot of *macha*, although you'll have to head to the Asian Art Museum to experience the real tea ceremony. Hagiwara Makoto and Sakurai Nagao brought their time-honored skills when they first immigrated to San Francisco, bringing with them their families and some specialized tools with thoughts of eventually creating a Japanese garden in the United States. Even though the garden was loved by all who discovered it, that didn't stop the U.S. government from interning the family that built and kept up the garden in World War II. These struggles wrought strife and unbelievable injustice, but somehow the garden and the family made it through, and the restored and well-kept wonderland is thriving today. Think about culture, politics, challenge, and beauty while you pace the garden paths. This magnificent, meditative place is probably my favorite single location in all of SF. Come early on weekdays to miss the crowds. SB

Learn

Courses, classes, and seminars of all sorts, and places to take on new challenges

Flexing your brain muscle is a great way to enhance a vacation or to prolong a visit to a place. Classes are also a great way to meet locals. My grandmother was never bored; at the ripe old age of 82 she took Chinese language classes, having no background in it at all. She always inspired me to listen up and see what I could learn.

 Norcal DJ Academy

2600 Van Ness Ave, Ste 190W
236.2084
www.norcaldjmpa.com

The science of spinning is becoming bigger and bigger for youngsters and oldsters alike. While I am satisfied to peruse record stores and just play the records, and watch my DVD of *Scratch* every now and again, it's comforting to know that the best of the best are making it possible for any Joe Schmoe to learn how to scratch properly. After-school programs for inner-city youth are an incredible outreach program of this academy. Take a onetime class, but be prepared to catch the bug. Once you're hooked, there's no going back—you'll spin for life. SB

Tante Marie's Cooking School

 271 Francisco St

788.6699

www.tantemarie.com

Call for classes, prices, and times

All cooking schools should be like this one. The intimate but ample kitchen provides students with an opportunity to communicate with the instructors, and avoids the common problem of many cooking classes that follow a lecture format. There are options for everyone, including guest chef demonstrations on topics like Vietnamese cooking and the handling of fish and shellfish. *JA*

Cell Space

2050 Bryant St

648.7562

www.cellspace.org

Daily 10a–10p, weekend closing time varies based on event schedule

Boasting a ten-thousand-foot performance space and nine individual art studios, there's literally something for everyone here. Silk-screening facilities are available for just $7 an hour, and you can use their darkroom for just $5. Lots of adult and youth classes are offered in a plethora of mediums like textiles and wood shop. Learn how to dance the tango, practice your welding skills, or catch a performance. At Cell Space there are just too many resources to count, and since it is largely community run, you never know what you're gonna get. Events include art exhibits, a farmers market, and a flea market to boot. Serena and I are regulars at their biannual SF Clothes Swap, where $5 will get you a free drink, plus tables of free clothes to sort through. Oh yeah! *MP*

San Francisco Conservatory of Music

50 Oak St

863.7326

www.sfcm.edu

For more informal concerts and to take lessons with masterful musicians, head to SF's Conservatory and get serious about your love of music. I can't wait until I make the time to do this myself. *SB*

Om Organics

3128 16th St. #109
205.9766
www.omorganics.org
Class schedules and events vary

Om hosts classes on many sustainable topics like composting, home gardening in the city, and seasonal cooking classes. Their web site has an insider's look at where the best fresh food can be found, as well as current events and info about farms and produce stands. This is one of the greatest SF resources for conscientious living, and the classes can't be beat. *SB*

Salsa classes at Roccapulco Supper Club

3140 Mission St
648.6611
www.roccapulco.com
Wed 8:30p–10:30p, Fri–Sat 8:30a–9:30p

Aside from being one of the best places to dance, this supper club also offers fantastic salsa classes. If you are looking for attention to detail, Wednesday is the best night to put on your dancing shoes. Two-hour classes are taught by Ciro and Mary Ann of La Evolucion Dance Company, and will only set you back $10. The first hour is for beginners, while the second hour provides more advanced training for intermediate students. Stay after class for an informal dance party. *MP*

Alliance Française San Francisco

1345 Bush St
775.7755
www.afsf.com
Hours and events vary

From classes to culture, wine to film, schmoozing to learning, Alliance Française is where you can actually learn French by immersing yourself in all things France, rather than just studying a bone-dry textbook. Learn about French drama, take philosophy courses in French, or just get a basic primer course—it is all here, offered at different times throughout the year. Check the web site for a course brochure. *SB*

Learning Annex

www.learningannex.com
Class locations vary, the web site is the best resource to start your search

Although the Annex proclaims itself as being the largest learning community in the world, in effect, it still has a local feel, at least in San Francisco. I have many a friend in the writing, traveling, and eating communities who have had wonderful experiences both teaching and learning here. Whether your interest is starting a small press, learning how to invest in the midst of the economic crisis, brushing up on high school French, or getting your foot in the door at a TV station, the adult ed classes here are affordable and worth your time. Plus, there are handy online courses if you won't be able to commute to school each week. I like meeting people in person, so I've opted for the stock investment strategies course in person, taken alongside a creative writing workshop in short poems. Ah, the Renaissance woman! *SB*

Cheese School

2155 Powell St, second floor
346.7530
www.cheeseschoolsf.com
Class schedule varies, call ahead

You don't have to be a snobby foodie to love cheese, or to become a bona fide cheese monger and impress all your friends. Sneak in a few sessions at the Cheese School of San Francisco and learn your Gruyère, Stilton, and Roquefort, your aged provolone and your buffalo mozzarella . . . mmm . . . Choose from tasty course offerings like "the cheeses of France," "Locavores' Cheese and Wine," or "Farmstead Cheese." Classes are mostly one-shot wonders, so plan for a couple hours of chees-u-cation! *SB*

New Conservatory Theatre Center

25 Van Ness Ave, lower level
861.4914
www.nctcsf.org
Call for shows, classes, and times

New Conservatory has been a valuable part of the San Francisco community for a quarter of a decade. In addition to their "Pride Season," which features plays that largely deal with LGBT issues, they house an excellent acting school for youth and adults alike. Their space holds three different theaters, allowing you three fabulous choices when you are in the mood for some culture. The shows tend to sell out due to the intimate nature of the performance spaces, so call ahead to secure your seats. *JA*

Sewing Classes

As someone who has benefited from a Waldorf education, I learned in kindergarten how to bake bread and how to sew a running stitch, and I've kept up both habits ever since. My honey is a great seamster too; he learned in Eagle Scouts, but what about you? Getting by in the world should involve some hands-on skills in my modest opinion, and sewing is at the core. Take a basic how-to class, or learn the ins and outs of pattern sewing. I took a semester off of university to take a textile class and a pattern-making class at an art school, and now I can not only envision new outfits but also retrofit thrift store finds, not to mention mend, mend, mend! Get with it and have fun in the same go at these two top-notch sew locales. *SB*

Sewing Workshop
2010 Balboa St
221.7397
www.thesewingworkshop.com

It's impossible not to get serious about sewing at the Sewing Workshop. Sewing Basics classes are taught practically every week, but the real gems here are their specialty courses, like the Cockades class, where you can learn to make intricate French hat decorations for ribbons and pins—amazing! Hand sewing, creating unique accessories, or sewing a perfect fitted jacket are also highlights on their full course schedule; some last one evening, some have repeat meet-ups, but all enable us to get in touch with our hands in a deeper way.

Stitch Lounge
182 Gough St
431.3739
www.stitchlounge.com

There are no classes here, but great supplies, so stop by and get buttons and good cloth scissors for your sewing delight. If you're a dyed-in-the-wool DIY-er, check out their two books at your local library: *Subversive Seamster*, about transforming thrift store finds into cool clothes, and *Sew Subversive*, all the tricks you need to be ultra-fashionable the DIY way.

Spanish Classes at Casa Hispana

110 Gough St #415
861.1223
www.casahispana.com

It is pretty important to have at least a working ability in Spanish when you're in a place settled by Spanish speakers and populated by many from a number of different nations. I like learning through discovery of culture—it makes the language stick better when I am involved in what is being discussed. Try the methods of Casa Hispana, where spoken Spanish is highlighted rather than the old-school rote style. You're on your way! I should go back so I can learn more than just how to order tacos from El Tonayense (see page 87). *SB*

Knitting Classes

San Francisco is an ideal knitting city—the mix of fuzzy fog, still-crowded streets, and a communal essence urge people young and old to create something with their own click-clacking needles and a ball of colorful yarn. Yerba Buena Center for the Arts recently featured a show of knitted imposter bags, from Gucci to Prada. If you still need inspiration to knit, then check the temperature; many months of the year, you'll be happy to have the hug of a scarf to warm you. *SB*

Noe Knit

3957 24th St
970.9750
http://noeknit.com

Move beyond the simple knit-one, purl-one scarf, learn to make cute cable hats, and even try your hand at felting. Noe Knit has more specialized classes so you can share your difficulties and successes with your fellow participants.

Atelier Yarns

 1945 Greenwich St
567.2535
www.atelieryarns.com

This is the spot to work on your dream sweater, whether in one of the seasonal "pattern play" classes or in an open workshop where you can bring in a project and be supervised to ensure success. Atelier has the most fanciful patterns; like a famed clothing shop or designer, you'll want everything in the pattern section to be made already, and on you!

Greenwich Yarn

2073 Greenwich St
567.2535
www.greenwichyarn.com

Perhaps the longest list of class offerings, all suited for beginners or intermediate knitters looking to learn the basics, color changes, or how to create an easy lattice.

SF Knitting Guild

100 Larkin Street, Main Branch SF Public Library; ask for specific room at info kiosk as it has been inconsistent

Not to be confused with the for-profit Knitters Guild of America, this casual, free group meets every month to chat, solve knitting dilemmas, and have a merry ol' time. Join in the fun at the library and if you have questions, e-mail ematsui@sfchronicle.com.

Imagiknit

3897 18th St
621.6642
www.imagiknit.com

Crafting is at its best at Imagiknit, a bona fide celebration of all things yarn. There are classes on designing your own pattern to fit perfectly on your bod, and even a course in how to knit ergonomically so you don't cause yourself injury.

Other knit-o-licious groups:

SF Knitters, Muddy's, 1304 Valencia St, 647.7994, every Wednesday, 7p
Crafty Bitches, Lexington Club, 3464 19th St, 863.2052, every Wednesday, 6:30p
Stitch and Bitch, Annie's Cocktails, 15 Boardman Pl, 703.0865, every Wednesday, 6:30p
Queer Knitters, Three Dollar Bill Café inside SF LGBT Center, 1800 Market St, 503.1532, every Monday, 7p
Men Who Knit, Café MacOndo, 3159 16th St, 863.6517, every Tuesday, 7p
Church of Craft, Atlas Café, 3049 20th St, 648.1047, group contact: 640.4224,every third Sunday, 12–6p

Get Inspired

Museums, installations, awe-inspiring exhibits, and anything that aims to enthuse

The West Coast art movement is led in large part by San Francisco. With a multitude of top-notch art schools, internationally acclaimed museums and galleries, and a general sense of design and style, getting inspired is practically made mandatory just by setting foot here. Underground filmmakers and modern sculptors have found a steadfast community of equals here. Playwrights and printmakers reside side by side. Screen printing workshops host spoken-word events. With citywide gallery crawls and a strong commitment to sustainability and reuse in art, there are many straight-ahead creative minds converging. Here is a listing of galleries, stages, and museums that bring to the surface the artistic integrity of this part of the world.

San Francisco Museum of Modern Art

151 Third St
357.4000
www.sfmoma.org
Mon–Tues 11a–5:45p, Thurs 11a–8:45p, Fri–Sun 10a–5:45p
Admission: $7–$12.50, free the first Tuesday of the month 11a–5:45p, half price every Thursday 6–8:45p

Elegant architecture with a bold striped motif sets the SFMOMA apart from other buildings downtown. The extensive permanent collections of modern painting and photographs are always accompanied by several special exhibitions and installations. There is a new library and research center for talks, and computer database access. Climb the stairs for an always-innovative top-floor show, often featuring the most incredible stretches of video and interactive art using modern technology. The Diebenkorn and Rothko in their permanent collection are particularly marvelous, as are their splendid photography collections and my favorite, *Kind mit Pudeln* (Child with Poodles), a room-size sculpture by Katharina Fritsch. Ah, poodles! *SB*

Yerba Buena Center for the Arts

701 Mission St
978.ARTS (2787)
www.ybca.org
Tues–Wed, Fri–Sun 12–5p, Thurs 12–8p
Admission: $5–$8, free the first Tuesday of the month

The modern art and resident artist exhibitions here always push the proverbial envelope. Named for San Francisco's first incarnation as a pre–Gold Rush port village, there is a diversity of performance art, film, and installations that often extend out in the surrounding gardens between the museum and the Metreon. A rich community asset uses resources to bring people closer to the world around them through art and through creative thinking. Join in a discussion, take a class, or hear a lecture after strolling through these unique galleries. This museum displays the best new art and the most tasteful media installations. *SB*

de Young Museum

50 Hagiwara Tea Garden in Golden Gate Park
750.3600
www.deyoungmuseum.org
Tues–Thurs, Sat–Sun 9:30a–5:15p, Fri 9:30a–8:45p
Admission: $6–$10, free the first Tuesday of each month 9:30a–5p

Even if your primary intention is to check out the view at the top of this museum's turret, you'll be easily suckered into an afternoon of art and culture—this place is just intoxicating! A real smorgasbord of art and artifacts, people seem to have a love/hate relationship to the new and improved de Young. As for me, I love the building's architecture and the Andy Goldsworthy entry. The collections are astoundingly diverse and really quite good. On the one hand, it is interesting to see the ritual artifacts of Oceana in the gallery next to collodion photographs and Haitian paintings, or Oaxacan stone carvings around the corner from art glass and works of Jasper Johns. On the other hand, there is little to no information about the artifacts; they are simply presented as art for art's sake, which may not respect the context in which the objects were produced or their purpose. Back on the plus side, the observatory tower rewards museumgoers with a great view all the way to the coast. The bimonthly special exhibitions are very well done. I say all this not to steer anyone away, but to open conversation about how museums are curated, and simply to take notes of the pros and cons of this innovative approach, which I think everyone will agree it is. Just pace yourself and plan for a tea break next door at the Japanese gardens afterward (which unfortunately have very rare free hours, usually in the early morning). *sb*

Last Saturday Art Walk

 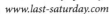

Last Saturday of every month, Soma neighborhood
www.last-saturday.com

There're six fabulous galleries to go to each final Saturday of the month in San Francisco's relatively new dual-gallery event. Each of the participating galleries have maps for free, so it doesn't matter which one you pick to start. My faves? Crown Point Press (20 Hawthorne St, see page 131); Aftermodern (445 Bryant St); and Gallery 16 (501 Third St). There's more: MM Galleries (101 Townsend St); Andrea Schwartz Gallery (525 Second St); and ArtHaus (411 Brannan St). So get marchin'! *sb*

Bucheon Gallery

389 Grove St
863.2891
www.bucheon.com
Tues–Sat 11a–6p

Next door to Citizen Cake, the bar-meets-restaurant-meets-patisserie, you'll be taken in by Bucheon. Full of something like a pop-art reincarnation, bright colors, loud textures, and readily sensuous art coats the gallery walls. I am surprised with the viewing ease these rotating shows manage, even in their youthful rashness. Take a peek in—there is always something bright and unusual to wrap your critical mind around. *SB*

SF Recycling

501 Tunnel Ave
330.1400
www.sfrecycling.com

A dump with artists in residence? Don't put it past San Francisco—this dump is one of my favorite places to explore. On the third Saturday of each month you can tour the artist studios, where trash is reformed, repurposed, and rewelded into the visions of whoever is currently creating there. Bring your recycling or a clean slate to cover with new ideas and inspiration from what else, but trash! *SB*

First Thursday Gallery Walk

First Thursday of the month, 5–8p
Various locations

I grew up following my artist mother around the streets of Philadelphia for that city's First Thursday event, the originator of a now-national phenomenon, so I am well versed in the lively goodness of coordinating openings. There's no wrong way to go about attending; stop by most any gallery in the Union Square general vicinity and you'll be handed a free sip of vino and be ushered in to the latest and greatest the place has to offer. Some of the standbys: Hackett-Freedman Gallery (250 Sutter St, fourth floor); John Berggruen Gallery (228 Grant Ave); Gallery Paule Anglim (14 Geary St); Robert Koch Gallery (49 Geary St, #550); Elins Eagles-Smith Gallery (49 Geary St); Brian Gross Fine Art (49 Geary St, #509); Mark Wolfe Contemporary Art (49 Geary St #202); Modernism Gallery (685 Market St, #290); Frey Norris Gallery

(450 Geary St); and 111 Minna (111 Minna St, see page 164). Make note, this is an array of mostly highly established galleries, with a few newbies strung in between, but this show is all about San Francisco's well-trodden art path, rich with famous names and soon-to-be famous newcomers. Go to Last Saturday (see page 127) for this city's softer art underbelly. *SB*

SF Camerawork

657 Mission St, second floor
512.2020
www.sfcamerawork.org
Tues–Sat 12–5p

San Francisco is home to some spectacular views—its hilltop neighborhoods provide ample opportunities for that perfect shot. SF Camerawork, a non-profit artist's organization founded in 1974, showcases six to eight major exhibitions each year, but seeing one is enough to have you aspiring to be a great composer in this remarkable medium. With workshops, conferences, critique sessions, a reference library, and more, Camerawork encourages emerging artists to delve into new directions in photography. *DL*

The Lab

2948 16th St
864.8855
www.thelab.org
Wed–Sat 1–6p during exhibitions

Playing a vital role in San Francisco's art community since 1984, the Lab is an interdisciplinary organization widely known for its presentation of experimental art from emerging and underrepresented artists. Simply put, art is creation by human endeavor; the Lab stays true to this definition by encouraging the evolution of artistic and social dialogue between artists and audiences. All genres and media are represented, from visual to performing to literary—and perhaps something unexpected. *DL*

Needles and Pens

3253 16th St
255.1534
www.needles-pens.com
Daily 12–7p

Where in SF do you go when you want a treasure trove of local 'zines? Needles and Pens, of course, where the always-interesting window displays will draw you in, and you'll find yourself wrapped up in imagination's wonderland for hours. All those ideas that rattle around in my brain find practical applications here, and I'm always inspired by the art hanging on the walls. Forget the fancy-pants art gallery scene and get real with artists who create like they breathe, as necessity and healing remedy. *SB*

Museum of the African Diaspora

685 Mission St
385.7200
www.moadsf.org
Wed–Sat 11a–6p, Sun 12–5p

As a one-of-a-kind museum, MOAD recognizes the full scope of the scattering of African cultures to new lands, through food, clothing, music, and personal narrative. The permanent exhibitions will leave you with many thoughts, both painful and inspiring; most eloquently perhaps are the slavery passages, told by the slaves who strived toward freedom's boundaries. The unique way this museum brings the story close to your heart by catching your curiosity makes it a must-see in SF. Transcend the common borders of culture, race, and religion, and open your heart to this meaningful and beautiful experience. *SB*

William Stout Architectural Books

804 Montgomery St
391.6757
www.stoutbooks.com
Mon–Fri 10a–6:30p, Sat 10a–5:30p

One of my favorite bookstores is a place where art and architecture are at the fore. Swiss architect Peter Zumthor, photography books by Kidder Smith, "The Air is Blue" from Mexico City's Lius Barragan, cutting-edge French interior design: this is where the movers and shakers hang out. No, I don't mean the suits you see traipsing around the financial district, I mean the ones that move culture forward, the ones whose creations end up dictating the market—the true trendsetters. For me, I don't like that kind of pressure, so I imagine myself in my tree-climbing outfit, lace-frilled dress with patent leather shoes, and I come and sit in one of their reading chairs, pretending my feet don't yet reach the ground and proclaim it picture-book day. You won't leave here without a plethora of witty and original ideas. *SB*

Lincart

1632C Market St
503.1981
www.lincart.com
Tue–Sat 12–6p and by appointment

Striving for interaction among artists, collectors, and viewers, Lincart has created an inviting and informal space that allows visitors to interact directly with the makers of the work. The gallery often features seemingly lighthearted works with deeper undertones to provoke discussion. Solo exhibitions are prominent, but I find the once-a-year group shows to be the highlight. Take, for instance, the 2006 show entitled "Boys Club," which presented themes inspired by the lyrics of James Brown, and keeping with the Lincart philosophy of interaction, mixed artists of various backgrounds and career stages. *DL*

Palace of the Legion of Honor

34th Ave in Lincoln Park
863.3330
www.thinker.org
Tue–Sun 9:30a–5:15p
Admission: $6–$10, free every Tuesday

Take one drawing pad, one pen, one pencil, and yourself over to the Legion and find a few subjects. This is my favorite game to play at one of the most incredible museums. Perched above the city, overlooking the wild currents of the Pacific and the crashing coast of the Marin Headlands, the Legion is a palace in many ways. It houses an organ, which you'll hear piping up each day and at evening performances, often accompanied by other instruments. Fully reconstructed rooms from historic structures are found throughout the otherwise white-walled museum, and a downstairs gallery of current revolving exhibits melds the rich fabric of the past with the present. *SB*

Crown Point Press

20 Hawthorne St
974.6273
www.crownpoint.com
Hours and openings vary

William T. Wiley is just one of the lucky artists to have been invited, and re-invited, to work at Crown Point Press, the world's most famous etching and printmaking studio. As I stroll through the public gallery I find one of his recent works with a short pondering:

"And so, the shadow of the whip. I remember reading a Zen story that said some horses respond to the shadow of the whip others respond to the first light tap and still others must be flogged until they feel it in the marrow of their bones and so which horse are you and for which horse does a Buddha have the most compassion." This quote rolls around in my head since the time I first saw it—and it seems each visit I make, another savored image or delicate string of words stays on my mind, like the most divine sort of residue. The two print shops spill the best work over into the gallery space, where you can also peruse the bookstore made up of Crown Point Press' own series of etching books, local treasures, and artist manuals. Frequent openings bring the printmakers from behind the scenes. As famed Crown Point veteran Sol LeWitt says, "Artists are mystics rather than rationalists. They leap to conclusions that logic cannot reach." Come see for yourself. *SB*

Mission Cultural Center for Latino Arts

2868 Mission St
821.1155
www.missionculturalcenter.org

Breaking this place down . . . 40 classes a week in all different disciplines, a stage where playwrights, choreographers, and filmmakers strut their stuff, and four floors of inspiration. This list, though impressive, doesn't begin to explain the powerful experiences waiting to be had. Learn capoeira, Aztec dance, Cuban salsa, flamenco, Puerto Rican salsa, and Afro-Peruvian dance techniques from masters of their art form, while meeting members of a rich and diverse community. Regular attendees are from every walk of life, all coming with an open mind to wax culturally creative. Music lessons on guitar, piano, and drums fill out the class schedule, plus a few silk-screening courses. Jam out any day of the week, then return to watch the stage light up with sound, color, and imagination. *SB*

Create

From beads to seeds, fabric to photos, these spots will enable your creative side for sure

I switched colleges my sophomore year to go to art school. I wanted to draw and paint and take photos all day instead of calculating chemical equations and studying political systems. Later, I changed my mind and went back for international studies and English, but what I learned from the experience was something that hadn't crossed my mind before: everyone can create beauty; everyone can be an artist. I saw people who had never taken their pencil out of the lines on a steno pad draw impeccable contour figures by the end of one semester. Their eyes and their hands had become one unit. With a little drive, anyone can contribute to the beauty in the world. I also feel that it is important to maintain a connection with handwork. If you haven't ever tried something like this yourself, the satisfaction of eating something you have grown or cooked, wearing a dress you have made, or a scarf you have knitted is astonishing. Your hands are the greatest machines.

FLAX Art & Design

1699 Market St
552.2355
www.flaxart.com
Mon–Sat 9:30a–6p

Whenever I need to put a smile on my face, I pop into FLAX to pick up a little something to brighten my day. Although the store is equipped for true artists, even a regular old paper junkie like me can get a very satisfying fix in this artistic supply shop. Check out the paper section at the back of the store, with large sheets of printed and unprinted paper in such delicious materials as silk, cotton, and wool. Looking for a beautiful journal or scrapbook, unique stationery, a really good set of art pens or even an artistic baby mobile? FLAX is your spot. If you are not sure what you crave, or you need advice on a decision, FLAX has an exceptional staff ready and waiting to meet your every creative need. *JA*

Oak Hill Farm Store

Ferry Building

Ikebana can be created even out of seemingly disconnected foliage. Sometimes you only need three stems to make an arrangement, other times you can use an armload of flora. I am such a fanatic. One of my favorite pastimes is creating these living sculptures; it is fun to continue working on them and learning more. Each finished display exhibits the nature of things as impermanent and always subject to change. At Oak Hill, the only completely organic flower stand in San Francisco, there are flowers that represent the seasons, something ikebana always seeks to interpret. Use organic and seasonal ingredients in your next floral creation, ikebana or no. *SB*

Beadissimo

1051 Valencia St
282.2323
www.beadissimo.com
Mon 12–6p, Tues–Wed 10a–6p, Thurs–Fri 10a–7p, Sun 11a–5p

Beads from around the world, in all shapes, sizes, colors, and variations, can be found in boxes and on strands at this designer's paradise. New findings, specialty metals, and chains give your jewelry creations new flair. The staff members are all talented designers, and can help give you options and inspire your ideas. Beadissimo is locally owned and operated and has reasonable prices. *SB*

Paper Tree Art Supplies

1743 Buchanan St
921.7100
www.paper-tree.com
Mon–Fri 10a–5:30p, Sat 10a–4:30p

Even if you know nothing about origami, I suggest a good-hearted rummage through the annals of Paper Tree, in the center of Japantown. Fine-tip glue dispensers, a wild selection of markers, gel pens, and calligraphy sets, and of course papers beyond your wildest imaginings. I tend to make my own stationery, and even with e-mail to connect with friends and loved ones, I still send letters as much as possible. I'm also part of a postcard club where each month every member sends handmade cards to all the others like flying art (sending art by airmail to someone else). Before I get down to it, I head here for a bit of a splurge to invigorate my collages. *SB*

Arch Drafting Supplies

99 Missouri St
433.2724
www.archsupplies.com
Mon–Fri 9a–6p

At last, a source for 0.9mm pencils, no more flimsy 0.5 lead snapping under my heavy-handedness. The tagline says it all—"Tools for designers, supplies for artists, inspiration for inquisitive minds." Arch offers supplies for just about any project you can imagine. In addition to their 10 to 40 percent marked-down prices, Arch offers discounts for all the starving students and underpaid faculty out there. Here's the kicker: I went into Arch looking to replace my favorite, but dirty and no longer functioning, pen to be taken aback by the existence of ultrasonic pen cleaning. By the end of the week I was happily gripping my favorite pen, restored to like-new condition. Remember a time when there was no need to buy a new tool as long as its broken or missing parts could be replaced? Arch carries a variety of parts so you won't have to break the bank replacing that expensive compass or technical pen. *DL*

Church Street Flowers

212 Church St
553.7762
www.churchstreetflowers.com
Mon–Fri 9a–7p, Sat 10a–7p

The most beautiful and interesting flowers and greenery can be found in this tiny little storefront in the Castro. While the store crafts beautiful arrangements of their own, they can also help you pick out the best selection of peonies, orchids, lotus blossoms, or any number of rose varieties for your own arrangement. All flowers are bought locally, so if it is not in season, they won't have it. Owners Michael and Tom are fully committed to community outreach, going so far as to provide free bouquets to couples marrying at City Hall during the brief legalization of gay marriages in San Francisco. *JA*

Patrick and Co.

1390 Market St
621.1477
Mon–Fri 8a–6:30p

A locally owned office supply store may not seem to be the place to wax creative, but then you haven't been to Patrick and Co., an old-school San Francisco financial district staple. Under low ceilings there are shelves of every knickknack, craft tool, or thickness of paper you can imagine, waiting to enter your stream of consciousness and funnel out into some material project. I love the little yard sale tags they sell, which make great bookmarks once I draw and collage on them. Or take a stack of metal widgets, otherwise bound for hinging some boring legal debriefing, and connect them to strings and flying paper sculptures in a mobile. Who knows what you'll make, but this unlikely spot is wonderful for the in-between ingredients that it takes to be an artist and a businessperson. Who says you can't be both? *SB*

Terra Mia Ceramic Studios

1314 Castro St.
642.9911
www.terramia.net
Sun–Thurs 11a–6p, Fri–Sat 11a–7p

We take for granted the little paint-your-own shops in towns strewn across the country, but in California, Terra Mia was the originator of the hand-painted craze. Decorate your own teapot with glaze in matte or glassy finish. Imprint your hands and feet in clay for posterity, then paint them in honor. Warning, if you are a close friend or relative of mine, there's a good chance your b-day present will be made by me here! SB

Casual Night Out
Dining and delighting in a relaxed atmosphere

There is always a time when you just want to kick back and have a relaxed evening out. The state of California is blanketed with a rich natural beauty, in combo with condensed epicenters of international culture and commerce. Go out, but go in comfort, with the divine purpose of repose. Good eats and good laughs galore lie ahead.

Absinthe

398 Hayes St
551.1590
www.absinthe.com
Tues–Thurs 11:30a–12a, Fri 11:30a–2a, Sat 11a–2a, Sun 11a–10p

It is hard to think of anything else after witnessing the San Francisco Orchestra's epic performance of Mahler's Symphony No. 8, also known as "the Symphony of a Thousand," much less where and what to eat. But there is always Absinthe, the corner brasserie around the bend from the Civic Center and the performance halls. Thanks to this reliable fixture, ideal for an après-concert munch, the music can still drift in my head while I immerse myself in the French-ness I love and the warm, delectable foods I desire. Opt for the daily soup special and try not to be confused by the number of menus served at different hours of the day. Charcuterie here is elevated to an art form, as are unique salads that seem to have pioneered ingredient combination trends in other eateries around the city. SB

Palace of Fine Arts

Lyon and Bay streets
563.6504

In the yellow glow that seems to emanate from the Golden Gate at sunset, the pillars around the Palace of Fine Arts are illuminated. In a moment where

everything in my life was up in the air, I took a long Saturday-night stroll weaving in and out of the pillars and waterworks, and all came clear. The deep quiet that can be achieved here, right in the middle of the city, is worth seeking out for tough decision making, or simply a timeless walk around the most picturesque structure in San Francisco. SB

$$ **Levende Lounge**

1710 Mission St
864.5585
www.levendelounge.com
Tues–Fri 5p–2a, Sat 6p–5a, Sun 11a–3p, Happy Hour Tues–Fri 5–7p

Amber lighting creates a warm glow and DJs pump down-tempo beats through the world-class sound system as I peruse the dinner menu of delectable, small-plate world-fusion cuisine. This stylish dig has been voted one of the best places for conversation, so strike one up with your neighbor at the bar while enjoying a cheese fondue duet. *DL*

$$ **Serpentine**

2495 Third St
252.2000
http://serpentinesf.com
Mon 11:30a–2:30p, Tues–Fri 11:30a–10p, Sat 6–10p

Slow Club's baby brother is most definitely worth mentioning in its own breath. Fresh salads start you out on the right foot, while fanciful dinners like braised local squid with heirloom tomatoes and indulgent savory bread pudding with fennel and nettle bring up the rear. Bookend your experience with one of Serpentine's delightful cocktails—the whiskey preparations are my faves. *SB*

Where Does All That Grease Go?

www.gotgrease.biz, www.sfgreasecycle.org

In San Francisco, there are several outlets for recycling grease, and many of the restaurants on these pages ensure theirs doesn't go down the drain. Grease from cooking is picked up by Got Grease and taken to San Francisco Greasecycle to be turned into biofuel. So when you chomp down on a Frjtz fry or savor a mouthful of goodness at Tartine, know that you are actually participating in the creation of clean fuel, at least indirectly.

Durty Nelly's

2328 Irving St
664.2555
Daily 11a–2a

OK, y'all might not think eating dindin at a pub is the best idea, but shun the thought when you head along the pastel streets of the Sunset to Durty Nelly's. Burgers, fish-and-chips, chicken curry, and beautiful shepherd's pie are all ideal casual dinners here, harmonizing with the Irish accents behind the bar and the fiddle players that sometimes stop by. Pints and drinks are

never far away, but I could just come here, sit by the fire, and split a meaty pie while considering the plus sides to a neighborhood bar in this unlikely spot in San Francisco, run by real Irishmen. *SB*

Katia's Russian Tea Room

600 Fifth Ave
668.9292
www.katias.com
Wed–Fri 11:30a–2:30p, 5–9p, Sat 5–10p, Sun 5–9p

Shameful! I wish I had urged my *bubbe* to teach me at least a bit of Russian so I could impress my honey when we saunter down Balboa Street toward Katia's. Ordering is the most fun when you choose tea service: pick four *zakuski* (little bites) and three sweets; the flow of traditional herbed Russian Tea keeps coming. The silver-cloaked podstakanniki teacups make me feel like a Russian princess. Blini with caviar, piroshki with cabbage and eggs, and pelmeni beef dumplings will be famous with everyone at the table, then finish with vareniki sweet cheese dumplings, black currant frangipani cookies, and syrniki patties, each their own authentic taste explosion. If you want standard dinner without the fanfare of a full tea service, order *golubtsi*, similar to the cabbage-wrapped beef in Poland, or classic poached sturgeon with creamy dill sauce slathered on top. Going to tea here is a fairy tale for my imagination. *SB*

Troya

349 Clement St
379.6000
www.troyasf.com
Mon–Thurs 5–9:30p, Fri–Sat 12–10p, Sun 12–9p

I've only yet been on taste journeys to Turkey, following my friend Carla into her fabric-cloaked kitchen to sample rosewater treats or sesame-coated *simit* bread right from the oven. But I've always been enticed by the complex spices and rich flavor combinations of this nation's edibles, and Troya is another testament to this fantastic foodway. Pastry-rolled chicken *beyti* is an all-time favorite, my honey orders extra *komposto* on his, a fruity savory sauce. Dolma and kebabs with spiced nut spreads cover my table—the affordable prices allow complete indulgence. Don't miss the Ottoman Empire–inspired rice, it is cooked with butter, olive oil, and a mix of dried fruits so the delicate flavors permeate each bite. Come before 7pm and you'll be privy to their excellent $5 wine and appetizer deal. I highly recommend the warm olives and the coriander zucchini cakes—finger-lickin' good. *SB*

Maki

1825 Post St
921.5215
Tues–Sun 5:30–9:30p

This tiny family restaurant is one of Japantown's best, serving authentic and simple Japanese dishes without Americanization. Ingredients are fresh and vegetables plentiful. Though the prices are a bit higher than other sushi joints, this place sets itself apart with quality and authenticity; there are clear reasons why this place is full every night. The menu must-haves are the *wappa*, steamed meat and bonito broth, the handmade udon bowls, and the lavish sukiyaki, served with a raw egg for dipping as it is in Japan. Daily specials keep the menu updated. If you are a Japanese food nut, you'll be coming back regularly. *SB*

$$ Pauline's Pizza

260 Valencia St

552.2050

www.paulinespizza.com

Tues–Sat 5–10p

If you've got an impromptu need for a celebration (scoring a great parking spot, for instance), head on over to Pauline's for a relaxed but positively scrumptious meal. A good percentage of the produce comes from Pauline's own organic garden, and many of the rest of their pristine ingredients come from local and organic purveyors. Pizzas sit on a sturdy yet soft crust and can be customized however you like them with any configuration of their many toppings. When they have it, the Meyer lemon puree is not to be missed. Once you try the bright citrus smeared atop your pizza, you will never look at pizza the same way again. Save room for the freshly churned ice cream that features ingredients from their farm, like strawberries or mint. *JA*

$ Y Ben House

835 Pacific Ave

397.3168

Daily 7a–3p and 5–9p

For stuffing your belly with inexpensive and delicious Cantonese-style dim sum, there's a large table at Y Ben waiting for you and your party. Signal the roving trays and be sure to gather up *har gao*, shrimp dumplings, bacon-stuffed turnip cakes, and pork taro balls, for which they are famous. Take this opportunity to walk on the wild side if you aren't used to the broad variety dim sum offers—the rarities are dependably authentic and perfectly prepared. But even if chicken feet, pig's blood pudding, or crispy pig skin aren't a delicacy in your mind, most dishes are composed of ingredients no riskier than grilled cheese, fish sticks, or minestrone. Get ready for a nice nap afterwards, the eating here is certain to warrant a bit of an après-feast snooze. *SB*

$$ Little Star Pizza

846 Divisadero St; 441.1118,

400 Valencia St; 551.7827

www.littlestarpizza.com

Tues–Thurs, Sun 5–10p, Fri–Sat 5–11p

Little Star is the deep dish winner! When it comes to delicious Chicago-style deep dish, this glimmer of a restaurant outshines the rest with local ingredients and secret dough tricks we may never get our hands on (we're trying!) The Classic, with sausage, onions, mushrooms, and peppers tucked inside the semolina crust and topped with tomatoes, is my choice, but the Little Star (with spinach, ricotta, feta, mushrooms, onions, and garlic) has quite the following as well. The pizza tastes equally delicious whether you eat in or take out, so pick whatever suits your mood. *JA*

$$ **Minako Organic**

2154 Mission St
864.1888
Wed–Sun 5:30–9p

If Minako and her daughter, Judy, knew I was writing this, they might never forgive me. Minako is one of the best-kept secrets of the Mission, serving delicate sushi and sashimi made with only the best fish and organic produce, and they like it that way. Judy is feisty, the music is loud, and the service is slow, but that's all part of the Minako experience. Don't pass up the tombo, and if you've got the appetite and the time, go for the five-course *kaiseki* menu. *JA*

$ **New Hong Kong Menu**

667 Commercial St
391.3677
Daily 10a–8p

Occupying a tiny crevice on the fringes of Chinatown, New Hong Kong Menu is good and cheap. Order a plate of chow fun or their famously seasoned chicken wings and for your $5 they'll also throw in two soups, one a savory soup du jour, the second a dessert soup that could include tapioca, mung beans, mango, or sugary seaweed. If you haven't had dessert soup, authentically Chinese style, don't turn up your nose at these ingredients; you'll be surprised at how tasty they can be. There's next to no English spoken here, and a once-over on the menu won't give you any sweet and sour, General Tso, or other Americanized options. Roll up your sleeves, prepare to get filled on $5, and dig into some real Chinese street food. *SB*

Tomasso's

1042 Kearny St
398.9696
www.tommasosnorthbeach.com
Tues–Sat 5–11p, Sun 4–10p

With so many Italian restaurants in North Beach, it's hard to distinguish the authentically good eateries from the brightly colored tourist traps. After doing a bit of detective work, I've found that Tomasso's trumps the competition. For more than 70 years, this charming little restaurant has been serving steaming plates of al dente pasta and brick oven pizza to the epicureans of San Francisco. The menu stays consistent, aside from weekly specials like the Parmesan pizza topped with a fresh bed of arugula. I opted for this choice the last time I dined here, and let's just say I was happy that we ordered a large. The Caesar salad comes close to the pizza in terms of deliciousness and should not be missed. It's generous and garlicky, topped with salty croutons and delicate flakes of parsley that add an irresistible twist. I imagine that not much has changed at Tomasso's since it first opened its doors, and in this case, that's a good thing. MP

Farmer Brown

25 Mason St
409.3276
www.farmerbrownsf.com
Hours vary, call ahead

Call me old-school, but it's taken a lot of convincing for me to exit my no-frills, hole-in-the-wall barbecue treasures and venture into the world of fancy ribs and brisket. But in the interest of open-mindedness, I cleaned myself up, put my white starched napkin across my lap, and dove into the plates at Farmer Brown. Sipping the tasty drinks got me in the mood for the surprisingly tasty vegetable jambalaya—meatless but full of flavor. Start with an apricot sidecar or a grapefruit gimlet, fruity drinks without the super sweetness that many restaurants pile on. Snack on complimentary peppered corn bread while you await free-range fried chicken in a dense, hard-to-top batter. Because of the epic side dishes and the classy ambiance, posh barbecue has forged a place in my foodie heart that all started with my night at Farmer Brown. SB

$$ Radio Habana Social Club

1109 Valencia St

824.7659

Tues–Sun 7p–12a (usually)

Radio Habana is a small place, with big sangria and more personality than you'll find at any other San Francisco hole-in-the-wall. The opposite of the less-is-more mentality applies here—funky tiles, wooden dioramas, mobiles, paintings, dolls, Christmas lights, and sculptures made from old crutches, paintbrushes, and leather jackets clutter the small space and endear it to me. Somehow they fit live music in, served with El Salvadoran and Cuban fare. I'm smitten. *SB*

$$ Pizzetta 211

211 23rd St

379.9880

www.pizzetta211.com

Wed–Fri 12–2:30p and 5–9p, Sat–Sun 12–9p

Tiny little Pizzetta is the needle in the haystack and you've just found it. Wedged into a residential block off of California Street, the thin gourmet pies are always of the season at this hopelessly romantic restaurant. My honey and I found ourselves here after a Bazaar Café folk music performance (see page 190) and were treated to an extension of our ideal evening. Roasted golden beets with a wedge of sharp and creamy goat cheese, butter-slathered flat beans, and a pie of prosciutto, pine nuts, and arugula made the night complete. It isn't bargain pizza, but there's nary a more loveable slice in the city. *SB*

$$ Al Masri

4031 Balboa St

876.2300

www.almasrisfca.com

Thurs–Sun 5:30–10p

Al Masri is unique not only for bringing a rare cuisine to the Bay Area, but also for providing dinner as it should be, an event to be shared with family and friends. As you dine on a delectable menu of meat and vegetarian dishes, you are treated to an authentic performance of Egyptian Raqs Baladi or belly dancing performed by graduates of the Sausan Academy of Egyptian Dance. The Academy was established by Al Masri's own executive chef and has put on performances around the Bay Area, including the grand reopening of the de Young Museum and the Legion of Honor's "Eternal Egypt" exhibit. Chef and PhD Hatem is a native of Egypt and has poured his heart into re-creating the most representational menu, with meat dishes from Cairo, vegetarian meals from Egypt's Coptic Christians, and the more sophisticated cuisine of the courts of Alexandria. Al Masri makes music and dance, as well as food, synonymous with cuisine. After all, some would say the Egyptians invented cuisine when they invented the oven. DL

Namu

439 Balboa St
386.8332
www.namubar.com
Daily 5:30–10:30p, Happy Hour 5–7p, late night with live music and DJs Wed–Sat 11p–1a
Typical of many newish eateries around town, Namu has a cool sign, cool oil paintings of natural-meets-industrial themes, and cool waitresses—but it isn't all about appearances at this Balboa Street favorite. Don't roll your eyes when you discover the menu is fusion: this is fusion at its best. Namu serves everything from burgers that nod to Asia with pickled diakon, to cold soba noodle salad, complete with both kimchee and pine nuts. I ordered an ocean salad of bright-red and deep-green sea fronds, the likes of which you'd find at any Japanese table, and was impressed with the complexity of textures and sweetness of flavor—both well beyond what you'd expect from your local sushi joint. The *banchan*, a complementary trio at Namu, are the traditional dishes of kimchee and other marinated vegetables served at Korean tables. Together with kimchee, the *ume* dressing-coated *wakame* tendrils in my salad were even more exciting—that bite of sour and spicy made each mouthful pop. From the raw menu—and there are six such sections of the tapas-centric list—my honey chose the hamachi, an almost exclusively farm-raised member of the amberjack family. Yellowtail amberjack has much healthier representation in the wild than tuna, mostly too small to make worthwhile for fishers, so I agreed and put my politics aside and enjoyed some of the best sashimi I've had in a long time. Slivered, but not too sparse, each slice of the buttery fish was crested with little twirls of sake-soaked konbu, dripped with house-infused chili oil, and escorted over

a fine half-moon of lemon, the flavor of which tingled the bottom of each piece of fish. I savored each bite, wishing for more.

The freedom of the menu is fun—bring a group and order several plates (they'll do double orders of the ika fry) and chat until one in the morning if you so desire, Thursday through Saturday nights. It is a great menu for talkers like me; you can pick at your food, enjoy each bite, and continue on in conversation over a pot of puer tea or a flight of specialty sakes. Stay for dessert and you'll be smitten with the fusion cupcake: a chocolate and azuke bean creation covered with chocolate drizzle and surprisingly bright yuzu crème anglais. *SB*

B44

44 Belden Place
986.6287
www.B44sf.com
Mon–Fri 11:30a–2:30p, Mon–Thurs 5–10p, Fri–Sat 5–10:30p, Sun 5–9p

Yummy tapas, in a warm and inviting atmosphere—there are good reasons why it's so easy to be care-free at B44. Classic jazz or Catalan sounds swing around the place, adding extra spice to the dishes. I come for the cured white anchovies, the warm octopus, the unbelievable Catalan salad, (complete with Serrano ham), the stuffed local squid, the outstanding Arros Negre, named for the squid ink that's added in the cooking process. The wine list makes the menu better, and if you are new to Spanish wine varieties they'll take good care to help you pick one to your liking. *SB*

Gitane

6 Claude Ln
788.6686
http://gitanerestaurant.com

Gitane is a rare newbie—one that feels like a San Francisco institution in all but a few areas. Entering in my favorite foggy city fashion, through the would-be back door on a downtown alley (between Kearny and Sutter streets), the high design (a fun mix of muraled flowers on the outside brick wall and sleek cabinetwork set around crocodile-texture wallpaper and designer lighting) and soft-spoken hostesses greet me. The bar is behind them, a masterpiece of after-work deliberation and fun-loving conversation, layered with suits, well-dressed women, and hair-gelled bartenders who shake their drinks quietly,

without show. The lighting is low, a starch-shirted somellier picks out a high-end Rioja from his cabinet as I am escorted up the narrow staircase, to a bubbling room of diners. My booth is tucked into a corner but I am still at the center of the event, next to an open window letting in a pleasant breeze and out of earshot of anyone else's conversation. The high-pile fabric on the facing benches is soft, the exposed brick lit up behind a wall of glass, and the table embellished with gypsy-esque patterns.

The menu is a stable mix of Spanish flavors, Portuguese delicacies, and modernized gypsy fare—a comfortable offering without too much diversion. Starting with a cool melon cocktail, the Ribera was a perfect accompaniment to the suave atmosphere with patxaran sloeberry liqueur, crème de peche, and blue ice vodka. Tajine and lamb shank were our entrée choices out of a varying list of main courses that included both pizza and filet mignon. The tajine came with warm couscous and a classic capped dish, full of moist chicken breast, poached prunes, and large succulent chunks of turnips, carrots, and zucchini. You can choose the vegetarian version as well and get the same robust meal. *SB*

Monday Night Out

Monday blues are bid good-bye at these eateries that stay open when all else seems shut.

It is hard to find a night out when all of SF is seemingly basking in the weekend. Lots of eateries are shut Sunday night, but more are closed Monday, which happens to be my favorite night to eat out. Places aren't as crowded, and it is a little way to keep the good times rolling. In fact, I often take Monday out rather than Friday or Saturday. We've found the best spots to start the week out with a yummy bang.

$$ Magnolia Pub

1398 Haight St
864.7468
www.magnoliapub.com
Mon–Thurs 12p–12a, Fri 12p–1a, Sat 10a–1a, Sun 10a–11p

On my last night in Lyon, I made a friend at a café who then took me on "a local's day in France." We began at the market where we had fruit for breakfast, then a café chat, then a walk in the park, then a lunch of *moules frites*. Ever since that wondrous day, I have chosen these steamed mussels and fries any time I see them on an American menu, with mixed results. Magnolia Pub is simply the best version in San Francisco, made three ways with shallots, Marsala, cream, tomatoes, or green onions. The prix fixe is never a bad bet and goes mighty well with their house brews and homemade sodas—when I have a sweet tooth I order the grape. Although Haight is a fun street, it lacks many good food choices, so Magnolia is my standby for a good meal in this neighborhood, or when I have my mind set on *moules frites*. The brews here vary from super strong to mild and hoppy, so take a good look at the menu and talk up a waiter before ordering. *SB*

$$ Limon

524 Valencia St
252.0918
www.limon-sf.com
Mon–Thurs 5:30–10:30p, Fri 5:30–11p, Sat–Sun 12–11p

When it comes to ceviche, there is one word on my mind: Limon. The fresh colors of this Valencia restaurant are echoed in the fresh flavors, plated in beautiful and authentic ways. Please take me with next time you go! *SB*

Woodhouse Fish Company

$$ $

2073 Market St

437.2722

www.woodhousefish.com

Mon–Thurs, Sun 11:30a–9:30p, Fri–Sat 11:30a–10p

There are plenty of places around SF for dressed-up seafood, but what about when you just want a beer and some crab, plain and simple? I head to Woodhouse, where they only serve seafood that has surpassed sustainability certifications, and steam, fry, and broil it right, without the lemon pepper that so many Wharf spots pour all over their crab. On Tuesday night, oysters are $1; Wednesday night, half a Dungeness crab is $7. Crabs are harvested carefully—no females and all mature size. Come for the basics and you'll be satisfied. *SB*

The Alembic

1725 Haight St

666.0822

www.alembicbar.com

Mon–Fri 4p–2a, Sat–Sun 12p–2a

With the simple mission to bring local food and homemade libations to San Franciscans, the Alembic wins over all who enter it. Behind the bar, drinks are mixed up using local brews, house-infused liqeurs, and neighborhood charm. Come in for a fizzy Ritz with sparkling wine, Cointreau, and maraschino liquor, or an après-dessert grappa made from Syrah grapes. Herbed gnocchi pillows, salmon cured three ways, and charred Monterey squid are the short menu's highlights, all sourced locally with love. The whiskey selection is phenomenal—all those I know in hot pursuit of a good whiskey in San Francisco point first to Alembic. Don't think twice after a film at the Red Vic, just hurry next door to discuss it over some great drinks and tasty bites. *SB*

$$$ SPQR

1911 Fillmore St
771.7779
www.spqrsf.com
Hours vary

I find that going on pack trips is helpful in reviewing restaurants. Let me explain: At the end of each trip (I try to get out for at least a trailside overnight every couple months), when I am sick of pan bread and trail mix, whatever dish is on my mind for that last couple of miles is the best one I've recently had. Let's face it—I eat out a lot, so I need the perspective once in a while. On more than one occasion, the only thing I could hold in my mind on the last few miles of trail was SPQR's carbonara, served old-school with a choice of either rigatoni or spaghetti (both made in-house). Other menu choices are delish, but I just have a hankering for the monster of pasta dishes after winding around switchbacks for the weekend. Brunch on Saturday and Sunday is out of this world if you've come ready for sophisticated belly stuffing. *SB*

$$ Café Pescatore

2455 Mason St
561.1111
www.cafepescatore.com
Mon–Fri 7–10:30a and 11:30a–10p, Sat–Sun 7a–10p

Café Pescatore is where I come time and time again for comfort food Italian-style: seafood, pasta, polenta, and wood-fired pizzas. Just a block from the Bay and the bustle of hucksters, buskers, cable cars, and Muni trolleys, is a quiet spot to enjoy a good meal. During warmer months there is outdoor seating for the most relaxed view of the wharf area. Dishes are created from very fresh local ingredients cooked with regional zest. Everything is prepared along a side wall in the main room, tiled in syncopated primary colors. The scents of the kitchen waft into the room giving a "mmm mmm" good attractiveness. The tiramisu is made on the premises and arrives like a leaning tower of Pisa with strawberry slices about to fall into a dash of extra mascarpone on the plate. The bar serves more locals than any other wharf restaurant, but also hosts out-of-town guests with great a cosmopolitan cocktail, interesting draft beers, and a full selection of liqueurs. *IB*

$$ Destino

1815 Market St
552.4451
www.destinosf.com
Mon–Thurs 5–10p, Fri–Sat 5–11p, Sun 11a–2p and 5–11p

A Peruvian friend of mine took me to eat at this incredible restaurant and I've been raving about it ever since. Executive chef James Schnek has a passion for food that comes through in every one of his creations. The fare is a contemporary spin on Peruvian cuisine, a fresh and innovative take on distinct traditional recipes. "More than just a restaurant," Destino organizes culinary tours of Peru and Argentina once a year. Fresh ingredients and well-thought-out dishes distinguish Destino as one of San Francisco's finest places to dine. The chicken empanadas—crispy turnovers stuffed with chicken, queso fresco, and Andean mint—are heavenly. In the Ceviche a la Peruana—a traditional medley of whitefish, cilantro, and aji amarillo pepper—salt and fresh lime preserve and enhance the flavor of each ingredient. For big appetites, opt for the three-course prix fixe menu. Whatever you decide on, wines from California, Spain, and South America complement any dish. *MP*

$ Thep Phanom

400 Waller St
431.2526
www.thepphanom.com
Daily 5:30–10:30p

Make a reservation if you plan to go to this ever-popular Thai spot in the lower Haight. Once you are firmly ensconced in a seat, order up a Thai beer or organic lemonade while you choose from their enormous menu. I can never pass up the crispy yam and taro root appetizer served with their creamy peanut sauce. The "some like it spicy" section is an excellent guide for heat junkies like me, and the "Thaitanic" beef is a customer favorite. If the vast selection isn't quite enough for you, go on a Sunday, Monday, or Tuesday for exclusive dishes not available on any other night of the week. *JA*

$ Nick's Crispy Tacos

1500 Broadway
409.8226
Mon–Fri 11:30a–9p, Sat–Sun 10:30a–9p

You'll find Nick's Crispy Tacos far from the Mexican Mecca of the Mission, but it's set apart from all others in my view. For starters, it's the only taqueria in the city that has plush red velvet booths, sparkly chandeliers, and fresh margaritas in one location. Nick's is committed to using high-quality ingredients like Niman Ranch meats, and it only adds to the tastiness of the offerings. While you will find all the usual suspects, like burritos, regular tacos, and quesadillas, heed the store name and order yourself a taco (or four) Nick's way. Your taco will be "made crispy" by placing a crisp fried tortilla inside a soft corn tortilla and it will include the addition of jack cheese and their creamy guacamole. I can't resist the carnitas taco, with pinto beans, pico de gallo, and melt-in-your-mouth pork. Of course, if I'm in the mood for more than one taco, the pescado's fresh-fried fish, cabbage, onions, salsa, and lime mayo are my next choice. Go here to fill up before a night on the town, or when you need a midafternoon pick-me-up. The kind staff is great about helping Nick's "virgins" choose their inaugural meal. *JA*

$$ Sociale

 3665 Sacramento St
 921.3200
www.caffesociale.com
Mon–Sat 5:30–10p, Sun 10a–2p

Young and fabulous chef Tia Harrison is my new hero. She has made her dreams into reality with an exquisite seasonal menu. The corn ground for her creamy polenta is grown specifically for Sociale to her specifications. Bone marrow with figs, beautiful handmade pastas, tender meats, and an overwhelming selection of rare vintages fill the bellies of the patio-lounging guests. But if you just want a scrumptious burger, this is still your place—just don't expect average greasy fries on the side. Slip in between two buildings down a brick staircase to this heavenly hideaway. *SB*

$$ Bar Crudo

 603 Bush St
 956.0396
www.barcrudo.com
 Mon–Thurs 6–10:30p, Fri–Sat 6–11p

Bar Crudo's name gives you perfect directions to the best seats in the house. While there are a few small tables upstairs in this teeny bistro, the real action is sitting right at the seafood bar where you can see the chefs at work. The mostly raw menu is constantly changing, but snatch up the uni when they have it. Chef/co-owner Mike Selvera dives for the spiky delicacy himself and serves it up fresh. As you'd expect, the crudo is the thing to get here. On any given night there are six crudos to choose from. You can always round out your meal with a selection of oysters, the excellent lobster and burrata salad, or a bowl of smoky seafood chowder. A concise but well-thought-out wine menu offers the perfect partners to the shining menu. *JA*

$$ Capp's Corner

1600 Powell St
989.2589
www.cappscorner.com
Daily 11:30a–11p

Going back in time doesn't seem like it would be easy. After all, your average somebody doesn't have a time machine in their rucksack. But a meal at Capp's Corner is a step into another era, where friendly service and "the family treatment" are mandatory accompaniments to the handsome main dishes. Start with a cocktail or a half bottle of champagne and ease into a communal meal. Salad is served on the table from a huge stainless bowl. Meat dishes— unbelievable osso buco the favorite—are rich and tender. Stepping into this wood-walled restaurant is a no-hassle time capsule, and a chance to go to another world with a different pace and more cheer than Christmas morning. *SB*

$ Miller's East Coast West

1725 Polk St
563.3542
www.millersdelisf.com
Daily 8a–9p

There are a short list of things I miss about the East Coast: snow days, real pumpernickel, mimosa trees, greasy pizza, cheesesteaks made with a Conchi roll, Indian food in Queens, and Valley Forge Park. But there is one thing that I go beyond missing to the point that I just can't live without it. That is a Jewish deli, of course, where egg creams are sipped while brisket, Reubens, latkes, and matzo brei are being prepared. Tuesday night, two eat for $15 for family night when you can choose between turkey, brisket, or meat loaf as your main course. To go along with whatever it is that you choose—and I'll tell you the choice isn't an easy one—get a cel-ray or an egg cream to go with it. At least try them once, celery soda and chocolate-soda-milk, respectively. These drinks complete the authentic Jewish delicatessen experience. An extra bonus is that they ship rye bread, half-baked, in from New York and finish it in their ovens, so fresh rye and pumpernickel are just like back east. Let's just say that this place was 85 percent of the draw of my Hyde and Clay apartment, and 95 percent of the reason I miss living there. *SB*

$ Spork

1058 Valencia St
643.5055
www.sporksf.com
Mon–Thurs 6–10p, Fri–Sat 6–11p

Poetic justice never rang truer than it does at this Mission spot. The restaurant serves local and sustainable food in a renovated Kentucky Fried Chicken restaurant (they even dug a KFC sign out of the attic to adorn their walls). Specialties like the inside-out burger with mashed-up "smashed" fries and the pot brownie, served with a spork, of course, are good enough to rub your face in. There are also some higher-end eats, like the Maine lobster poached in red curry and the nightly sashimi special. Tables fill up fast, but I prefer sitting at the counter where I can admire the little Martian men adorning the wine shelves. *JA*

$ Los Pastores

3486 Mission St
642.5385
Mon–Sat 7a–9p, Sun 8a–7p

Located in the outer Mission, Los Pastores is a hidden gem. Chef and owner Irma Calderon treats her customers like her children, dishing up fresh salsas, *agua frescas*, and warm hugs as soon as you plant yourself in one of her seats. This is where I go with friends when our wallets are hurting but we're still looking for some great chow. I adore the chilaquiles. Los Pastores is supported by La Cocina, a community kitchen that helps food-based businesses owned and run by women. *JA*

$$ A16

2355 Chestnut St

771.2216

www.a16sf.com

Lunch Wed–Fri 11:30a–2:30p, Sun–Thurs 5–10p, Fri–Sat 5–11p

I can't decide what I love more at A16: the comforting and delicious Southern Italian menu or the incredible wine list featuring unique bottles from the same region. A16's chefs have been certified as pizzaiolos in Naples, and it is evident in their pizzas. The thin, elastic crust is the perfect base for each unique pie, all of which can be topped with prosciutto, arugula, an egg, or house-cured pancetta. Ask for their homemade chili oil to drizzle on top for a little extra bite. *JA*

$$ Taste of the Himalayas

2420 Lombard St

674.9898

www.tasteofnepalsf.com

Mon, Wed–Sun 11a–2:30p and 5–10p

Tibetan and Nepalese delicacies are brought to life at this gem of a hole-in-the-wall off Divisadero. Join locals in a momo feast, the Tibetan-style dumpling, steamed or panfried for vegans or meat eaters. Nothing will brighten your day better than a momo feast, trust me on this one. *SB*

$$ Baker Street Bistro

2953 Baker St

931.1475

www.bakerstbistro.com

Mon 5–9:30p, Tues–Fri 11:30a–2:30p and 5:30–10:30p, Sat 10a–2:30p and 5:30–10:30p, Sun 9:30a–2:30p and 5–9:30p

After beginning another hectic week, I have no sense of guilt over treating myself to the works at Baker Street. Whether I choose the comfortable indoor setting or a table beside the beautifully painted exterior, my stomach is prepared for a feast that will send me home satisfied and ready to tackle the remainder of the workweek. A mouthwatering soup du jour, a plate of goat cheese, Morbier and fruit, a delectable duck breast with pomegranate bigarade . . . Be sure to bring a dining partner to share in this smorgasbord of delicious French delights. There's also a special three-course Valentine's Day prix fixe, just a tip. *DL*

La Taqueria

2889 Mission St

285.7117

Daily 11a–9p

This is the taqueria for the purists out there. Burritos at La Taqueria are as bare-bones as they come. You are given no bean choice (pinto only), no tortilla choice (flour only), and no rice (at all). Salsa is gratis, but you'll have to pay extra if you want cheese, sour cream, or guacamole. So why is it that this taqueria is consistently chosen as making the most desired burritos in the city? Well, my friends, that would be their meat. Carnitas that melt in your mouth, carne asada, and divine *lengua* hit the spot. *JA*

Shanghai Dumpling King

3319 Balboa St

387.2088

Mon, Wed–Fri 11a–9p, Sat–Sun 10a–9p

This restaurant's name will tell you just about all you need to know. They specialize in dumplings—you'd be crazy to miss out on the Shanghai dumplings themselves. While SF has lots of excellent Chinese food, I have yet to taste a Shanghai dumpling that rivals those of the King. You get no fewer than 10 (!) of the eponymous dumplings for $4. I will forever remember my first bite of one of these dumplings; the delicate wrapper yielded to a gush of hot broth and spiced minced pork. I remember feeling elated at my new discovery and disappointed that I had lived in the city for so long without ever having tried these wondrous bite-sized creations. While you are there, sample a few of the other dumpling choices, or the excellent green beans and green onion pancakes. *JA*

Hotel Utah Saloon

500 Fourth St

546.6300

www.thehotelutahsaloon.com

Mon–Fri 11:30a–2a, Sat–Sun 1p–2a

A tradition in San Francisco revels, this vintage building has seen all manner of city residents and passers-through since the Gold Rush. Get a pint at this old bar, with a gaggle of regulars young and old, and you'll be drinking in history. Come for the open mic on Monday, one of San Francisco's best lively events on this unpopular day. *SB*

Old Jerusalem Restaurant

$

2976 Mission St

642.5958

Mon–Sat 11a–12a, Sun 11a–10p

According to my well-traveled friends, there is nary a falafel around town that outdoes those at Old Jerusalem (yes, I was the one in Hebrew school whose mother wouldn't let me go to Israel—"too dangerous"). But I did have a proper New York upbringing, and in the process ate a good many of these little balls of love. Chickpea flour is a divine substance, all too often mistreated, but no matter what our credentials, the vote is in, and Old Jerusalem is the place to be. *SB*

Imbibe
Where to sip and swill with a local feel

Drinking, ah drinking. It is so wrong, yet it is so right. I go for spots that offer mocktails and cocktails—it is rare that I am down for too much alcohol, but that doesn't mean I can't appreciate it. I love a good whiskey or bourbon, I just can't take more than one drink most of the time. But don't mind me, go and prove you're more robust at one of these ideal spots, and if you don't drink at all, no worries—most serve creative nonalcoholic bevies next to their strongly intoxicating ones.

Americano

8 Mission St

278.3777

www.americanorestaurant.com

Mon–Fri 6:30a–1a, Sat–Sun 7:30a–1a

Take in panoramic views of the bay and sip on sophisticated cocktails like the Kumquat Caipirissima, a delightful twist on the mojito. Just being here will make you feel important. Located on top of Hotel Vitale, this lively bar and restaurant boasts the largest outdoor patio in the city and it pulls in a handsome crowd. The kitchen serves a contemporary fusion of Californian and Italian fare, like crusty shrimp pizza and roasted beet salad. The outdoor patio, which serves a limited bar menu until 1am, is what separates Americano from the multitude of San Francisco hangouts offering gourmet eats and fancy drinks.

Around sunset, the view is absolutely breathtaking and the outdoor heat lamps will keep you toasty well into the evening. *MP*

21st Amendment Beer Café

563 Second St
369.0900
www.21st-amendment.com
Daily 11:30a–2a

Blowing away the competition of Northern California breweries is no small feat, but little tough guy 21st Amendment has got a thing about outdoing them all. Let's begin with a can (yes, a microbrewery that still uses them!) of watermelon wheat IPA. Between the sizzling hops and bready undertones, your taste buds won't know how to thank you for this one. Feast from the big, huge, all-American menus, only a bit more upscale. *SB*

Bitter End Pub Quiz

441 Clement St
221.9538
Mon–Fri 4p–2a, Sat–Sun 11a–2a, Quizzy: Tues 9p

This place is either quiet or rowdy, but whichever extreme, it does both well. Come with friends for a heart-to-heart over pints of cider or to reminisce about your college days with Jack and Cokes and a few too many games of pool. The crowd gets organized on Tuesday, when quizzy descends, teams buddy up, grab pitchers of cheap brew, and get busy. (No, not that kind of busy, though you'll find this is a place easy to get hit on.) They get brain busy, trying to remember which character on *The Simpsons* wore that wig that one time, or which president was allergic to vegetables. It's nothing important, but it's more fun than sitting there twiddling your thumbs, waiting for something interesting to happen at an Irish pub. *SB*

Orbit Room
1900 Market St
252.9525
Daily 8a–2a

Why aren't all bars like Orbit Room? They really all should be. Neighbors gather around inexpensive draft beers or the best cocktails in town for the price. Lavender, hot peppers, and herbs infuse their vodka selection, and together with Cajun spices, rosewater, and all kinds of fresh fruits and vegetables, the bar comes alive beyond the standard bottles. The Bloody Mary is a meal in itself, made as spicy as you can handle with half an avocado perched on top. The small bar hosts a collection of chatty locals, and inverted-triangle tables offer floor-to-ceiling views of a particularly interesting block of Market Street. Read the philosophic blatherings in the cleaning closet-cum-bathroom, talk to strangers, and sip something delicious without losing your mind or your money. *SB*

The Grove

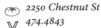

2250 Chestnut St
474.4843
Mon–Thurs 7a–11p, Fri–Sat 8a–11:30p, Sun 8a–11p

I always love trying a new wine, and I am working on honing my taste buds, but I've never enjoyed the vending machine-style wine bars scattered throughout the city. Get a real person to answer wine questions and pour the perfect glass for an afternoon spent reading and lazing on the patio. A perfect recipe for stress reduction is a good novel and a half-shade, half-sun seat at this posh, eco-friendly café. *SB*

Dogpatch Saloon

2496 Third St
643.8592
Mon–Thurs 4p–12a, Fri–Sun 12p–2a

My search for an impromptu hangout is becoming a lost cause as I find myself traveling through a desolate neighborhood east of Potrero Hill. A lone sign looms overhead; "Dogpatch Saloon," it reads. Generally, I'm suspicious of any bar with "saloon" in its name, so I enter with few expectations, but my suspicions are immediately put to rest. Offering an eclectic group of regulars and a free lunch on Thursday when you buy a drink, Dogpatch doesn't disappoint. My advice to you when on the prowl: first, remember your Shakespeare—"What's in a name?"—and second, go to Dogpatch! *DL*

Bloodhound Bar

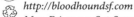

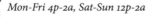

1145 Folsom St
http://bloodhoundsf.com
Mon-Fri 4p-2a, Sat-Sun 12p-2a

The owner, Ben, has an energetic pit bull/lab mutt. Jared shows me adorable photos of his over-sized Boston. I give a good ear scratch to a friendly bull terrier. My little poodle sits in my lap home. I am at the aptly named Bloodhound, a bar that welcomes dogs. This is a friendly, simple bar that feels like a part of the neighborhood, another great place to hang out in the SOMA area. The atmosphere at Bloodhound is better than most: antler-like air plants stud the walls between Far Side–esque oil paintings and wall veneers made from re-purposed wood that was once a barn in Indiana. Bare bulbs with artsy rusted cages provide dim enough lighting to give faces a healthy glow without exposing too much redness after a few drinks. The flapping blackbirds painted on the ceiling look almost real, as if they'd been rustled up by a big, sloppy hunting dog, flying to safety on a nearby branch.

Order from their unique and very local specialty cocktail menu—the Bloodhound, like a Salty Dog without the Salty and with a splash of Compari, is made with Hangar One Vodka from nearby Alameda and the whiskey drinks get a couple shakes of house-made grenadine if you ask nicely. There's a respectable beer collection including California IPAs and Belgian bottles if you're not in the mood for the strong stuff, and a hunting-themed arcade game to keep you occupied when you're sick of petting dogs and chatting nonsense. *SB*

Terroir Natural Wine Merchant

1116 Folsom St
558.9946
http://terroirsf.com
Mon-Fri 10a-12a, Sat-Sun 10a-2a

I'm happy to have discovered Terroir, a self-proclaimed natural wine store that specializes in hard-to-find biodynamic blends and varietals.

Deagan, the co-owner, is perched behind the small bar hovering over his interested customers. I am out of earshot but I bet they are entranced in some story of a far-off vineyard or a nearby urban vintner. I'm satisfied to sit on the sofa up in the cozy loft area, reading, sipping, and giving my eyes a rest once and a while by checking out the slide show projected on the wall. There are organic and biodynamic wines, as well as those from small farmers who aren't certified but are conscientious in their methods, displayed in a way so you aren't overwhelmed. *SB*

Elbo Room

647 Valencia St
552.7788
www.elbo.com
Daily 5p–2a

This is one of my favorite places to kick back in the Mission. There are two levels, which are so distinct it's like going to two bars in one. For a small cover—usually no more than $10—make your way upstairs to listen to bands. Downstairs, there's another bar area with pool tables. Quick bartenders make stiff libations, so there's never much of a wait. Two more words: photo booth! MP

Yield Wine Bar

2490 Third St
401.8984
www.yieldsf.com
Mon–Sat 5p–12a

Yield is San Francisco's first posh and green watering hole, and boy is it one to write home about. The entire menu of tasted and tried vintages comes from small family operations, biodynamic farms, and organic wineries. That means each is serious about good wine while doing their part to maintain a healthy watershed, healthy soil, and healthy workers in the process. On my last trip here I was studying up on local wines, having just returned from a prolonged exploration of Sonoma and Mendocino County regions, and found that the chèvre-stuffed dates and the caramelized roasted Brussels sprouts paired perfectly with the familiar wines we chose. Each month, the wine list shifts up, but you can be sure to find reds from Argentina, France, California, New Zealand, and even China sharing the pages. Yield looks under every rock to find these special wines, made with care, and brings them to their sweet San Francisco spot. SB

Persian Aub Zam Zam

1633 Haight St
861.2545
Daily 1p–2a

Walk into a spice jar, albeit a tiny one, at well-loved Zam Zam's for what many would consider the closest thing to Rick's in Casablanca at home in

San Francisco. The crowd gets raucous quickly with the strong drinks served here, at times a little too raucous for my taste, but then again, isn't Haight Street supposed to be at least a little out of line? *SB*

Art Bars

Creative cocktails inside creative spaces

San Francisco has an established art scene, with galleries popping up around every corner. The locals also enjoy their bevies with a bit of foodie flair; it isn't rare to find muddled herbs, grated spices, fresh fruit juices, and small-batch liquors mixed into a colorful cocktail. Combining both a love of art and fine drinks, these spaces are a popular city hybrid, frequented by all types of San Franciscans.

Space Gallery

 1141 Polk St
377.3325
www.spacegallerysf.com
Mon–Sat 1–5p

Sangria, salsa band, stylin' people—Space is the place when you're looking for inspiration in Nob Hill. This gallery is made for artists, with a hip owner who'd rather make his bucks from the bar than take a huge commission, and crowd-pleasing music and sake-tinis. Catch up on the news and a few more modern artists so you can hold a discussion with the interesting intellects that show up here for openings. Local artists from every genre make a splash with each new show—I haven't been let down yet. *SB*

Madrone Lounge

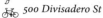 *500 Divisadero St*
241.0202
www.madronelounge.com
Sun–Mon 6p–12a, Tues–Sat 6p–2a

When Madrone calls itself an art bar, it means it: spoken word, photography, spinning vinyl, collaged menus, painting, film and video, and interior design are some of the art forms this creative space covers. The relaxed atmosphere is much more my speed than the other art bars around SF. You can bring in or order food from around Divisadero (where there's great pizza, soul food, and sushi), and there's a café addition to their bar of house-infused vodkas. *SB*

111 Minna Gallery

111 Minna St
371.0414
www.111minnagallery.com
Gallery: Tues–Fri 12–5p, times vary for nightly events

My first trip here was for a media party, where my friend Nha Vinh and I schmoozed with other publishers, writers, radio hosts, and columnists in this most wonderful bar. This space transcends anything you would think of as the typical bar scene; it is a flux of cultural influences, a work in progress created by the people who set foot inside. On some nights local artists come and scribble while onlookers can ask questions and get involved in the new art. Photography and mind-bending art exhibits are always pushing the boundaries, and the drinks keep everyone happy. A calendar of events shifts the mood each night, so check what's on and get ready to make social history. This place gets my vote for best art bar. *SB*

Varnish Fine Art

77 Natoma St
222.6131
www.varnishfineart.com
Fri 11a–11p, Tues–Thurs 5–7p and by appointment Tues–Sat

Varnish is the shiny smooth contingent of San Francisco's art scene. The paintings and sculptures are the main draw; walk around the elevated gangway to take in the mounted artworks and the colorful crowd below, sipping on an Eel River organic amber ale or a nice dry rosé. The happy hour at Varnish is like an art opening four nights a week. Order a couple of cheeses, like raw cow's milk red Leicester, and the scene is complete. *SB*

83 Proof

83 First St

296.8383
www.83proof.com
Mon–Tues 2p–12a, Wed–Fri 2p–2a, Sat 8p–2a

Join the mob of freewheeling party people six days of the week around the bar at 83 Proof. The bartenders are ready to whip up anything under the sun—if you start looking confused, they'll interject like mind readers, mixing a special concoction with your name on it. Keep out a keen eye as you walk by—there's no signage on the outside, just a warm and welcoming watering hole. *SB*

Mighty

119 Utah St
626.7001, info line: 762.0151
www.mighty119.com
Thurs–Sun 10p–4a

I am definitely a sucker for local hip-hop, like Hieroglyphics and the Oakland Faders, Euro DJs, and new-cool bands like Audiofly and Rogue Element. Here I can get it all—great wall art, a contemporary if not über-cool ambiance, and frilly incarnations of my favorite booze: Campari or Frenet Branca. Get out your snazzy digs and hit up the most sensational music and art scene. *SB*

Gallery Lounge

510 Brannan St
227.0449
www.thegallerylounge.net
Mon–Wed 4p–12a, Thurs–Fri 4p–2a, Sat 7p–2a

The Gallery Lounge is a glitzier version of SF's other art bars, more focused on high-powered conversations and a frenzy of chic outfits and chic people. Yes, the gallery space is inspiring, so you don't have to be alcohol-influenced to start up interesting conversations with strangers. Only go if you are in for the long haul, 'cause this place has the vibe of candlelit entrapment. You'll relish getting wrapped up in this SoMa scene. *SB*

Film Buffs

Movies a go-go

A night out at the movies is a mandatory pastime even in this exciting city. But part of San Francisco's culture is silver-screen oriented, so skip the big movieplex and head for an art house theater to see an old favorite or a new great from across the world.

The Roxie Theater and Little Roxie

3117 16th St; 863.1087
3125 16th St; 431.3611
www.roxie.com

The Roxie is a mainstay, one of those experiences that San Franciscans all take part in, across all social barriers. The day traders and dot-commers come out from behind their computers, the stockbrokers bring their significant others, students and artists cough up their last dimes, and Mexican chefs catch flicks here after they've wrapped their last burrito for the day. Playing mostly independent films, including screenings for many of the fests listed in the Calendar chapter (see page 250), the Roxie isn't glam, but it still warms the heart of all who pass under its billboard. *SB*

 Movies in Dolores Park

Dolores Street at 19th Street
Free second Thursday of the month April through October, 8:30p

A San Francisco staple, this night transforms Dolores Park into the neighborhood living room. Bring a blanket, wine, and snacks to share! Cozy up to your loved one or mingle with the crowd around you. It's a great excuse to watch such classics as *The Goonies* and *Airplane* on a Thursday night in the summer. Put on by local residents (so it's free for you and me!), even the neighborhood Tamale Lady makes an appearance with her delicious eats. Too bad it's only once a month! *JA*

San Francisco Cinematheque

145 Ninth St
552.1990
Screenings at various times and locations, stop by the office for current information

Experimental film? "What's that?" you ask. "What is it about?" Somewhere between an installment of ideas and a breeze of technological color, experimental film is born. I look at it as a visual concert, a musing for my eyes. Come check it out for yourself at Yerba Buena Center for the Arts, and also at screenings at California College of Art in Potrero Hill. *SB*

SF Movie!

Whether you want to get into the zone to prepare for your next trip to the Foggy City, or you're sitting around with friends debating where a certain movie scene was shot in your hometown of SF, it is always a good idea to rent something (from a local video store of course!) that takes place in this great city. After all, some of my favorite films are included in the following list, all SF-related titles: *The Birds* (1963), *The Barbary Coast* (1935), *The Maltese Falcon* (1941), *The Conversation* (1974), *San Francisco* (1936), *A View to a Kill* (1985), *Vertigo* (1958), *Golden Gate* (1994), *Dirty Harry* (1971), *Days of Wine and Roses* (1962), *The Presidio* (1988), *The Dark Passage* (1947), *Bullitt* (1968), *Basic Instinct* (1992), *Haiku Tunnel* (2001), *Freebie and the Bean* (1973), *48 Hours* (1982), *Invasion of the Body Snatchers* (1978), *Harold and Maude* (1972), *The Joy Luck Club* (1993), *The Lady from Shanghai* (1949), *Pacific Heights* (1990), *Pal Joey* (1957), and *Petulia* (1968). There are others I am leaving off this list, hoping you won't notice . . . *Star Trek IV* (1986), *Mrs. Doubtfire* (1993), *Murder in the First* (1994), *40 Days and 40 Nights* (2002), *The Rock* (1996), and *The Princess Diaries* (2001).

Red Vic Movie House

1727 Haight St
668.3994
www.redvicmoviehouse.com
Showtimes vary throughout the week
Admission: $6–$9, four-admission punch card $30

I'll bet you didn't know that the director of the *Lord of the Rings* films did a zomedy (zombie/comedy) flick back in the '90s. When I saw this film on the Red Vic calendar, I was at the box office in a nanosecond. With its comfy sofas and eclectic schedule of cult films that you won't soon find playing anywhere else, this collectively owned and operated cinema combines the social aspect of your living room with the experience of the big screen. Through all the ups and downs, the Red Vic has stayed true to its cinema-savvy mission. As indie movie theaters go, this one is pretty outstanding—beer and sofas, popcorn and classic films, foreign films and an easy-to-use web site—it has all the perks your little heart desires. You may find yourself here for a screening of

Annie Hall or the newest winner of the Seattle International Film Fest; it just depends on the night. Waltz down Haight Street and window-shop before you plop down at the Vic. DL

Castro Theatre

429 Castro St
621.6120
www.castrotheatre.com
Shows and times vary
Admission: $6–$9

Designed by famous Bay Area architect Timothy L. Pflueger to be reminiscent of a Mexican cathedral, the Castro remains one of the few 1920s movie palaces in the country still in operation. The lavish interior borrows concepts from around the world. The walls are covered in classic-motif scraffito murals, conveying a fantasylike grandeur. Cult films, cinema classics, and film festivals galore—suffice to say you'll enjoy many a night out at this city landmark. Perhaps the most notable thing about this theater is a film festival called Midnight Mass that runs for approximately eight weeks July through September and has been running for more than 10 years. The festival consists of cult films ranging from *Creature From the Black Lagoon* in 3D to *Showgirls*, and is hosted by Peaches Christ, one of my favorite drag queens. The preshows are always amusing and there is always some interesting people-watching to be done among the sold-out crowds. DL

Balboa Theater

3630 Balboa St
221.8184
www.balboamovies.com
Daily 11:30a–10p

Balboa Theater is near perfect. The old movie-house feel and the handpicked films from every genre are unbeatable, then add the neighborhood charm and the proximity to Al Masri (see page 145) and you've got a winner. A big winner. Back in 1926 it was the hub of western San Francisco. Each year there is a preview of the Cannes picks, hosted by the knowledgeable Gary Meyer—follow his lead to the best new cinema from around the world. SB

San Francisco Film Society, Sundance Cinemas and Film+Club

www.sffs.org/events

Throughout the year, there are film festivals cluttering every San Franciscan's calendar, but of all of them, the SF International Film Fest is most adored. But the Film Society, the ones behind the International Fest (see page 255), are busy throughout the year too. Filmmaker events are on every month—go to hear Mike Relm (famous for his mash-up DJing and video mixing) speak, see a series of films from Quebec, or discover new Italian cinema. Most of these ongoing events are in the heart of Japantown, at Sundance Cinemas (1881 Post St, 929.4650), some at Opera Plaza Cinemas (601 Van Ness Ave, 267.4893), and the live events are most often held at Mezzanine (see page 195), one of my favorite clubs in the city. Film+Club hosts some of the coolest cutting-edge films, often accompanied by a chance to meet filmmakers and cultural icons of the future, in an environment fit for a party. *SB*

Volunteer

Fun, quick, and easy ways to give back to the city

Volunteering is the best way to meet locals. Unite in a common cause to make a positive impact in some area or another, and you're sure to make fast friends. San Franciscans are eager volunteers, so it follows that there are some interesting opportunities for helpers. Volunteering is a must-do activity for a trip to the foggy city, and something I incorporate into all my travels with much success. Roll up your sleeves!

La Cocina Community Kitchen

2948 Folsom St
824.2729
www.lacocinasf.org
Estimated time: long-term commitment, 2 hours a week

I adore La Cocina because they provide a win-win opportunity that gives me the warm fuzzies whenever I think about it. They support local women who are launching food-based businesses on low incomes by giving them access to a commercial kitchen outfitted with energy-efficient appliances, and by providing any training or technical help they might need. That's the win for the ladies that are lucky enough to receive their services, but there's also a win for you and me because the food that comes out of that kitchen is divine. JA

St. Anthony's Foundation

150 Golden Gate Ave
592.2726
www.stanthonysf.org/volunteer/volunteer.html
Estimated time: long- and short-term activities

Imagine an organization whose sole purpose was to see to it that everyone's basic needs were met; a charity that provided food, housing, and even counseling and employment training for people looking to improve their condition. That place exists and it's called St. Anthony's. For more than 50 years, the foundation has provided an array of crucial services to San Francisco's less fortunate. Every day, scores of homeless and low-income people make their way to the dining room to sit down to a hot meal. The St. Anthony's Free Medical Clinic is staffed by licensed doctors and provides a full range of specialized services. The amazing work the foundation accomplishes would not be possible without the help of volunteers, who give their time, talent, and compassion. Check out their web site to see how you can help. MP

Glide Memorial

330 Ellis St
674.6080
www.glide.org/volunteer
Estimated time: long- and short-term opportunities

Probably the most famous church in the city, Glide Memorial offers a number of ways for you to lend a good deed to the community. I like coming for the awe-inspiring gospel choir, and to stay afterwards to help with one of their community projects. Mentor a kid from an at-risk community or work as a receptionist in one of their many offices. Volunteers with specialized skills are especially needed for the health services clinic and employment training program. Long-term and short-term opportunities are available, and extra help is always needed around the holidays, when the church serves festive meals to homeless and low-income people. MP

826 Valencia

826 Valencia St
642.5905
www.826valencia.org
Daily 12–6p

The next generation of leaders and inventors will determine the direction our little ship of a world goes in, so best treat them right and give them as many tools as they can fit in their toolboxes, right? 826 Valencia is a one-of-a-kind resource for the children of San Francisco—especially the Mission district—teaching, tutoring, and taking kids 6 to 18 on field trips. No learning is quite like the experiential type, so seeing the wide world—and believe me, the Bay Area has a good concentration of it—is the best way for the education to stick. Volunteer your time doing any number of things; there is an easy form on the web site. You can also shop at the Pirate Supply Store—the proceeds all go to 826's Valencia great programs. You'll find many a T-shirt sporting locally inspired designs, and a treasure chest of publications like *Seeing Through the Fog*, an amazing San Francisco guidebook written by the students of Gateway High School. A big Arrrrr! to 826 Valencia for their passion and energy keeping kids away from the tube and tuned in to the fun of knowledge. *SB*

Alemany Farm

100 Crescent Ave
261.2705
www.alemanyfarm.org/index.html
Estimated time: 2-hour commitment

This urban oasis is dedicated to growing healthy, organic, local food for distribution to the low-income communities that surround the farm. It's worth taking a trip just to view this gem, but you can also check their web site for "Farm Work Days," when anyone can dig in and help tend this community garden. The farm sits in the shadow of a windmill, which provides excellent photo ops as well. *JA*

San Francisco Food Bank

900 Pennsylvania Ave
282.1900
www.sffoodbank.org
Estimated time: long-term or onetime 2-hour commitment

I usually can only volunteer at the food bank once a year, but it's not because I don't want to be there more. Believe it or not, this volunteer opportunity is so popular that it books up well in advance. Call as soon as you know you want to partake in this fun and fulfilling opportunity. The food bank's employees are friendly and always carefully explain the tasks they are assigning. They also explain why each task is being done, and where their food comes from. For example, on my last visit, we sorted apples not cosmetically fit for a supermarket but perfectly good for consumption. The Food Bank distributes to many local organizations, like Project Open Hand, a meal service for people living with AIDS. Volunteer opportunities include sorting and packing food, distributing food boxes to clients of the food bank, special events assistance, and administrative help. JA

Other Resources

San Francisco and the Bay Area are full of charitable organizations in need of energetic, community-minded volunteers. Here are some more opportunities to get involved with; some are resources that connect residents and visitors to great volunteer tasks. The projects range from petting and walking puppies, learning how to whitewash, garden, cook, or climb around parks fixing trails. You never know where volunteering will take you, but one thing's for sure—you'll meet some great people and have a good time giving back. SB

Volunteer Info Center

www.volunteerinfo.org

LightHouse for the Blind

214 Van Ness Ave
694.7371
www.lighthouse-sf.org/help/volunteer

Project Open Hand

730 Polk St
447.2300
www.openhand.org

Volunteer Match

385 Grove St
241.6868
www.volunteermatch.org

Rocket Dog Rescue

4040 24th St and 501 Castro St (adoption locations)
642.4786
www.rocketdogrescue.com

San Francisco Garden Resource Organization

235.4292
www.sfgro.org

St. Martin de Porres

225 Potrero Ave
552.0240
http://martindeporres.org

Bay Area Volunteer Information Center

www.volunteerinfo.org

The Volunteer Center

1675 California St
982.8999
www.thevolunteercenter.net

Fort Point Historic Site

The end of Marine Drive in Presidio, Building 201
561.4395
www.nps.gov/fopo

SF Heart

660 Market St, Ste 401
263.8949
www.sfheart.com/volunteer.html

SF Connect

60 Spear St
385.7778
www.sfconnect.org

One Brick

237 Kearny St. #209
246.4321
www.onebrick.org

Dress Up

Don your shiny shoes and head out to one of these fancy
places—not all come with a huge price tag

There are those occasions where you just have to dress up—
something inside you wants to put your good foot forward and go
all out. San Francisco has a definitive ritzy side, all done up and
tied with a bow. But this is the West Coast we're talking about,
so a laid-back attitude comes into play even in these posh places.
If you are looking for the best food, or just an opportunity to take
your new dress shoes out on the town, these places are your best
bet. Not everywhere requires big bucks, though some are pricier.
Remember, drinks are usually the culprit for amping up your dining
bill, so if you are careful in that department you can make even the
more expensive places affordable.

Le Colonial

20 Cosmo Pl
931.3600
www.lecolonialsf.com
Sun–Wed 5:30–10p, Thu–Sat 5:30–11p, lounge: 4:30p on

If Le Colonial were a man I would give him my heart. He is respectable, well
put-together, incorporates diversity into his wise perspective on life, and is
fine in his tastes, his dress, and his intellect. Vietnamese is a cuisine inspired
by the practices of haute French culinary techniques, and whether or not you
are versed in this type of dining, Le Colonial whisks you to a private island
where everything is made just to your liking. Bo Luc Lac, a garlicky-cubed
beef, Du Du Tom, poached prawns and papaya, and crispy Cha Gio spring
rolls are served as they would be to an empress. Treat yourself to a night at
this eco-conscious restaurant that has found a way to balance sustainability
within the lap of luxury. It's hard to eat at a place like this without baring
your soul in conversation, so be careful who you bring here. *SB*

$$$ Coco500

500 Brannan St
543.2222
www.coco500.com
Mon–Thurs 11:30a–10p, Fri 11:30a–11p, Sat 5:30–11p

Imagine going to one of the premier dining spots in the city for the exquisite food, and then discovering that they also have one of the most exclusive cocktail menus in all of San Francisco—you'd be at Coco500. On the hunger side, you can find anything your heart desires on the seasonally rotating menu. There is something for everyone, from the casual fried green beans to creatively delicious pastas to the elegant catch of the day. The Cocomole "tacos" are cute as can be with bits of beef cheek piled on individual tortilla chips, but don't eat too many as the dessert menu is not to be missed. *JA*

$$$ Woodwards Garden

1700 Mission St
621.7122
www.woodwardsgarden.com
Tues–Sat 6–10p

In the shadow of the historic amusement park, this exquisite kitchen has been creating beautiful seasonal menus for some time now. Duck under the Bay Bridge overpass to find chocolate torte with fleur de sel shavings, tender roasted duck, and the best version of pear, blue cheese, and toasted pecan salad this city has to offer. All ingredients pass the test for locally grown, mostly organic, and sourced from the highest quality producers. *SB*

$$ South Park Café

108 South Park
495.7275
www.southparkcafesf.com
Mon–Fri 11:30a–2:30p, Tues–Sat 5:30–10p

Beside a grassy plot in the middle of the financial district, South Park is a French bistro that hasn't been "Californicated." If you know how to manage this, the service is better—make decisions in your head before saying anything, observe with a keen eye and ask for something when you want it, don't wait around humphing and expect your server to "get it." Don't take it personally, the elegant seasonal menu and unbelievable chocolate creations of chef Little are always worth it. Just relax and pretend you are in France, because everything around you will make you believe it is so. P.S., the chef is actually in his restaurant, cooking nearly every night it is open, a rarity in the midst of San Francisco's snooty chef culture, so don't pass "French" off as snooty, *s'il vous plaît*! SB

Sebo

517 Hayes St
864.2181
http://sebosf.com
Tues-Sat 6p-10p, Izakaya Sun 6-11p

I come to Sebo with a chip on my shoulder; it's been a long day and even though I've heard great things I am still skeptical about shi shi sushi. I start with sake to wet my appetite, and end up learning about a tiny brewery Beau has just discovered, the same Beau behind True Saké (see page 231). The waiter lets me in on some juicy tidbits about the fish protection programs in which Sebo engages, like the one at Kindai University, where they are cultivating fish in new ways in order to maintain wild populations. He can even find out what fishing practices the boat used that brought in my kohada (shad) and ishigarei (flounder) nigiri. Not only that but the taste is supernal, it is easy to tell this fish is fresh. Don't miss the glorious nine-piece chef's selection sashimi, the cucumber and pickled umé plum maki rolls and, if you are up for something completely different, the try ankimo, monkfsh liver delivered several times a week from Boston. Come back for Japanese pub-style dishes served Sunday nights, Izakaya pig out! Hard-to-find authentic grub is abundant and inexpensive: for $5 each I had grilled mochi, classic sautéed burdock (prepared the same way I was taught by my Obaasan taught me when I lived in Kyoto). Fried squid and marinated shortribs are $7, grilled salt sweetfish and chicken veggie hot pots are $9. All are elevated with an Orion beer. No more shi shi sushi skepticism at Sebo. Say that three times fast! SB

Spruce

 3640 Sacramento St
931.5100
www.sprucesf.com
Mon-Fri 11:30a-2:30p, Daily 5-10p

Mark Sullivan, the wonderful chef at Spruce, likes to get his way. So much so that he sources many of his ingredients from the restaurant's own farm, SMIP Ranch, just south of the city. The result is undeniably phenomenal, in fact, Esquire magazine named Spruce the best new restaurant for 2008, and there was some pretty heavy competition. To rise above the rest, the menu features courses where the taste of the central ingredient is elevated. Citris makes roasted fennel glow, foraged mushrooms and muddled herbs make an earthy base for gnocchi pillows, the classic combination of rabbit and lentilles de Puy, with their peppery flavor, goes beyond typical folded in fazzoletti (hankerchief) pasta with delicate braised mire poix. Desserts seem meaningless from reading the menu, a sundae, some cheese, some ice cream, some cookies... but don't be fooled, each order of après-dinner treats is a guarantee that there will be a sculpture placed on your table. *SB*

Ozumo

161 Steuart St
882.1333
www.ozumo.com
Mon–Wed 11:30a–2p and 5–10p, Thurs–Sat 11:30a–2p and 5:30–10:30p

Ozumo serves traditional Japanese cuisine with an edge. Choose from customary dishes like tempura, or if you're feeling adventurous, order something from the tasty plates menu like the Dohoyo, a layered jewel box of mackerel, avocado, and tofu. The fish is always fresh and delicious, and if you're not in the mood for sushi, the kitchen offers lots of other choices, like an array of grilled meats from the Rabota grill. The atmosphere is fun and hip, and on the weekends, they have a DJ spinning records. There's a reason why the *San Francisco Chronicle* consistently places Ozumo in the top 100 restaurants. *MP*

Jai Yun

923 Pacific Ave
981.7438
http://menuscan.com/jaiyun
Fri–Wed 6:30–9:30p

A leap of faith is required when dining at Jai Yun, a gem tucked away in the heart of Chinatown. This is the brainchild of chef Chia-Ji Nei, who owns and operates the restaurant with the help of his wife and son. The nontraditional menu features no food, only prices ranging from $45–$150 per person. Don't get suckered in, though, as the $45 menu features a banquet fit for a king. The delicate egg whites and abalone, winter melon with spicy pork, and fragrant whole fish with citrus and herbs will make you swoon with delight. One of the craftiest tricks you'll encounter is "mock duck"—tofu prepared and smoked as if it were a cold duck appetizer. Jai Yun is an excellent choice for celebrating a special occasion with a small group of people, as the family-style dishes lend themselves to sharing. The interior is simple, boasting strings of Christmas lights and a soda cooler, but the food is anything but, so be sure to make a reservation. And just in case you need more convincing: every time I've eaten there the chef has come out to a standing ovation in the dining room. *JA*

$$$ Chapeau!

℞ *1408 Clement St*

🛵 *750.9787*

Ⓥ *Tues–Thurs, Fri–Sat 5–10:30p, Sun 5–10p*

I admit I am supremely partial to French cuisine without the influence of other cuisines. While I agree French techniques can be applied to all food preparations, when you say you're a French restaurant, you better bring the goods. This tiny gem has perfect steaks, divine appetizers, and soups made the gut-wrenchingly time-consuming French way. The best part is the three-course early-bird special; priced at only $24, this might just be one of the best deals in SF. Come on—salmon tartar, roast point loin with mashed chestnuts, and handmade profiteroles for that price? I like a place that never disappoints, takes me back to France, and also gives me the option of inexpensive haute cuisine or a done-up meal with courses of food and wine that last the whole night through. Excuse me as I drool from the memories. *SB*

$$ Hayes Street Grill

🍴 *324 Hayes St*

℞ *863.5545*

Ⓥ *www.hayesstreetgrill.com*

Mon–Thurs 11:30a–2p and 5–9p, Fri 11:30a–2p, 5–10p, Sat 5:30–10:30p, Sun 5–8:30p

If I could eat only one thing for the rest of my days, it would be fish. So where will you find me on nights when I deserve a treat? Hayes Street Grill, of course, where fish is the main affair, poached, grilled, sautéed, baked, fried, and skewered.

The rest of their menu isn't shabby, but their forte is clear. Most of their fish and shellfish are sustainably caught, and side dishes feature many local ingredients. I have been here many times and I have never been let down. *SB*

$$ 1550 Hyde Café and Wine Bar

1550 Hyde St
775.1550
www.1550hyde.com
Tues–Thurs 6–9:30p, Fri–Sat 6–10p, Sun 5:30–9:30p

Get cozy inside this adorable postage stamp-sized wine bar and restaurant. Trick your dining companions into giving you a seat facing the window so you can watch the cable car trudge up the tree-lined street for a true SF experience. A good way to enjoy the vast wine list without breaking the bank is by ordering one of their featured wine flights that consists of three 3-ounce pours. I stick to the appetizers when it comes to my meal, like grilled peaches and cucumber with mint, basil, and Taleggio, or scallop crudo with avocado and citrus. *JA*

$$ Top of the Mark

1 Nob Hill
616.6916
www.topofthemark.com
Mon–Sat 6:30a–2:30p and 5p–1a, Sun 10a–2a

This is one of those must-do experiences, whether or not it's on the typical tourist itinerary. And since residents are regulars at this sky-high bar lounge, you can mingle among them rather than the token gawkers. Order from an extravagant list of specialty martinis, including the Candy Bar, a Frangelico-laced version that was a major part of my 21st birthday initiation. Friday and Saturday nights, there is live music, and surprisingly good salsa music brings a crowd of talented dancers, always a feast for the eyes. Come early for happy hour and grab a seat looking out at the city and surrounding bay, and stay into the night for high-class cocktails and hot dancing. *SB*

$$$ Zuni Café

1658 Market St
552.2522
www.zunicafe.com
Tues–Sat 11:30a–12a, Sun 11a–11p

When it comes down to it, the simplest things seem to be the hardest to truly master. In eating out, fusion cuisine sometimes muddles the skills it takes to prepare something simply but correctly. Zuni is anything but simple in ambiance, being a be-seen type of eatery and bar, but their fine menu rings loud and clear. The best entrée is the roast chicken. Please take this opportunity to reassess what you previously considered to be the quintessential hen. For me it was like rediscovering pie after using a Julia Child recipe. A perfect blend of fresh herbs tucked under the skin, served with au jus that elevates the doldrums. Start with local oysters and a choosy vintage from their extensive wine list. Sit downstairs for a window view, or climb the stairs and find yourself in an intimate dining room. Chef Judy Rodgers is a pioneer in the local food movement and she makes an effort to serve only sustainable products (right down to the cornstarch straws in the drinks). Zuni has something for everyone at almost every hour. *SB*

$$$ Delfina

3621 18th St

552.4055

www.delfinasf.com

Mon–Thurs 5:30–10p, Fri–Sat 5:30–11p, Sun 5–10p

I was lucky enough to wander into Delfina just after it opened in 1998, and nothing has been able to keep me away from the restaurant since. It's my go-to place for all things: celebrations, disappointments, or the average day when I don't have a proper excuse. I am so in love with Delfina that during a trip to Italy I made a pilgrimage to its namesake and inspiration, Da Delfina, in the Tuscan countryside. The food is enough to keep me pounding at the doors, but Delfina rises to the top for so many other reasons. Owners Craig and Annie Stoll have managed to maintain the feel of a comfortable neighborhood restaurant despite being nationally recognized as one of the best restaurants not only in SF, but in the United States. Servers are relaxed but still at the top of their game, answering every culinary inquiry with a warm smile. The menu changes each evening, but there are a few staples you can always find, like the spaghetti with plum tomatoes—the epitome of what a spaghetti with tomato sauce should be—the *insalata di campo*, which marries bitter greens with salty pancetta and Parmesan with walnuts and balsamic, and the flatiron steak adorned with a dollop of bone marrow and served alongside Delfina's well-known french fries mingled with fried herbs. Sformatino, a savory flan, often makes a revelatory appearance. I'm most partial to the soups and the pastas, and I often end up with too much on my table when I'm there on a night featuring the chickpea soup with paprika oil and the incredible wild nettle tagliatelle. Desserts are all winners, especially the buttermilk panna cotta, whose tanginess provides the perfect counterpoint to your meal. Make a reservation as soon as you know you want to go, as they book up in advance, or go at 5:30 and try to snag a seat at the counter. JA

$$$ Range

842 Valencia St
282.8283
www.rangesf.com
Sun–Thurs 5:30–10p, Fri–Sat 5:30–11p

Eating at Range provides the unique vibe of electricity and excitement while still seeming cozy and inviting. If you are lucky enough to nestle into one of their U-shaped booths, you may never want to leave. After you've sipped one of the innovative cocktails, like a Green Lantern composed of gin, Viognier, kiwi, and lime juice, you can start the difficult process of narrowing down what to eat from their very tasty menu. I enjoy the manila clams, steamed in whatever broth they fancy that day and served with something delicious like chorizo or fennel sausage. Entrées are spot-on and the constantly changing menu can feature gems such as flaky sautéed cod with Peruvian beans or slow-cooked pork chops with hearty corn and kale stew. Range doesn't insult vegetarians by offering the ubiquitous pasta or risotto. Instead, they offer a vegetarian selection that is interesting, balanced, and full of protein, like barley and pecan-stuffed piquillo pepper. I've often been tempted to order dessert first, just in case I might get full, since Range's desserts are some of the best in the whole city. Trust me when I say that a peach and raspberry crisp with rich coconut ice cream or a bittersweet chocolate and Armagnac soufflé will dazzle you. JA

$$ Slanted Door

1 Ferry Building Marketplace #3
861.8032
www.slanteddoor.com
Sun–Thurs 11a–2:30p and 5:30–10p, Fri–Sat 11a–2:30p and 5:30–10:30p

Once upon a time there was a boy named Charles Phan whose family fled from Vietnam to Guam and ultimately ended up in the Mission district of San Francisco. That boy decided to open a small neighborhood restaurant in the Mission, serving modern Vietnamese cooking and employing just about everyone in his entire family. That restaurant was the now famous Slanted Door, which has grown from its neighborhood roots to mythic proportions. The Mission restaurant no longer exists, but Slanted Door still does, making its current home in a sleek, hip corner of the Ferry Building with sweeping bay views. Although the vibe of the restaurant has changed over the years, going from small and intimate to large and boisterous, the food has remained consistent. They also do an exceptional version of pho, with fresh, local chilies and herbs to toss into your broth. There is a whole fish served nightly, which usually comes with a yummy sauce that inspires diners to leave nothing but the bones on the platter. My tofu-hating friends have changed their tune after sampling the deeply flavorful lemongrass tofu. When it comes to dessert, bypass the usual suspects (crème brûlée, chocolate cake) and go for the unusual Asian-inspired desserts like Thai basil panna cotta served in a mango soup or the ginger tapioca, which is my choice every time. When I am under the weather, nothing makes me feel as good as a to-go bowl of their pho and some chic flicks. *JA*

$$$ Jardiniere

 300 Grove St
 861.5555
www.jardiniere.com
Sun–Mon 5–10p, Tues–Wed 5–10:30p, Thurs–Sat 5–11:30p

Imagine being whisked away to one of Citizen Kane's dining rooms, where the sole aim of every suavely dressed server is to please you and you alone. Short from risking life and limb in a weird scientist's time machine, Jardiniere is the only way I can think of to relive the decadent experience of this memorable character. The unparalleled service, the devastatingly gorgeous food, the internationally respected wine list, the sweet hum of the Steinway Grand, and the film noir lighting are all geared toward making your party feel like royalty. Even the spacious design of the restaurant yields to this higher calling, allowing enough space between romancing couples, upscale birthday toasts, and many theatergoers. Chef Traci de Jardin has led the pack of

conscientious chefs toward sourcing locally grown, high-quality ingredients that are in keeping with responsible practices. Her duck breast with
bok choy and candied ginger, her duck confit teamed up with rillet, her
cabernet-infused short ribs and caviar-dolloped salmon tartar are all constructed of sustainable meats and produce prepared with the finest of French
cooking methods. When I am in need of a mini-celebration, I come for a glass
of wine and the unparalleled *bonne-bouche* dessert platter—a fun selection of
mini treats like a tiny madeleine, little chai crème brûlée, and baby lemon tart.
Because there is a spacious bar it is easy to be a part of the elegance without
eating a full meal; waitstaff are happy to indulge smaller appetites from the
chic high stools. Jardiniere soars above the rest of San Francisco's fine dining,
never stoops to snooty service, and provides the quintessential San Francisco
fare while maintaining a green business model. *SB*

$$$ La Folie

2316 Polk St
776.5577
www.lafolie.com
Mon–Sat 5:30–10:30p

La Folie is four-star dining the way it should be. The cozy dining room in
warm hues of burgundy invites me to settle in and get ready for the culinary circus. Chef Roland Passot has created a bargain with his flexible menu,
allowing you to choose three, four, or five courses for $70, $80, and $90,
respectively. This includes luxe ingredients like foie gras and lobster. Service is refreshing—friendly and comfortable as opposed to stuffy and rigid.
Treat yourself to a glass of bubbly, or better yet, choose a wine off of the "one
and only bottle" list that holds wines of a limited quantity. I was thrilled to
find that these wines started at bargain basement prices. You'll leave La Folie
happy, sated, and comforted by the fact that there is still enough left in your
bank account to begin planning a return visit. *JA*

$$ Greens

Fort Mason Center, Building A
771.6222
www.greensrestaurant.com
Mon–Sat 5:30–9p, Tues–Sat 12–2:30p, Sun 10:30a–2p and 5:30–9:30p

Known for decades as a bastion for haute vegetarian food, Greens is a prime restaurant in a prime location. Come for dinner and watch as the sunsets and vegetables get romantic all of a sudden. Fresh pastas like green pea ravioli and creative plates like phyllo-wrapped cremini mushrooms and artichokes are marked by an air of sophistication. I'm positively smitten with their fixed-price menu, served Saturdays, and many of the regular items are in the restaurant's cookbook. I recommend taking a deserving date here, then grabbing the book and re-creating the meal at home. *SB*

$$ Foreign Cinema

2534 Mission St
367.4432
www.foreigncinema.com
Mon–Thurs 6–10p, Fri 6–11p, Sat 11a–11p, Sun 11a–10p

Foreign Cinema is probably the only restaurant in town with ceilings this high, and there's good reason—they need to fit the movie screen just so, where diners can savor fine meat, fish, and vegetable dishes and also get a good view of the mostly foreign art films, both new and old. Visit nightly for a different menu and movie to go alongside. Don't worry, the volume isn't so high that you can't tell your dining buddy how much you love your meal! *SB*

$$ Medjool

2522 Mission St
550.9055
www.medjoolsf.com
Mon–Thurs 5–10p, Fri–Sat 5p–2a

Of all the good reasons to explore the Mission, Medjool is really as close to the top as it can be. The only reason it isn't the clear numero uno is that it is too pricey for an everyday thing, but if I had a million dollars, I'd be there every night. There are several ways to enjoy this spot: come early and sup on gussied-up Med cuisine from the rooftop tables, come for a cocktail at the alluring bar, or dance into the night to the sounds of exotic DJs. I say mix it up, the food, drinks, and ambiance are all stellar, so best to try them all. *SB*

$$$ **Millennium**

580 Geary St
345.3900
www.millenniumrestaurant.com
Hours vary

Millennium is many things to many people. For lifelong vegetarians it hosts celebrations like special anniversaries and memorable romantic moments. For foodies it offers a different way to savor San Francisco's bounty. For us who save up our pennies for a bit of haute cuisine, no vegetable is more inspired than at Millennium. They offer seasonal fixed-price menus, plus "frugal foodie" menus, three courses for just $38, compared to the usual high price tags for this fine food. Maple-glazed, smoked tempeh with spring garlic mashed potatoes and grilled asparagus in a cabernet reduction; stuffed truffled roulade made from French black lentils and chantrelles; black truffles; smoked pimenton cream . . . No other haute eatery honors vegetarian cuisine like Millennium. *sb*

Listen

Any auditory experience you can imagine, from concerts to theater—it's all here

Well-strung notes can carry every shade of human emotion. I like to close my eyes and let my other senses go when I catch wind of some magical melodies. My mother used to say you can't listen with your mouth open. But some of these places promote listening while you eat scrumptious meals and guzzle microbrews. San Francisco is full of both music lovers and music makers. Whatever your ears perk up to, it is essential to enjoy the sounds and indulge in aural distraction as often as possible.

$$ **Jazz at Pearl's**

256 Columbus Ave
291.8255
www.jazzatpearls.com

The history of this business reads like one of San Francisco's many crooked streets or steep hills, but today this velvet-shrouded jazz club is as hopping as ever, with nightly acts featuring local stars and touring musicians. I've heard

Hammond organ played here while sitting a few feet from the stage and eating a four-course menu. It's hard to imagine a better night out. *SB*

 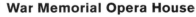

War Memorial Opera House

301 Van Ness Ave
861.4008
www.sfopera.com

Home of the San Francisco Opera since opening night in 1932, the War Memorial Opera House is one of the last Beaux Arts structures built in the country and employs the Roman Doric order in its colonnade of paired columns. A magnificent, high barrel-vaulted and coffered ceiling covers the grand entrance hall, and a massive aluminum and glass panel chandelier hangs from a mystifying blue vault in the theater space. The state-of-the-art lighting system is one of the most sophisticated in the world, and an extension behind the main stage provides enough storage space to accommodate three different performances on successive nights. Standing room is only $10, and affordable tickets are available the day of the show. *DL*

Stern Grove Concerts

Stern Grove Outdoor Amphitheater, 19th Ave
www.sterngrove.org
Free 2p Sundays, mid-June through August

The nonprofit organization that hosts this yearly festival has been bringing world-class performing arts to the Bay Area for free since 1938. A few I've seen in the last couple years: Huey Lewis and the News, Haitian drummers, and John Santos, and they've all gotten me shaking my booty. Each concert is a unique experience, and since it's free, why not attend as many as possible? Get there early and you'll have great seats for the show. SB

Bill Graham Civic Auditorium and Presentations

99 Grove St and presentations at other SF locations
www.billgrahamcivic.com

Bill Graham, the famous Holocaust survivor, philanthropist, and backbone of 1960s counterculture in San Francisco, left a legacy to the city's present-day residents. His foundation continues to benefit causes from civil rights to AIDS research, and the auditorium in his name has become a mainstay for music and events of all types. The Dalai Lama recently gave teachings here on "dependent origination," the interrelatedness of all things, and weeks later there were political debates, a society fund-raiser event, and a few rock concerts. The purpose of this space and the events put on by Bill Graham Presents are all aimed at taking music and culture to the next level, and benefiting people and their rights as free beings. It is a landmark in SF's Civic Center, across from City Hall, where you'll find any number of events. SB

The Fillmore Auditorium

1805 Geary Blvd
346.6000
www.thefillmore.com

Janis Joplin, Otis Redding, and the Doors are among the legendary acts that have graced this world-famous music hall. And you can feel the history beaming from the walls as soon as you enter. Greeters personally welcome each guest, and during select shows, collectable psychedelic posters are passed out to anyone lucky enough to attend. Intimate intricacies like these preserve a tradition that has kept this place going strong for a good part of a century.

General admission allows patrons to get within feet of their favorite performers without paying absurd amounts for front-row tickets. Balcony seating is available for those who prefer to kick back and enjoy the show. MP

Rassela's On Fillmore Jazz Club

1534 Fillmore St
346.8696
www.rasselasjazzclub.com
Mon–Fri 5–10p, Sat 5–11p

Ethiopian food goes great with live jazz. Order zesty *doro wat* (chicken) or *tibs wat* (beef) doused in authentic ginger and cardamom red sauce to savor while live blues lulls you a little closer to your loved one. On fiery Latin Jazz nights, it'll be hard to stay seated with hot beats and fine cocktails luring dancers to the floor. In between grooving and chatting it up with fellow jazz lovers, grab a lentil or ground beef sambussa pastry pocket, for the most delicious bar food around. SB

Buddha's Universal Church Concerts

720 Washington St
982.6116
http://bucsf.org/play
Performances Sat 2p
Admission: $12

Take a first hand look at classic Chinese musical drama, with make-up that I'm sure every fashion designer would envy. I like to see the show in the original Cantonese, but there are English versions as well. Monastic and village music, costumes from different periods in Chinese history, and cultural traditions come together at the biggest Buddhist temple in the United States. SB

Do Re Mi Karaoke

1604 Post St
771.8884
Daily 3p–3a

Skip the stage and head to your own private karaoke booth Japanese-style. When I lived in Kyoto I got to experience "live karaoke" where all the regulars at the bar also played instruments—mind you they were not what I would call musicians, but the amorphous group formed ensembles any time someone requested a song. My friend Liz and I found ourselves in many a karaoke booth while we lived there, each time with a different group of friends, all united in song. With fond memories of both band and booth karaoke, minus the booze, I get my fill of reminiscing about my time in Japan at this cornerstone of Japantown entertainment. Bring a crew of friends and sip virgin highballs until the sun comes up. *SB*

SF Playhouse

533 Sutter St, second floor
677.9596
www.sfplayhouse.org
Box Office: Tues–Sat 11a–3p by phone

One of the best theaters on the West Coast brings quality live performance to the Bay Area with a yearlong schedule of shows. Modern and up-and-coming playwrights showcase their new works; classics like *Faust* and *Macbeth* share the stage with Broadway favorites acted by top stage actors. Subscribe to an entire season if you are in San Francisco for a while, volunteer to help around the theater, or just spend an evening taking in a new theatrical story. *SB*

San Francisco Symphony

Louise M. Davies Symphony Hall, Grove and Van Ness streets
864.6000
www.sfsymphony.org

With Michael Tilson Thomas at the helm, this orchestra has risen to new heights and is well known as one of the best performers of Mahler, a favorite of mine. On my last trip to their stunning theater, my honey and I witnessed Mahler's Symphony no. 8, the famous "Symphony of a Thousand," where the room reverberated with a chorus of that size. No trip to the orchestra has ever been so memorable. The Fratelli Ruffatti organ also makes performances here truly unique. The beautiful concert hall was designed and constructed by women. *SB*

Aquarius Records

1055 Valencia St
647.2272
www.aquariusrecords.org
Mon–Wed 10a–9p, Thurs–Sun 10a–10p

I like all kinds of music, just as long as it is good. However, on my last road trip, my friend Perrin called me out after an excruciating mixed-tape session heavy with Boyz II Men and other blasts back to my childhood. Time for a major rummage at Aquarius (coincidentally, my sun sign), where the bad music has already been weeded out. This place makes it easy for me to get back my rep as a groovy tune hound. *SB*

Bazaar Café

5927 California St
831.5620
www.bazaarcafe.com
Mon–Fri 9a–10p, Sat–Sun 8a–10p, showtimes vary

No matter what the big record companies say or do, whether or not covers are allowed to be performed, Bazaar Café is practically immune as a result of the fresh up-and-coming talent they gather through their doors. My cousin Raina Rose is among them, a singer-songwriter who packs a crowd into this cozy coffeehouse and lulls them into her world with grooving melodies and skillful guitar harmonies. The baristas never let the steamer go during songs, and the hot chocolate still rivals any in the city. Come for a vegan scone, a slice of home-baked pie, and a pleasant evening of musicians on their way to greatness. *SB*

The Rickshaw Stop

155 Fell St
861.2011
www.rickshawstop.com
Wed–Thurs 5p–12a, Fri–Sat 5p–2a

Local beat-box crews, art student fashion-show parties, disco blasts, and international DJ acts fill up the small Rickshaw Stop every night it's open. The upstairs has a chill-out space with get-stuck sofas, and the hopping dance floor is lined with rickshaws, presumably from India. This space is a major supporter of local civic pride and hosts many benefit functions—not the kind that CEOs would go to, except a GrassRoutes CEO, of course. Creative ways to promote peace and messages of free will are alive and well at this small but well-loved SF nightspot. Saturday nights are nonstop bhangra! *SB*

101 Music

513 Green St
(CD-focused sister store is on Grant Avenue, vinyl is on Green)
392.6368
Daily 12–10p

OK, so I am not a "digger." Well, not in the typical sense of the word. I don't have turntables, just one plain record player, and I got most of my record collection as a consolation prize for my parent's twisted divorce. I still manage only a few records per trip to 101. But that is not because they don't have the goods, it's just that I have yet to find a comfy way to bike around SF with records on my back, and, probably, that I feel like a wannabe in a place where all the cool DJs hang out, digging for their next vinyl treasure. There are some eighty thousand records in this basement, and whatever you find is just $5. Come in search of nothing in particular and find the source of your desire on the shelves, racks, and stacks of records at 101. *SB*

DNA Lounge

375 11th St
626.1409
www.dnalounge.com
Events and cover charges vary

Not just another industrial looking dance club with some interesting interior design, DNA Lounge maintains several unconventional features, such as an open wireless network and a large scrolling LED sign with a publicly accessible web interface. The regular events here are some of the most innovative (albeit unusual) around, and cater to any musical genre you can think of. Take Remedy, the weekly deep house and hip-hop dance night, or Meat, where you can listen to industrial music while enjoying some free barbecue. My personal favorite is Bohemian Carnival, where eclectic dance music is accompanied by circus performances. For the nostalgic child of the '80s, try New Wave City; and for you wallflowers, Pop Roxx features live alternative and indie rock bands. Now all I need is a burrito—wait, they have those too! *DL*

Bay Area Theatre Sports (BATS)

B350 Fort Mason Center
474.6776
www.improv.org

Going to a BATS show is sure to leave you sore and aching from laughter. The hilarity of the performances combined with the incredible talent executing said performances will have you rolling in the aisles. Each show is entirely improvised, and you may find you've become part of the action, as audience suggestions and participation are strongly encouraged. If you are in town for a while you can look into taking a class with the nonprofit company (usually four to 12 sessions. There are occasionally onetime specialty classes offered, so it's worth checking even if you are only here for a short trip). *JA*

ODC Theater

3153 17th St
863.9834
www.odcdance.org

Aside from the heterogeneous mix of people in SF, one thing's for sure—we all love to dance. Even if we ourselves aren't adept at suave moves or intricate steps, it is something we can all enjoy and appreciate. SF's premier school and stage for modern dance is ODC, where some lucky San Franciscans get the training and take to the stage. Inexpensive tickets make this a great dinner and performance date, or just a chance to admire the expression of bodies moving in a coordinated scheme. *SB*

The Orpheum

1192 Market St
551.2000
www.shnfs.com

From several blocks away, the triumphant lighted sign evokes visions of the carefree Roaring Twenties nightlife. As I enter the elaborate palace that is the Orpheum, I take a moment to ogle the ornate arches and mythical figures of Spanish folklore all around. A magnificent sun illuminates the theater as I make my way to a seat; soon the lights dim and I imagine it's the 1920s all over again. This historic city landmark has gone through two major renovations and has featured several genres of entertainment over the decades since it opened in 1926, from vaudeville to silent films to musical comedies and presently a playhouse for touring Broadway productions. DL

The Independent

628 Divisadero St
771.1421
www.theindependentsf.com
Box Office: Mon–Fri 11a–6p

This latest incarnation of a neighborhood staple, which has been showcasing music for over 30 years, offers performances ranging from hip-hop to indie rock. The box office is open on weekdays and one hour before show time so you can avoid the so-called convenience charges associated with online ticket purchases—not very convenient if you ask me. No food is served at this venue, but you'll find several dining choices just a block away around Divisadero and Fulton. Following the show, go one block west to Alamo Square, where you can take a leisurely stroll while the music lingers in your head. DL

Intersection for the Arts

446 Valencia St
626.2787
www.theintersection.org

The first time I visited Intersection for the Arts, an actress friend of mind took me to see *Hamlet: Blood in the Brain*, an urbanized version of the Shakespeare classic, set in the darker side of 1980s Oakland. We arrived an hour early but the show was already sold out. Because shows tend to sell out at this truly intimate theater, they have a waiting list system set up, and we were the first to be placed on it. We ended up securing a few unclaimed tickets to what ended up being a first-rate performance, and the wait gave us plenty of time to catch up over hot cider at a nearby coffeehouse. Hailed as San Francisco's oldest art collective, the Intersection for the Arts houses every medium of creative expression imaginable. Exhibits range from the bizarre, like an intricate model dog made entirely from dog hair trimmings, to the intriguing, like an entire series of projects—both performance based and visual—that explore the human consequences of the prison industrial complex. Check out a local author's work during a reading, or listen to the sounds of Bay Area–grown jazz. The common tie is that everything produced and displayed at this venue will force you to think. *MP*

Great American Music Hall

 859 O'Farrell St
885.0750
www.gamh.com

My punk college roommate introduced me to hardcore music at this palace-like venue in the heart of the Tenderloin. I'll never forget the surprising amount of courteousness in the mosh pit; if you lost your balance there were 10 people already hoisting you up to your feet before you knew what happened. The hall's interior is stunning with beautifully decorated balconies and frescoes, and the acoustics are top-notch for any genre—bluegrass, punk, you name it. It's quite possibly the best place to hear live music in the city if you ask me. Great American Music Hall is also a partner in the Recycle Hear campaign to promote recycling at San Francisco's popular music venues. *DL*

Bottom of the Hill

 1233 17th St
621.4455
www.bottomofthehill.com
Doors: 8:30p, shows and ticket prices vary, Happy Hour: Wed–Fri 4–7p

The neon sign glows with an eerie blue light outside of this hip venue for up-and-coming acts at the bottom of Potrero Hill (hence the name). The tight interior space is reminiscent of a house-party gig where your best friend's band would play—there's even a patio out back and a kitchen to complete the picture. Everything from alternative, rock a billy, punk, and hardcore to folk, funk, and pop is played here. The web site lists all visiting bands and the dates they've played since 1997, so when your friend's band makes it big you can say, "I saw them at the Bottom!" *DL*

Slim's

 333 11th St
 255.0333
www.slims-sf.com

Where can you thrash to punk rock, jam to R&B, or be serenaded by the sultry sounds of a down-home blues singer? Ever heard of a place called Slim's? The acts featured at this nightclub are as eclectic as the career of the owner, R&B artist Boz Scaggs. Big acts like Nine Inch Nails and Blues Traveler have passed through this place, and it's one of the few venues where you can still enjoy a show within arm's reach of your favorite artist. Don't expect anything posh though—the venue, like the vibe, is unpretentious. More warehouse than music hall, the fantastic sound system and undeniable talent is what draws the crowds. Shows are known to sell out, so it's a good idea to buy tickets in advance. A modest dinner menu is served nightly on the upper level, and bar food is always available. *MP*

Mezzanine

444 Jesse St
625.8880
www.mezzaninesf.com

In these days of overstimulation and über-productivity, it is not enough for a club to be just a place to come and shake your booty. There has to be another draw, or several things going on at once: a great bar, a projection screen, bands and fashion events, movies and a backstage and a balcony. Mezzanine has it all. Once a month new art films are screened for the early crowd, and there's a regular lineup of groovy events, like a Mos Def show or a fashion show, complete with poodles, to benefit leukemia patients. The dancing is at its best on Thursday and Friday nights. Dress to the nines and you'll be in good company—I make it my venue of choice to premier new outfits or makeup concepts. Slither around the back streets between Mission and Market and you might even find parking before you head up the red carpet and into this chic space. *SB*

Café du Nord

217 Market St
861.5016
www.cafedunord.com

Nestled beneath the Swedish American Hall on the north side of Market Street, this diamond of a café dishes rockin' live music, savory treats, and stiff drinks without draining your pocketbook. The classic Victorian architecture gives Café du Nord an almost tranquil ambiance and it is not hard to believe this place was once hailed as a notorious speakeasy during Prohibition. Even as the place gets packed, the vibe stays miraculously mellow. The cover is usually around ten bucks, featuring nationally acclaimed artists as well as the best up-and-coming indie bands. The kitchen also offers a fantastic selection of food late into the evening, so come hungry and make a night of it. On my most recent visit I ordered several items from the appropriately titled "tasty plates" section of the menu. The hummus plate came with generous portions of smoky eggplant, sweet heirloom tomatoes, steaming pita bread, and garlicky hummus. The mini-corndogs, my personal favorite, consist of thick juicy franks coated in crispy cornbread batter that go perfectly with my favorite strong Belgian beer, Grande Reserve Chimay. Café du Nord offers a fantastic selection of brews; I would argue that the beer selection is reason enough to give this place a try. The fully stocked bar also carries several premium wines by the glass. Between the great food and drinks, and romantic decor, seeing a concert here is a real treat, and a perfect date spot to boot. MP

Amoeba Records

1855 Haight St
831.1200
www.amoeba.com
Mon–Sat 10:30a–10p, Sun 11a–9p

This is by far the best record store in the city because it is run by the smartest music lovers in San Francisco. They stock thousands of CDs, LPs, and DVDs, and can help you track down even the most obscure of musicians, maintaining local flare by promoting unsigned musicians in their store on a consistent basis. Don't be surprised if there's an in-store performance or a sign detailing the nonprofit organization or rainforest preservation fund your purchase is going toward that week. SB

San Francisco Playlist

1. The Dodos: "Red and Purple"
2. The Botticellis: "Who Are You Now"
3. Jefferson Airplane: "Somebody to Love"
4. The Grateful Dead: "Uncle John's Band"
5. Janis Joplin & Big Brother and the Holding Company: "Piece of My Heart"
6. Steve Miller Band: "Rock'n Me"
7. Black Rebel Motorcycle Club: "White Palms"
8. Dead Kennedys: "Holiday in Cambodia"
9. Counting Crows: "Mr. Jones"
10. Faith No More: "Epic"
11. Huey Lewis and the News: "Do You Believe in Love"
12. Journey: "Lights"
13. Santana: "Oye Como Va"
14. Third Eye Blind: "Semi-Charmed Life"
15. 4 Non Blondes: "What's Up"
16. The Beau Brummels: "Just a Little"
17. Aphrodesia: "Bus Driver"
18. Sly and the Family Stone: "Thank You (Falettinme Be Mice Elf Agin)"
19. Oona Garthwaite: "Trouble"
20. The Charlatans: "The Shadow Knows"
21. Invisibl Skratch Piklz: "Ah One, Two, Three, Cut"
22. Mike Relm: "Tron"
23. Foxtails Brigade: "The Hours"
24. The Frail: "Floated Away"
25. Michael Musika: "The Traveler Loses Possession"
26. John Vanderslice: "The Minaret"
27. Maus Haus: "We Used Technology (But Technology Let Us Down)"
28. Loquat: "Swingset Chain"
29. Chanticleer: "Revenna Sanctus"
30. Lord Loves A Working Man: "The New Hat"
31. Michael Tilson Thomas, conducting the San Francisco Symphony: Mahler Symphony No. 7 and 8
32. DJ QBert: "Redworm"
33. Jawbreaker: "Gutless"
34. Train: "Meet Virginia"
35. Deerhoof: "Twin Killers"

Queer Scene

The LGBT scene is hot and hopping, no matter which way you swing.

Everyone knows San Francisco is a Mecca for lesbian, gay, bisexual, and transgender populations. What local can forget Gavin Newsom's milestone legislation legalizing same-sex marriages? And did you know SF is the only city that will pay for the sex-change operations of its transgender employees? Ideas that seem absurd to the rest of the country are the status quo here. This freedom to live freely openly has allowed a rich counterculture to develop that is very much a part of San Francisco's diversity and uniqueness. The Castro, the center of San Francisco gay culture, was once a rundown neighborhood before a population made up of largely gay men reclaimed the community as their own. Now it flourishes with bars, restaurants, organic markets, theaters, and hair salons. The Mission district has an emerging lesbian community, and it shares many similarities to the early days of the Castro, and just across the Bay, Oakland boasts the largest lesbian population in the world. Whether you are gay or straight, San Francisco's queer scene has a lot to offer. You don't need to attend a Pride Parade to experience it either. Enjoy a quaint lunch at a cafe in the Castro, or practice your dance moves at one of the many gay or mixed dance clubs that abound.

Mecca

2029 Market St
621.7000
www.sfmecca.com
Tues–Thurs 5–11p, Fri–Sat 5p–12a, Sun 12–8:30p

Yes, there's a menu, but unless you reserve a table in advance and go with the mission to eat, you should just head for the bar. Mecca is a glam gourmet twist on the bar scene, where everything looks good—the staff, the food, the cocktails, and the people. Dress it up and plan to splurge on the tastiest drinks around. My favorite is the raspberry puree pineapple martini, made with top-shelf vodka even if you don't ask for it. Fine stuff! *SB*

SFGay.org

An all-in-one resource for San Francisco's mixed LGBT community, this always-current site has all the info you need for queer contra dancing, lesbian reggae, book readings, performances, new clubs, and all the juicy tidbits. Some of the best events in the city are featured here, so check back regularly. *SB*

Trax

1437 Haight St
864.4213
www.traxsf.com
Daily 12p–2a

With drinks for less than $3, Trax's thrifty happy hour rivals the Holy Cow. Visually, I imagine not much has changed at Trax since it first opened in the 1940s—and that's all part of the charm. Friendly customers and friendlier bartenders provide a mellow alternative to some of the more high-strung venues in the Castro. *MP*

Harvey's

500 Castro St

431.4278

Mon–Fri 11a–2a, Sat–Sun 9a–2a

Harvey's is a great place to enjoy diner-style food, like spicy chicken wings, and people watch. Located in the middle of the Castro, it's a popular meeting spot for locals and tourists alike. Brunch is served until three in the afternoon daily, and most evenings, DJs and classic cocktails get the party started. Hearty burgers and golden fries are served 'til two in the morning and are great for thwarting an imminent hangover. If you're lucky, you may just stumble in on a drag queen show. This place wears many hats, and they all seem to fit. *MP*

Mint Karaoke Lounge

1942 Market St

626.4726

www.themint.net

Daily 12p–2a

This karaoke bar is the best good-time watering hole around. After a night of singing and general camaraderie, you'll be friends with everyone in the place. It is by no means an exclusively queer experience, though a steady Castro crew rolls in on most nights. Gather round a stage-side table and sing to your heart's content without the competition of other karaoke bars or the nervousness of singing in public—everyone is just here for a laugh and a smile, so come and build up your endorphins. *SB*

Wild Side West

424 Cortland St

647.3099

Daily 1p–2a

One of the city's best-kept secrets will make you wish you'd been coming here all your life. The Wild Side West is the bar that lets everyone in and treats you like you've always been there. It's like the older, wiser sister, the Lexington Club—a longtime lesbian hangout and watering hole—but with a far more relaxed and hands-off atmosphere. The real secret? The hidden garden/jungle in the back, where you can hide away with your sweetie and a cocktail and pretend like nothing else matters. *MP*

Theater Rhinoceros

2926 16th St
861.5079
www.therhino.org

The longest-running queer theater in the world is here in San Francisco, hosting classic LGBT plays like *Bent, What the Butler Saw,* and *Lilies.* Come check out a new performance or one that's stood the test of time. *SB*

Lexington Club

464 19th St
863.2052
www.lexingtonclub.com
Mon–Thurs 5p–2a, Fri–Sun 3p–2a

You won't find too many Y chromosomes at this classic girl bar, making the Lexington a much-needed anomaly in San Francisco's male-dominated gay scene. Church pews for chairs and burgundy red walls lined with local art add a touch of romance. Pool tables and pinball machines provide plenty of entertainment, while the music selection is limited to whatever's on the jukebox. *MP*

Transfer

198 Church St
861.7499
Mon–Fri 12p–2a, Sat–Sun 8a–2a

The best nights to come are Monday and Saturday, when the bar gets super busy and the pool table morphs into a platform for attention-seeking dancers. DJs spin hip-hop ballads and pop/rock mash-ups. Male and female go-go dancers get the mixed crowd riled up. On slower nights, it's a great place to shoot pool and mingle with regulars. *MP*

The Café

2369 Market St
861.3846
www.cafesf.com
Mon–Fri 4p–2a, Sat 3p–2a, Sun 2p–2a

If you're looking for a dance party, look no farther than The Café. It's probably the most famous gay dance club in the area, and it rivals The Metro as the largest gay club in the city. Nightly drink specials—like $2 Tuesdays, when all well drinks are $2—keep the crowd nice and wet. And since this is a dance party, an ample dance floor doesn't stop patrons from cutting a rug wherever they please. MP

Phone Booth

1398 South Van Ness Ave
648.4683
Daily 12p–2a

This smoky dive boasts super strong drinks at prices that will leave you with plenty of extra cash to shoot pool and play your favorite Motown ballads on the jukebox. Weeknights are best, when the bar fills up with a mixed crowd and lots of regulars—free popcorn to boot. MP

Martuni's

4 Valencia St
241.0205
http://martunis.ypguides.net
Daily 2p–2a

Somewhere at the intersection of vamp and camp sits Martuni's, the place in the city to sing your heart out with a cocktail in hand. Pick out a tune and one of their custom martinis, and let your inner Judy Garland shine for the evening. JA

Café Flore

2298 Market St
621.8579
www.cafeflore.com
Sun–Thurs 7a–11p, Fri–Sat 7a–12a

Café Flore has been called the most relaxed gay atmosphere in the world, and for good reason—it feels more like Paris than the Castro. Outdoor seating amidst the most beautiful botanical garden is great for spring and summer, and an indoor fireplace keeps it toasty all through the winter. I love coming here in the mornings and reading the paper over a bowl of their homestyle hot cereal, served with cream, fruit, and pure maple syrup. Dishes like eggplant crostini and spinach salad sprinkled with goat cheese will leave you feeling satisfied and revived. They also have great desserts and strong cups of coffee. If you're looking for a refuge from the hectic pace of city life, let Café Flore be your oasis. MP

Holy Cow

1535 Folsom St
621.6087
www.theholycow.com
Thurs–Sat 9p–2a

I dare you to find a thriftier happy hour. On Thursday night, they serve $1 well drinks 'til 10, and the entire bar is half off 'til 12! There is never a cover, and the place fills up with college-age kids and other bargain seekers. The music is a mix of radio reruns and flashback ballads you can sing along to. Love it or hate it, it's been a city staple since the '80s, it's run by the same local guys, and you can always count on a dance party. MP

Stay Up Late

Where to find midnight snacks, 24-hour businesses, and casual late-night drinking, dining, and dancing

Staying up late to dance and dine and relax is something everyone does at least once in a while, so here are the best places around to get in touch with your nocturnal side.

$$ Globe

 290 Pacific Ave
391.4132
Mon–Fri 11:30a–1a, Sat 6p–1a, Sun 6–12p

A staple of the financial district, this little shoebox of a restaurant is known for its late hours, even attracting some of the city's top chefs after their own restaurants have closed. Dine on succulent grilled fish with farro (yes, my new favorite, farro!) salad, but be prepared for an energetic ambiance. If you prefer your meal with lots of decibels, then sit back and enjoy this city restaurant. DL

$ The Grubstake

 1525 Pine St
673.8268
www.sfgrubstake.com
Mon–Fri 5p–4a, Sat–Sun 10a–4a

There's always room for a little burger and fries to cap off a night of drinking and dancing, but at Grubstake, housed in an old Oakland-to-SF streetcar, you'll find Portuguese fare as well. Salads with meat, burgers with cheese and mushrooms, a basket of something fried—these are all appetizing at 3am with Jack and Coke still coursing through your veins. Classic *caldo verde*, or clams and garlic, or codfish with potatoes and seasonings, are hard to come by in the wee hours, so have a mini-vacation to Portugal, a piece of SF history, and a filling meal whenever the time is right. *SB*

Sam Wo's

813 Washington St
982.0596
Mon–Sat 11a–3a

Most of SF strictly closes at 2am. But not Sam Wo's—it is open until 3am. Order at the narrow ground level, right from the kitchen, then head up the thin stairs to the third floor where you can gaze down at Chinatown in the moonlight. Steelhead fish soup, barbecue wonton soup, and the raw fish salad appetizer are crowd-pleasers at this 100-plus-year-old restaurant. Don't be stingy—after all, the food is cheap and it is made to be shared with everyone around the table. I like treating it like tapas and ordering several menu items for all to share. This is my favorite late-night hangout; whether I've been out dancing or up late writing, I can always count on the delicious handmade wontons at Sam Wo's. *SB*

Beauty Bar

2299 Mission St
285.0323
www.beautybar.com
Mon–Fri 5p–2a, Sat–Sun 7p–2a

Get your nails done and indulge in a scrumptious cocktail like the Conditioner, a cleverly coined mixture of vanilla vodka, ginger ale, and fresh-squeezed lime juice for just $10. Decorated in a glut of throwback hairdryers and 1950s glam memorabilia, this neighborhood dive bar is like a "Cheers" for hipsters on weeknights. Thursday through Saturday, the party takes off as the evening commences with martinis and manicures. The monthly Gemini Disco Party, a bash of bright lights and crazy costumes, is probably the most happenin' Sunday night in the mission. It's also home of the monthly Ms. Beauty Bar Pageant. It's a ball and you can witness hopefuls showcasing vintage getups and bizarre talents to score a spot in the Ms. Beauty Bar pinup calendar. MP

The Mexican Bus Salsa Tours

Various locations
546.3747
www.mexicanbus.com

There are a plethora of party buses in the city to choose from if you're looking for a preplanned night of drunken fun, but this one ranks on top. For $38 you get door-to-door service to some of the most fun dance halls and salsa clubs in the city, and you get to ride on this loud and swanky bus. Adorned in tropical colors and trinkets, a jamming PA system and tequila shots keep the party going between stops. For large groups, an entire bus can be rented for about $500. For an extra fee, dance lessons, live performances, and catering can also be arranged, and if you're on a budget, you can always BYOB. MP

$ The Tamale Lady

The Mission—keep your eyes out!

Tamale Lady Virginia Ramos is the fairy godmother of the drunk and hungry. Late in the evening, she roams the Mission with her coolers filled with delicious tamales of all varieties. She can be elusive, but she almost always stops at Zeitgeist to tend to the sloshed masses. I know of people willing to sell their soul for one of the cheese tamales, and the pork tamales will avert any imminent hangover. If the tamales aren't a big enough draw, Virginia herself is a treasure, doling out hugs and hot sauce with a smile. JA

Blondie's Bar

1540 Valencia St
864.2419
www.blondiesbar.com
Daily 2p–2a

This place is probably best known for its 16-ounce martinis—yes that's right, 16 ounces of booze in just one drink. If you're feeling dangerous, delve into a Dagwood, a signature Tanqueray martini with sausage-stuffed olives! Or play it safe with a Jackie-O-Cosmo, a fruity mix of orange vodka, triple sec, fresh lime, and cranberry juice. The central location also makes it prime for barhopping, with the Casanova, the Beauty Bar, and Bruno's just footsteps away. *MP*

$ The Bus Stop

 1901 Union St
 567.6905
Daily 10a–2a

 If you're in the Marina and you're looking for a place to watch your favorite game, then park your tail at the Bus Stop. If the 20 flatscreen TVs aren't a draw, then the $5 Grey Goose martinis should surely be. Absurdly cheap drink specials and heaps of grilled and deep-fried bar food make it easy to stay at this place much longer than planned. My favorite thing about this place is that the kitchen stays open until 2am, making the Bus Stop a great place to start or end a night in the Marina. *MP*

$ Yuet Lee Seafood Restaurant

 1300 Stockton St
 982.6020
Wed–Mon 11a–3a

This is the kind of place that I would believe only exists in fantasies had I not had countless meals there. Besides serving authentic Hong Kong–style cuisine, Yuet Lee manages to squeeze in diners until three in the morning, all while providing helpful suggestions to those of us clueless about the menu, without being condescending. It's a dream come true for folks who want to try new things but don't know what to ask for. The salt and pepper squid, fried crispy after being drenched in the title ingredients, is the best I've had anywhere, and each bite is filled with the perfect amount of seasoning. Seafood is always fresh, and I challenge anyone to leave a bite of the clams in black bean sauce behind. Round out your meal with the steamed Chinese greens—what you'll end up with is expertly cooked bok choy delicately laced with fresh minced garlic. If it's a busy night, you may be asked if you'd like to share a table with another party. Take them up on the offer, as it's a great way to see what other people order and make new discoveries about the menu. *JA*

$ Nopa

560 Divisadero St
864.8643
www.nopasf.com
Daily 6p–1a (bar opens at 5p)

Nopa takes its moniker from the neighborhood it resides in, and the restaurant has been rapidly making the same neighborhood a bona fide dining destination. The high-energy environment features funky murals depicting San Francisco, and houses two floors to maximize the number of lucky folks who get to eat there nightly. When I'm catching up with friends over one of their superb cocktails (such as the Washhouse, which features organic vodka, basil, and lime juice), I like to sit on the second floor and watch the all the action from above. Although the menu changes nightly, I'm a big fan of their baked pasta dishes and the soups. If you happen to see the little fried fishes on the night you dine, snatch them up immediately. The crispy, whole smelts are the perfect predinner snack. Desserts, especially the fluffy donut holes, also aim to please. The only thing that can keep me away is the noise level, which can soar on busy nights, so go ready to use your outside voice. *JA*

$ Hemlock Tavern

1131 Polk St
923.0923
www.hemlocktavern.com
Daily 4p–2a

Where is it possible to take major names like Gillian Welch and Cat Power off their pedestal and see them rock out in their original context? Why, the Hemlock Tavern, of course. Their back-door music room, lovingly entitled Club Silencio, is the coolest micro-venue in the city, where bands from near and far, bands established and fresh, get on stage at least five nights a week. Circle around the centrally located bar and chat it up with fellow music lovers before the show. Happy hour is 4 to 7pm daily, with a buck off well drinks and brewskis. When your tummy starts rumbling, grab a bag of smokin' hot peanuts to munch on while you rule over your billiard competitors. *SB*

Zeitgeist

199 Valencia St
255.7505
Daily 9p–2a

Rows of picnic tables, pitchers of beer, and an outdoor barbecue. This dirty bar is perfect anytime, any day. The picnic tables force you to share any available space and conversation with characters you'll not soon forget. It self-identifies as a biker bar, due more to the plethora of bicycles than to the amount of hog riders. Black is the color du jour, and a cloud of smoke usually covers the backyard, making it an ideal place for dive-bar lovers who love their beer more than their reputation. Rumor has it the grilled cheese sandwiches and the Bloody Marys are to die for, but, honestly, this is the type of place where everyone has a pitcher in hand. Plus, if you stay long enough, the Tamale Lady will walk up to you just when you were getting hungry. What better way to spend a sunny afternoon in the city? Don't go if you either look like or are a yuppie—you'll never feel more out of place. *MP*

Orphan Andy's

2370 Market St
864.9795
24-7

The whole "awake during the day, asleep at night" thing doesn't work for everyone. Some of us feel that our creative juices get going only after everyone else is asleep. I've been known to have my greatest artistic ideas at odd hours, and sometimes the project extends so long that I need a meal to sustain my flow. The cutesy kitchen at Orphan Andy's is ready for me at any hour, be it a 5am cup of coffee and crumb cake or a 1am steak and eggs. Coffee is served like it should be, with bottomless refills, but I seem to always order hot cocoa instead. Whatever your tastes call for, if it can be found at a roadside diner, it can be found at Orphan Andy's, at any hour. *SB*

Blasthaus

www.blasthaus.com

Some of the most provocative events in the city are planned by Blasthaus, a group of tech-savvy creative types who plan digitally enhanced installations and parties all over town. If you are a DJ, chances are it is your dream to spin for a Blasthaus event, like their famous New Year's Eve parties. Venues vary, sometimes Vessel hosts, sometimes The Concourse, but each evening is an inspiring mix of beats, videos, and interesting people, and a creative conscious that lasts into the wee hours of the morning.

The Endup

401 Sixth St
646.0999
http://theendup.com
Hours vary by event, usually Tues–Sun 7p–5a

Music lovers unite! This bar is a regular late-night destination for musicologists and mixologists, male models, and moderates alike. Everyone in search of a local band's rhythms will have found his or her match at the Endup. 'Nough said. *SB*

$$ Bissap Baobab and Little Baobab

2323 Mission St; 826.9287
3388 19th St; 643.3558
www.bissapbaobab.com
Tues–Sun 6–10:30p, club open until 2a (closed Sundays)

I don't think it is fair to refer to Africa as one big mass; most generalities about the big continent don't hold, and the depth and variation of cultures between each of the many nations there make it impossible to sum up as a continent. So skip over to Mali and Senegal, on the cusp of the world's largest desert, to a place where West African cuisine is savored. Bissap Baobab serves up *sonome* (squashed potatoes, slightly fried and mixed with corn and spices, then drizzled with avocado sauce) and yuka fries (a Senegalese mainstay made from the tall yuka plant you can see growing all over California)—and that is just to start. Chicken *mafe*, a Mali staple, is my favorite entrée, dripping in not-too-spicy peanut sauce and resting on fluffed rice, but it is hard to resist the onion-slathered fish dibi, the coconut tilapia, or the marinated chicken yassa, doused in garlic mustard sauce. The mix of people is as important to my high opinion of this place as the food. Stay late, and travel less than a block around the corner to Little Baobab, where you can hear the music play on—the bar gets busy and the crowd takes to its feet. *SB*

$ El Farolito

2777 Mission St

826.4870

Daily 12p–3a

Appearances can be deceiving here at little corner-stop Farolito. Get in line, listening in to the bubbling Spanish interchanges between regular customers and skilled burrito-makers, and pick a super suiza carne asada quesadilla, probably the most-ordered item on the long menu. It comes with tender beef under a blanket of gooey cheese, slathered with sauces. It is big, big enough for at least two hungry eaters. *Lengua* burritos are divine—if you haven't tried beef tongue before, I sincerely urge you to try it. Vegetarians can get their fill too. Come earlier rather than later if you don't want to be crowded out by tipsy folks. SB

Stay In

The best take-out and take-home activities in town

Sometimes I try to pack too much into a day. By evening, all systems are not go. But taking in the town can be done inside, too. There are many great restaurants that specialize in to-go food, delivery, or places where the seating isn't as comfortable, so you can choose one of these low-energy nights to have an in-hotel or in-home dinner. While you're at it, why not rent a flick and make a cozy night of it?

Fayes Video and Espresso Bar

3614 18th St

522.0434

www.fayesvideo.com

Mon–Thurs 7a–10:30p, Fri 7a–11p, Sat 8:30a–11p, Sun 8:30a–10:30p

I am one of those people who forget the names of films and the name of actors in the same moment. "You know that movie with that actress in it?" I forget how dumb I sound when the words leave my lips. But sure enough, as soon as I see the title staring me in the face, the story floods back to my memory. At Fayes, I try and take a peek at their top 100 list, so I can go with a mission. And if I forget the name or the actor on the walk over, I can always get a cappuccino to fog my glasses while I try and capture the title. Monday, all films are $2, and on Wednesday are two for one. SB

$ Escape from New York Pizza

1737 Haight St and other locations
668.5577
www.escapefromnewyorkpizza.com
Mon–Thurs and Sun 11:30a–12a, Fri–Sat 11:30a–2a

It is hard for a New Yorker to find Brooklyn-style droopy pizza on the West Coast. And while the search might still be on, Escape offers some pretty hard-to-resist slices. The most popular is the potato pie, with fresh herbs, garlic, and thin-sliced potatoes. The local chain delivers to most of the city; their Haight Street location is right near the Rec Vic Theater, and nothing beats pizza and a movie. *SB*

$$ Delessio

302 Broderick Street
Market St
552.5559
www.delessiomarket.com
Mon–Fri 7a–7:30p, Sat–Sun 8a–9p

I don't eat junk food. After years of culinary lessons and experiences, I just can't get the stuff down my gullet. But there are thoughts, on lazy days, of ready-made foods, things I can reheat in the microwave for veg-out sessions. Pick up all the entrées you please at this ready-to-go deli with the best hot bar in town. All the dishes are made in-house from locally sourced ingredients— the scalloped potatoes, roast chicken, and inventive veggie plates are the best. Also, this is an ideal place for diners on dietary restrictions, as each item is carefully labeled with signage indicating if it is vegan, vegetarian, wheat free, contains nuts or dairy, etc. No guesswork here as you pile your plate higher. It's hard to steer away from the dessert selection without a truffle or two; save room for a miniature cupcake or some of their chocolate "bubble wrap." If you care to stay put with your meal, you can sit at one of the sidewalk tables and watch the passer by drool as they eye your lunch. *SB*

$ Marcello's Pizza

420 Castro St
863.3900
www.marcellospizzasf.com
Sun–Thurs 11a–1a, Fri–Sat 11a–2a

One of my favorite things about New York is the pizza. Its heavenly thin-crust pies are permanently etched in my memory. When I get a New York craving, I call Marcello's. Tangy tomato sauce, the perfect amount of cheese, and skinny crust that you can fold make this pizza almost East Coast worthy. Sub sandwiches, chicken wings, and salads are also available. The entire menu is posted online so you can decide on what you want before you call. They also do free deliveries on orders over $7, which is great because parking in the Castro can be a pain. If you're feeling really indulgent, add a few of their mini cheesecakes to your order. In addition to making great food, Marcello's uses eco-friendly boxes, and they recycle and compost. So even if you feel guilty about your meal, you can feel good about supporting a green business. *MP*

 ## Blackwell's Wine & Spirits

5620 Geary Blvd
386.9463
www.blackwellswines.com
Mon–Sat 10:30a–9p, Sun 12–6p

Off Geary, there's a great little secret: Blackwell's wines, where all those pricey Napa and Sonoma vintages you tasted on your last trip to the North Bay are a fraction of the cost. Knowledgeable staff help make a selection, so pair something with your next meal or surprise your friends at the next dinner party, without dropping a bunch of cash. Bring a bottle or two home, or to a friend's, and stay in for the night. *SB*

Four Star Video

402 Cortland Ave
641.5380
www.4starsf.com
Daily 11a–10p

One of the best selections of off-the-beaten-track videos is here at Four Star. I love getting random foreign titles and being positively surprised or laughing at my unresearched choice. Peruse the shelves while you wait for your take-out from one of the restaurants around the block. *SB*

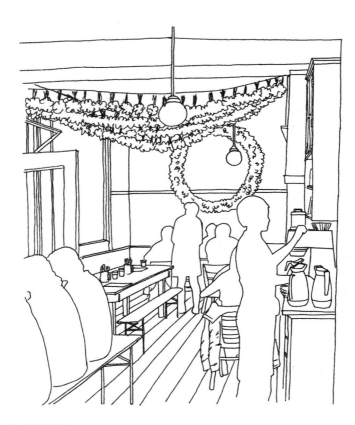

$ Goat Hill Pizza

300 Connecticut; 641.1440
715 Harrison St; 974.1303
525 Howard St; 357.1440
www.goathill.com
Sun–Thurs 11:30a–10:30p, Fri–Sat 11:30a–11p

So here's the deal: Goat Hill is the best delivery pizza in town. It is the only "all you can eat" restaurant you'd want to eat at. And it is arguably one of the first, if not the first, to Californicate pizza, as I'd put it, i.e., put sundried tomatoes on a pie made from sourdough. So even though now there are oodles of fancier pizza spots, this tasty slice still holds strong as the pillar of San Franciscan pizza eating. Monday nights at the Potrero Hill location (300 Connecticut St), you can eat all you want in pizza and salad for $10.95 a person; on Howard Street that deal stands every day, for dining in. Delivery from all three locations is swift and dependable—I get the Greek Gourmet (red onions, green olives, tomatoes, feta, and fresh rosemary)—and a bowl of their divine minestrone to share with my honey. *SB*

$$ Sparky's 24-Hour Diner

242 Church St
626.8666
24-7

Let me lay this out clear and simple—the reasons to love Sparky's are three: locally owned for a long, long time; big monster menu of American addictive substances; free delivery. Gooey grilled cheese and a strawberry milk shake? Crispy french fries and a heap of green salad? None of these combos are a problem, they are all a matter of minutes from your door or hotel room. Need I say more? *SB*

Pamper

Shelters from the hustle and bustle, simple enjoyments, and all things feel-good

Part of the whole pampering process is good, hot comfort food. The classic is chicken soup. But I find most places load their chicken broth with salt, as a substitute for slow-cooked flavor. This is bad news for the body; instead of pampering you get seriously dehydrated. So, in this chapter, I've given special attention to not only the in-the-moment effects, but the aftereffects as well. Here is a selection of feel-good foods, restful spaces, and of course, spas and salons, to refresh, re-energize, and restart your engines.

$$ Suppenkuche

525 Laguna St
252.9289
www.suppenkuche.com
Mon–Sun 5–10p, Sun 10a–2:30p

For a dose of German healing, head to Suppenkuche, where a tall pint of perfect Bavarian booze and a hearty portion of schnitzel will set things right again. Owned, cooked, served, and savored by the burgeoning German population of SF, this place remains un-Americanized. Warm your bones with a bowl of their soups, and don't forget to ask for their special mustard; it tastes good on everything. *SB*

$$ Blue

2337 Market St
863.2583
Mon–Fri 11:30a–11p, Sat–Sun 10a–10p

Rich mac and cheese, hearty chicken potpie, and tasty healthful salads make Blue, ironically, the best place to be cheered up from the inside out. Traditional American comfort classics are made with local ingredients, minus the hefty price tag. Don't miss the root beer menu that ranges from sweeter renditions to more barky bitter versions. *SB*

Westwood Beauty Supply

1524 Ocean Ave
586.1421
Hours vary

The best place to peruse inexpensive body lotions, hair potions, and makeup is this expansive shop near SFSU. If you can get by the owner's Chihuahua, you'll be on your way to pamper paradise, for a fraction of the cost any downtown store would have you pay. *SB*

Lavande Nail Spa

113 Carl St; 566.5333
2139B Polk St; 931.7389
www.lavandenailspa.com
Mon–Wed 10a–7p, Thurs–Sat 10a–8p, Sun 10a–6p

My mother-in-law refuses to let anyone touch her feet unless she's visiting me and I take her to Lavande. The blissful pedicures always include a sea salt scrub and lengthy massage, leaving you feeling relaxed and gorgeous. The nail technicians won't let a smudge sneak past them even if, like me, you are notorious for bumping a nail immediately after polishing. If you are hard to please, never fear—Lavande has an enormous polish selection, including Zoya polishes with no harsh chemicals or formaldehyde, and designer shades from Chanel and Yves St. Laurent at no extra cost. Your tootsies will be a perfect 10. *JA*

Union Street Apothecary

1764 Union St
771.1207
www.usapothecary.com
Tues–Fri 10:30a–6:30p, Sat 10a–5p

This is the place for the all-out skin splurge. Divorce, family matters that are taking over your life, serious business—you need to secure a good reason to have the "team" at the apothecary take care of you. Once you've got it, just relax and know that no matter what bags or sags are under your eyes, the stress will be gently relieved from your face. High-quality sunscreens and other top-notch products are in stock for a quick pass through this posh shop, but for a real feel-good makeover look no further. *SB*

Habit

1905 Union St, Ste 1
441.3332
www.waxhabit.com
Daily hours vary, call ahead

If you should happen to find yourself in SF during one of our warmer moments, you may have a need for a bit of (ahem) hair removal. My first visit to Habit was so pleasant that I couldn't wait to return—not a frequent sentiment after a waxing experience, right? Owner Carrie Maxwell's space is decked out in old apothecary style. She makes you feel right at home with a comfy spa bed, a glass of wine (or water), great music, and seasonally fla-vored taffies. If that weren't enough, Carrie has a "wax bar" with nine differ-ent waxes; she chooses the right wax for each body part and skin type. Prices can be steep, but it's worth every penny. *JA*

International Orange

2044 Fillmore St, second floor
888.894.8811
www.internationalorange.com
Mon–Fri 11a–9p, Sat–Sun 9a–7p

Heavenly facials, soothing massages, and revitalizing yoga classes are the name of the game at this day spa. It takes its moniker from the paint color used on the Golden Gate Bridge. If you decide to take a yoga class before your spa treatment, you will have the benefit of downward-dogging in the city's only completely green yoga studio. The men's and women's lounges have lockers with plush robes, perfect after a jaunt in their steam room. While you wait for your treatment, you can sip water or tea and munch on antioxidant-rich dark chocolate and dried fruit. The facials are pure magic and all of IO's therapists explain the benefits of every luxurious product they slather on your skin before kneading your troubles away during a head and neck massage. For more massage, IO has a myriad of choices, including Thai massage, prenatal massage, and an indulgent four-handed massage. The employees are friendly, knowledgeable, and skilled at their craft. While IO provides the ultimate pampering experience, they are also fiercely committed to being environmentally sound by using PVC-free yoga mats and local, organic, and natural beauty products. *JA*

Moishe's Pippic

425 Hayes St
431.2440
Mon–Fri 8:30a–4p, Sat 9:30a–4p

In the thick of Hayes Valley is this understated Chicago-style deli, where simple ingredients go into some fantastic lunches. I am not a huge fan of hot dogs, but if I am in the mood, the Vienna beef franks at Moishe's would be my choice. Add sauerkraut, relish, and some fontina cheese, and you've got one dressed-up dog. Pastrami sandwiches and fluffy scrambled-egg sandwiches fill out the two-sided paper menu at my favorite SF hole-in-the-wall. Their soups are perfect for pampering. *SB*

Turtle Tower

631 Larkin St
409.3333
Wed–Mon 8:30a–7:30p

The cities of the South Bay have SF beat where pho is concerned, but that doesn't mean you can't find a mean bowl of the Vietnamese soup within our city. In fact, when my friend Kathy's Vietnamese parents are in town, they refuse any pho that isn't generated in Turtle Tower's kitchen. There are nine varieties of the beloved soup, each under $6. PSA: This pho is served Northern style, which means no fresh herbs to toss in your broth. *JA*

Secret Garden Tea House

721 Lincoln Wy
566.8834
www.secretgardenteahouse.net
Tues–Fri 12–6p, Sat–Sun 11:30a–5:30p

The institution of afternoon tea has been all but lost on this side of the Atlantic, a harsh reality for me, a person who would seriously consider picking up, riding BART to the SFO international terminal, and flying over the pond for high tea at Fortnum & Mason. With the discovery of Secret Garden, which shares the name with one of my favorite childhood books, I don't need to max my credit card for such an elaborate and ridiculous trip. The mint and cucumber sandwiches, the hand-painted bone china, and the rich double Devon cream smeared on a fresh-baked scone will do just fine. For less than $20, you can share a full tea course with a friend. Take turns picking treats off the stacks of the tea tray while you catch up on good times gone by and dreams to be fulfilled. *SB*

Avra Organic Spa

505 Beach St, Ste 130
351.1500
www.avraorganicspa.com

Really, there's no reason to put anything other than natural, purifying substances into your body. You've only got one, after all! Avra's illustrious body wraps heal you from the inside out, and only contain the most pristine ingredients. Facials based on your specific *dosha* (the ancient Ayurvedic concept) detoxify your urban pores—say good-bye to the soot of the city. *SB*

Kabuki Springs and Spa

1750 Geary St
922.6000
www.kabukisprings.com
Daily 10a–9:45p

I'm back in Japan at Kabuki's clean and comfortable communal bathing tubs, washing away my worries for a song. When I feel more indulgent, I'll try their spa packages, all inspired by Pan-Asian healing techniques, like Nirvana, a body polish, private bath, and Swedish or Shiatsu massage. *SB*

Sweet Tooth

All things sweet converge here, and these are the best places to discover your soft spot for sugary treats

Even the healthiest of us crave a sugar rush every so often, a task San Francisco's bakers, chocolatiers, pastry chefs, and dairy gods and goddesses have heartily taken up. Pack your toothbrush and brush in between licking ice cream cones, munching handmade caramels, seducing your senses with a truffle, or smothering a cupcake. (My uncle the dentist told me to tell you that.) I figure as long as I keep shuffling through the Get Active chapter and taking Uncle Rob's advice, I can enjoy all the wonders herein.

$$$ Citizen Cake

399 Grove St
861.2228
www.citizencake.com
Hours vary

On a few occasions in my little life, I have wound up at a grand hotel buffet, overflowing with baskets of fresh-baked goodies, slabs of tender meat, and trays of main courses and salads. I don't know where to start, and soon I find our table loaded with gargantuan proportions of who knows what. What was once painstakingly decorated cakes and slow-roasted game hen becomes a disaster of taste to behold. Citizen Cake sorts out my dilemma by editing the menus of those epic brunch buffets to only the choicest dishes, both sweet and savory. Poached eggs over bacon and wilted organic spinach, chanterelle scrambles, homemade plum donuts with glaze, and a heaping assortment of signature cakes and petites fours are given the attention they deserve instead of being caught in the shuffle. Somehow, the best grits in town are found at the place with the best sweet treats—don't leave without a lemon sandwich cookie. *SB*

Stella Pastries

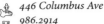

446 Columbus Ave
986.2914
www.stellapastry.com
Mon–Thurs 7:30a–7p, Fri–Sat 7:30a–12a, Sun 8:30a–7p

After a few too many aperitifs at a North Beach bar, complete your Friday night with a sweet nothing at Stella. For me there's no decision: the cannoli here is the best in the city, filled with the ricotta-based mixture right at the time you order. Amaretti cookies absolutely melt in your mouth; I can't leave without taking a bushel home for crumbling into almond pastry dough for tarts. I save the amaretti paper wrappers and light them on fire—the flame dies away quickly and they float upwards like I'd imagine a fairy would. If you have more time, stay for coffee and a napoleon, which you can eat while taking in the hustle and bustle of the North Beach scene. *sb*

Eastern Bakery

720 Grant Ave
433.7973
www.easternbakery.com
Daily 7a–3:30p

Mooncakes are a prized treat in Chinese culture, filled with traditional ingredients like lotus root, taro, sweetened winter melon, and black bean paste. I've long adored these scallop-edged buns that seem to be both rich and light in flavor at the same time. When you purchase them from stores, strong preservatives interfere with flavor and are actually dangerous to ingest. At Eastern Bakery, where master bakers and workers are paid a good wage, all their goods are baked fresh daily, including their sought-after mooncakes. Look no further for Chinese baked goods—you will love these. *sb*

Bittersweet Chocolate Café

2123 Fillmore St (second location in Oakland)
346.8715
www.bittersweetcafe.com
Sun–Thurs 10a–8p, Fri–Sat 10a–10p

The best cure for any chocolate jones can be found at this two-story café in the heart of the Fillmore. This offshoot of the Oakland location acts as both a café and a retail store, allowing you to indulge in whatever your heart desires. The store features chocolates from around the world, like Fran's gray salt caramels and specialty boxes from Vosges. I prefer to stay and linger in the café, with my chocolate Thai iced tea, one of nine chocolate drinks Bittersweet offers. In colder weather, I go straight for the classic hot chocolate complete with a homemade marshmallow (whipped cream is also an option). When I can't resist an edible treat, I devour the decadent pear chocolate ginger muffin or one of the featured cupcakes. Or a brownie. You get the picture. If you can't decide, ask the staff what they would suggest—they've never steered me wrong and I've often ended up discovering something truly amazing this way. *JA*

$ Moscow & Tbilisi Bakery

5540 Geary Blvd

668.6959

Daily 7a–9p

Use your Internet connection before heading to this classic Russian bakery so you can learn a few words in Russian. Few non-Russians enter this place, but, in my opinion, more should. The tasty and inexpensive treats here aren't always served with a smile, unless of course you've gone ahead and followed my advice. This particular bakery is more authentic and delicious than the others on Geary, so follow your nose to Moscow & Tbilisi. For a few bucks, a piroshki, a poppy seed roll, or a Danish-like cheese tart will make it worth your while. Skip the more sugary pastries and stick with the real Russian ones. Even though my *bubbe* was Russian, I still can't get in with this crowd—and I want to be "in." After you find this spot, you'll want to be "in" too. *SB*

$$ Petite Patisserie

1415 18th St

821.9378

www.petitepatisserie.com

Tues 7a–3p, Wed–Sat 7a–7p, Sun 8a–12p

This tiny blink-and-you'll-miss-it organic bakery is the perfect place for carb loading. I have to physically restrain myself from gobbling up more than one of their buttery croissants in a sitting. Check out the day's shortbread selection—the choices include delectable varieties like Mexican chocolate, cardamom, and good old vanilla. Petite Patisserie will also make cakes to your liking (including wedding cakes) in flavors such as coconut and mango or hazelnut. Their light, golden challah is the ideal choice for your French toast recipe or simply on its own. There is nowhere to sit inside the micro-sized store, so make sure you have enough hands to carry out your perfect pastries. *JA*

Destination Baking Company

598 Chenery St
469.0730
Mon–Fri 6a–6p, Sat–Sun 6a–4p

Pucker up for the lemon tarts or satiate your tummy growls with a savory cheddar cheese scone. Destination has got a myriad of treats to meet your every desire. Breakfast pastries are two for one after 2 pm, but don't worry if they run out—you can always grab a piece of their moist carrot cake to make it all better. Destination uses only local, organic ingredients, and all of their wholesale clients are local as well. Even though they have loads of goodies to prepare for their own store, they share their baking space with the kids from Mission Pie (also in this chapter) to help them in their initiative. That's some pretty sweet stuff. *JA*

Bi-Rite Creamery

3692 18th St
626.5600
www.biritecreamery.com
Sun–Thurs 11a–9p, Fri–Sat 11a–10p

This is gourmet ice cream at its finest. The creamery is housed on the same block, but on the opposite side of the street as its parent establishment, Bi-Rite grocery. On a nice day you will likely find a significant line, but it is definitely worth waiting for. Bi-Rite starts with fresh, local, organic ingredients to create their clamored-for ice cream. They boast traditional flavors, like the extraordinary mint chip, pure vanilla, and a deep rich chocolate (there is also a soy chocolate flavor for the lactose intolerant). If you are feeling adventurous, try one of their signature flavors, like the popular salted caramel or the mellowing honey lavender. There is a selection of sundaes, but I like to make my own so I can choose the sauce and a topping like candied pecans or grains of fleur de sel individually coated with chocolate. *JA*

Miette Confiserie

449 Octavia Blvd
626.6221
www.miettecakes.com
Mon–Sat 11a–7p, Sun 11a–5p

For an instant dose of childhood glee, pop into Miette Confiserie and stroll amongst the gumdrop topiaries to pick out the perfect bonbon. The store is decorated like an old European candy shop with shelves piled high with multiple colors of malt balls, jelly beans, and M&M's, plus an enormous selection of organic and fair trade chocolates from around the world. If you are looking for something a little more local, try Kate's caramels, a divine creation made by a friend of the owners who moonlights in candy making. You can also buy the cupcakes and baked goods made by the shop's sister store, Miette Patisserie. The staff is friendly and extraordinarily helpful, making sure that if you leave with nothing else, you still leave with a smile. *JA*

Swensen's Ice Cream

1999 Hyde St
775.6818
Tues–Thurs, Sun 12–10p, Fri–Sat 12–11p

This classic ice cream shop has been a corner store at the heart of several generations of San Franciscans. Swivel around in the soda-fountain chairs and, after a root beer float, hike up Hyde to view Alcatraz from the tippy-top of Russian Hill. *SB*

Yoogo Gelato

601 Broadway
398.2996
Daily 10a–11p

China and Italy border each other in SF, so it only follows that a gelateria perched on the line between these converging worlds would feature durian and black sesame as their flavors. But let's get something straight here— durian is an acquired taste. I mean that. Without major loads of sugar, this sought-after delicacy tastes like sour cherry chicken, or something very new to the Western palate. In a creperie-boba-gelateria shop, you can find the best of both worlds, often in strange combinations. I come because it is the only locally owned gelateria in the city (excepting places that serve gelato but are primarily a café or restaurant, and most of those don't make it themselves). I also come because they have Budweiser, stracciatella, pumpkin, and lychee flavors, in addition to the aforementioned versions. Come for something creamy, taste before you buy, and be rewarded with a huge serving of gelato, sweet or not. *SB*

$ Mission Pie

2901 Mission St
282.1500
http://missionpie.com
Mon–Thurs 7a–9p, Fri 7a–10p, Sat 8a–10p, Sun 9a–9p

Building a bridge may not be as hard as we all thought. (Although the new Bay Bridge has taken long enough to finish!) The virtual bridge between Pie Ranch Farms (in Davenport) and the Mission district is impenetrable at Mission Pie, where eating pie is a religion. This is country pie in the city, made by urban families who foster local food knowledge for their kids and the community. Apple and pumpkin are my top picks, but I am a classic girl, after all. Order the pear raspberry or the plum frangipane when they're in season; every day there is a new menu of what's available. *SB*

$ Kara's Cupcakes

3249 Scott St; 563.2253
900 North Point St; 351.2253
www.karascupcakes.com
Daily 10a–6p

Kara played her cards right, she sure did. Something inside her must have been fixated on childhood dreams, because her creatively delicious cupcakes are delightfully un-grown up. One of the first kitchens to resurrect the cupcake as a chic dessert, the selection at her growing number of retail outlets (she's now in Napa's Oxbow Market and planning to open in Oakland's new California Harvest Hall) is mind boggling. Java and banana are divine in the morning, and lunchtime favorites are Kara's Karrot or the best stand-in for a PB&J sandwich, a peanut butter ganache cupcake. For an after-dinner treat, tantalize your taste buds in classic sweet vanilla and sweet chocolate. Every meal could be that much better with one of Kara's now-famous single-serving cakes. *SB*

$ Maggie Mudd

903 Cortland Ave
641.5291
www.maggiemudd.com
Mon–Fri 3–11p, Sat 11a–11p, Sun 11a–9p

Move over meat eaters, dairy eaters, all you vegan haters! Ice cream is rein-vented at Maggie Mudd. A Waffle Bowl Banana Split shared with my honey means our bellies won't be a-grumblin' during our movie. My friend Char-maine likes getting the Orange Cremesicle, but I swear by the Coconut Road, complete with vegan marshmallows. There are many dairy flavors and sher-bets too, but the spectacle has to be the easily digestible dairy-free flavors, that never taste as though they are missing a thing. sB

$$ Tartine

600 Guerrero St
487.2600
www.tartinebakery.com
Mon 8a–7p, Tues–Wed 7:30a–7p, Thurs–Fri 7:30a–8p, Sat 8a–8p, Sun 9a–8p

All organic, all tasty, all fancy pants—this bakery is hands-down the best in the city, known around the globe for their rich bread pudding (thanks, Mar-tha!). Don't skip a loaf of the country wheat with walnuts for later, and grab a double chocolate cookie and a lemon tart to down right at one of the steel tables outside—that is, if you can fit in the door. Come early on weekdays for the best selection and the least congestion. Amen, ovens! sB

$ Polly Ann Ice Cream

3138 Noriega St
664.2472
Daily 11a–10p

Sweets aren't relegated to the Mission and SoMa! Take a bus ride, reading a good cookbook or guidebook on the way, to the Sunset and Polly Ann's wall of flavors. After all, there are no fewer than 500 reasons, 49 served each day. Arab's Lunch, Alligator Pear, Whiskey Flip, Sarsaparilla, King of Heart, the list even includes strange flavors like avocado and vegetable. Adjust your desire buttons appropriately, select a few to taste, then choose a sundae so you can savor spoonfuls of several flavors. My favorite? Strong Italian Cof-fee, Zest Ginger, and, my standby since I learned the wonders of ice cream,

Black Raspberry. Celebrate Obama's victory with Bush's Delight—his days as a flavor may yet be numbered. If you've been hankering for a new hobby but didn't know where to turn, you can purchase all the tools to be Popsicle maker extraordinaire here, too; just request a catalog when you get to the counter. *SB*

$ Mitchell's Ice Cream

688 San Jose Ave
648.2300
www.mitchellsicecream.com
Daily 11a–11p

Before all the nouveau, froufrou dessert palaces sprinkled San Francisco, my father and his cousins were eating Mitchell's—still a diamond in the crown of this city's ice cream scene. Mint chocolate chip at Mitchell's just can't be topped in my opinion, and from what I gather, my honey is the reigning expert on that flavor. I opt for a mix of white peach and passion fruit sorbets—there's really no better way to cap a day of urban exploration. *SB*

$$ Crown and Crumpet

900 North Point St, in Ghirardelli Square
771.4252
www.crownandcrumpet.com
Mon–Thurs 10a–6p, Fri 10a–9p, Sat 9a–9p, Sun 9a–6p

English tea isn't the dusty old traditional cliché here at Crown and Crumpet. The couple behind the teapots makes the experience fun and modern, with bright pink mod furnishings and excellent loose leaf teas, served with delightful cakes and tarts. For lunch, order toasted crumpets with Welsh rarebit and organic tomatoes, or head straight for the high tea. Tea for two includes your choice of endless tea, the aforementioned crumpets, eight homemade sweets, and eight tea sandwiches, plus fresh jam and clotted cream. Butter me up! *SB*

Buy Me

A unique take on shopping from artichokes to zippers

Andy Warhol really was on to something when he equated department stores with museums. Indeed, the way to appeal to shoppers is an artful task, and well represents our most modern takes on design and cultural signing. So whether you have a practical purpose, need a little retail therapy, or just want to gaze at the most modern of museums, these spots should fulfill your aims, while also being community- and environment-friendly businesses.

 Flight 001

525 Hayes St
487.1001
www.flight001.com
Mon–Sat 11a–7p, Sun 11a–6p

This design-forward travel store can streamline the packing stage of your next flight, eliminating some of that pretravel stress. We've all had our share of experiences having to run around town for maps and medicine; Flight 001 (they like to emphasize the pronunciation of 001 as "One") brings all travel-related items and accessories to a single convenient location. With all of their innovative products, hauling awkward luggage around the terminal is a thing of the past. *DL*

 Best In Show

545 Castro St
864.7387
www.bestinshowsf.com
Mon–Fri 11a–8p, Sat 11a–7p, Sun 11a–6p

My cat's custom-made fish collar is perhaps one of the silliest purchases I've ever made, but I adore it and he looks so chic wearing it. Best In Show also features jars of exciting toys for all your animal companions, as well as designer doggie transport bags and politician chew toys. On weekends they often play host to various animal shelters looking to adopt out their adorable charges. *JA*

Dollhouse Bettie

1641 Haight St
252.7399
www.dollhousebettie.com
Mon, Wed 1–7p, Thurs–Sat 11a–7p, Sun 12–6p

My two favorite adjectives: naughty and elegant, together at last. Dollhouse Bettie is the best lingerie store in SF, no contest. And it's not just because of their frilly '50s-style undies, their strappy teddies, comfy and cute bras, or wild stilettos. They will make a corset fit to your body, just for you. Design your own with unique colors and lace, in the shape you desire—these aren't the crack-your-ribs, short-of-breath corsets from centuries ago, but modern, wearable, sexy ones that flatter any figure. Get smitten with yourself! *SB*

Queen of Sheba

110 Sutter St
567.4322
Daily 9a–9p

Middle Eastern goodies abound at this neighborhood market. The prices are excellent, and there are lots of food options ready to be eaten with minimal preparation. This store is perfect if you are planning a dinner party and you want to impress your guest with an exotic meal, but you don't have a lot of time to prep. Choose from an abundance of hard-to-find cheeses like Nabulsi (a firm cheese made from goat's milk), plenty of hummus-like dips, and a variety of soft flat breads. In addition to lots of vegetarian options, they have a great selection of halal meats. The rack of lamb is a steal at less than $5 per pound, and their cucumber yogurt dip goes great with any meat or veggie dish. For dessert, try the date and fig cookies; they are sweet, sticky, and instantly comforting. They also sell Kefir, a traditional Middle Eastern drink that's something like a cross between milk and yogurt. It comes in a variety of fruity flavors, and I can never resist picking up a few bottles of the peach for later. *MP*

My Trick Pony

742 14th St
861.0595
http://mytrickpony.com
Tues–Sat 11:30a–7p, Sun 12–5p

My favorite little collection of screen-printing artists congregate at My Trick Pony, a place where you can make your own designs into groovy screen-printed wearable art. Browse the shirts and other knit jersey gear of their own creation, or talk with one of these artists about your own project. I try and make it to as many Movie Nights as possible, where you can catch classics like *The French Connection* and *Jaws* while hanging with other artists. *SB*

Wishbone

601 Irving St
242.5540
www.wishbonesf.com
Daily 11:30a–7p

Wishbone is the perfect cure for gift block—when you need a gift for someone now but have no idea what to get. The store holds treasures like adorable Bee-house teapots, soy candles, original jewelry, Paul Frank duds, gorgeous artisan stationery, Demeter fragrances, and hip baby onesies. You can embellish your gift with one of their many trinkets, like mini-magnets or retro buttons. Grab a gift for yourself while you are at it since the store also carries a wide range of interesting and funny books, most of which are from local authors. *JA*

Archive

317 Sutter St
391.5550
www.archivesf.com
Mon–Sat 10a–6p

I have a problem, not a big problem, but a problem just the same. My boyfriend hates shopping. For me, he'll happily tag along, if only to see me smile and try on different outfits. But for him, no way, José. That was until we stepped, hand in hand, me tugging, him dragging his heels, into Archive. There's something supremely stylish and at the same time ultimately masculine about this Sutter Street boutique, where a pile of cash transforms into the most handsome outfit around. Find independent Japanese and Italian labels mixed in with a few local designers. Even beer-drinking Niners fans can get excited about clothes without the fear of going metrosexual. Manly man style morphs into something wearable and distinct. *SB*

Rainbow Grocery

1745 Folsom St
863.0620
www.rainbowgrocery.org
Daily 9a–9p

When I moved only two blocks away from Rainbow, I did a happy dance and then ran over to pick up some provisions for unpacking. This grocery is a co-op and only houses products that are organic, natural, or fair trade. Search parties have been enlisted to come find me when I venture into the enormous bulk section for tea, pretzels, oatmeal, coconut, or any number of pastas and cereals. Still, my preferred spot is the cheese section, which is one of the most well-stocked and well-priced in town. Talk to the employees working that day, as they always find me a new and unusual cheese to add to my dairy repertoire. *JA*

Lucca Ravioli Company

1100 Valencia St
647.5581
www.luccaravioli.com
Mon–Sat 9a–6p

Growing up, my absolute favorite dish was my mother's linguine with pesto sauce, which I called "green noodles." Lucca offers the closet thing to home-made with their kitchen-prepared pastas and sauces, not to mention their trademark ravioli, stuffed with cheese, spinach, or beef, and turkey during the holidays. Perusing the fresh-cut meats and cheeses with the rustic wooden floor beneath my feet makes me forget about the existence of the supermarket. Everything you need to make a deliciously filling Italian meal can be found at Lucca. *DL*

You Say Tomato

1526 California St
921.2828
www.yousaytomato.biz
Tues–Fri 10a–7p, Sat–Sun 10a–5p

Ever since I lived in London I've been trying to get the word out that the food really isn't that bad there—well, not all of it. In fact, I can't get enough of some of the staples I used to stock. I can get them again at You Say Tomato and satisfy my love for all things British. I head to this shop on a regular basis. Grab all the favorites—Pim's, biscuits, brown sauce, even canned haggis—well, that might not be a favorite. *SB*

John Campbell's Irish Bakery

5625 Geary Blvd
387.1536
Mon–Fri 7a–10p, Sat–Sun 7a–8p

How could it be that the most known culinary fact about Ireland is the potato famine? It's easy to forget the hardships of history when faced with a windowful of traditional raisin soda bread, crusty loaves, plain and currant scones, and Belfast Bep's. There's something fresh from the oven for every Irish dish—my favorite combo is lamb stew with Campbell's soda bread dipped in for a lingering moment. *SB*

New World Market

5641 Geary Blvd
751.8810
Mon–Sat 9a–9p, Sun 9a–8p

Every time I come here I can feel a little something on my shoulder, and I'm sure it is my *bubbe* directing me to the best herring and the honey-filled chocolates. All the Russian delicacies are here—the farmers cheese, the almond-flavor cookies (perfect for dunking), the cherry preserves, meats, and pepper spreads. I get hungry just thinking about it. Come to fill your picnic basket or to switch it up for your weekly groceries. I like to go to a different ethnic grocer each week and get inspiration for food and culture all in one go. This market is the place to go for all things Russian, plus the bakery across the street is a treat pre- or post-shopping. *SB*

True Saké

560 Hayes St
355.9555
www.truesake.com
Mon–Sat 12–7p, Sun 11a–6p

It is crucial to get sake fresh. Unlike vodka, rum, or wine, sake isn't aged in the same sense, so get yours from a place that has a wide selection and a quick turnover. Choices baby! True sake has the know-how and the selection to bring people from all around the Bay Area, so they always have the fresh stuff. Talk over your decision with one of the knowledgeable staff members—they really know their stuff. After a lesson or two, you'll know your likes and dislikes and can take a trip to Japan Center, another place with quick turnover, albeit not as high quality as True Saké. Ginjo is well polished and tasty, but once you have a Diagingo, you'll be coming back for more. Sebo, the GrassRoutes girls' favorite spot for swanky sushi, gets their rare sake from the "secret room" here in Hayes Valley. *SB*

Little Otsu

849 Valencia St
255.7900
www.littleotsu.com
Wed–Sun 11:30a–7:30p

Once removed from the original all-vegan clothing store Otsu, this über-popular shop supports healthy shopping at all levels. All of the products are made by people who were paid well. There's no leather, and tons of adorable local finds, both practical and pointless. You'll love the remixed and recycled materials used to make notebooks, jewelry, stuffed animals, and wallets—a great place for gift shopping. *SB*

Cheese Boutique

666 Chenery St
333.3390
Mon–Sat 10a–7:30p, Sun 10:30a–6:30p

Not even a mild affliction of lactose intolerance can keep me away from this place. Not only do they have the best Brie, they also carry garlicky homemade hummus, Toscano salami, soft English biscuits, and plenty of other goodies. The prices are also much better than what you would find for similar items at the grocery store. If you're looking for instant gratification, try the tomato and mozzarella sandwich on baguette—the only downside is that it's sure to illicit cravings down the road. The super-friendly owner hand picks the hard-to-find inventory, and he offers plenty of advice and samples if you can't make up your mind. Your stomach may punish you after a visit to this place, but the consequences are well worth the bliss. *MP*

My Boudoir

2029 Fillmore St

346.1502

www.myboudoir.net

Boobs may be fabulous, but they are also flabbergasting. They change shape and size frequently, and are downright hard to pin down. I want a mix of comfort, practicality, and flair when I choose a bra, and the bottom line is finding a good fit. Not only do the helpful workers at Boudoir set up the ideal situation for relaxed boob talk, even for the timid, they can hook you up with bras from local designers that were made just to fit your body—at least they feel like they were. Any time I get frustrated with my chest, I find the solution here. *SB*

Samiramis Imports

2990 Mission St

824.66555

My exclusive distributor of tahini, Samiramis has a Middle Eastern spread that'll make you want the war to end even more so you can be more celebratory about this rich culture than worried. Taste the seeds and nuts that pack in snacking proteins, or try a strong feta or traditional farmers cheese, sold at the counter next to the flavored tobaccos ripe for one of the many hookahs in San Francisco. *SB*

Super Mira

1790 Sutter St

921.6529

Of all the fabulous Japanese markets around San Francisco (just stroll Japantown's streets and you are sure to find a great example), I find Super Mira to be the most consistent. It is one of the only markets to sell exclusively organic produce. Organic burdock root, lotus, and organically grown sushi rice are in high supply. Try sautéeing thinly sliced burdock root, pretty slices of lotus, chopped carrots, and enoki mushrooms for a healthy homestyle Japanese meal. *SB*

La Palma Foods

2884 24th St

647.1500

www.lapalmafoods.com

Nothing inspires me about potatoes. Sometimes I think I am the only one, but honestly, I am rarely wowed by these starchy staples. There are a few spots around this city where this generality goes out the window—Millennium (page 185), Frjtz (page 82), Chapeau (page 178)—and I add this outstanding Mexicatessen to the list for its homemade potato chips. I am suckered in no matter what mission I am on when I walk through these doors—I often come to score a stack of hot tortillas, chorizo sausage for lazy weekend omelets, or *horchata* mix for an upcoming picnic. Resist the urge to be self-controlled, grab these chips, and you'll fall in love with potatoes for good. SB

Shop with your Eyes

There are a few pockets in America where the upper crust comes to fill their homes. They want the "right" things for their menagerie, the best examples of high-style furniture, sculptures, and housewares. San Francisco is home to many well-known shops with know-it-all shopkeepers fit to treat these wealthy ones just so, but you don't need to be a famous actress to take a peek at the goods. Here are a few spots where your eyes won't go hungry:

Busacca Gallery

2010 Hyde St
776.0104
www.busaccagallery.com
This is the best place to peruse the history of fine furnishings, where museum-quality items are accessible to all those in-the-know enough to find the entrance to Busacca.

Eurasian Interiors

1861 Union St
775.1610
www.eurasianinteriors.com
Prized beauties from Eurasia are collected in this impressive showroom. The colorful glazes on pottery sculptures and the fine carvings are especially worth a look.

Camerin USA

2 Henry Adams St
621.2551
www.camerinusa.com

A place where art and function are in graceful harmony, these famous designs are the keystones of furniture as an expression, not just something to sit on.

Modern Past

677 Chenery St
333.9007
http://modernpast.com

Funky furniture, lots of great '20s- and '30s-era looks with eccentric tendencies.

Conor Fennessy Antiques and Design

801 Columbus Ave
673.0277
www.conorfennessy.com

Wallace Berman prints and a proud array of oil paintings shine on furnishings fit for a king or queen—or someone who just got a fat paycheck.

Blackman Cruz

2021 17th St
934.9228
www.blackmancruz.com

The most inspiring of all these shops is the rather exclusive Blackman Cruz, where haunting images are all-of-a-sudden desirable objects. Don't be surprised if a skull-motif sculpture or a flying bat find their way into your heart, or ogle some of the most fabulous chairs ever.

Naomi's

1817 Polk St
775.1207

More of a museum than a shop, Naomi's (as in Martha Stewart's buddy, a he, who goes by the alias Naomi Murdach) is a sight to behold. Recall decades gone by through the most beautiful vessels, pottery, china, and dinnerware, including the most colorful collection of teapots under the sun. If you want to learn anything about American pottery, here's your gold mine. Come with clear and crystallized questions to have your best results with this wise man with a dry humor. *SB*

Painted Bird

1201A Guerrero St
401.7027
www.paintedbird.org
Daily 11a–8p

The rain is an especially good excuse for a trip to Painted Bird for a dip into the rainbow of affordable vintage colors on display. Consult one of the SF local fashion gurus who work and hang out at this epicenter of discount fashion to create a unique look that combines the old with the new. Shifting selections and the opportunity to sell back what your closet is ready to expunge are an added bonus. Is this hip corner of SF just recirculating its wardrobe through the doors of Painted Bird? *SB*

Paxton Gate

824 Valencia St
824.1872
http://paxton-gate.com
Mon–Fri 12–7p, Sat–Sun 11a–7p

My favorite shop in San Francisco is a place of oddities—the natural kind, of course. Whether you find yourself ducking under the stuffed cougar in search of a unique tea blend, a fossilized tooth for an art project, or the ingredients for a succulent garden, there is no way you'll leave Paxton without creative inspiration and a newfound love of the natural world. Get out into the wilds of the Mission! *SB*

Eco Citizen

1488 Vallejo St
614.0100
www.ecocitizenonline.com

Green translates to the shop-happy citizens who hover at one of the newer additions to the city's green scene. Find stylish home decor and clothing, like fancy dresses from Larsen Gray and Linda Loudermilk (red satin, here we come!). Jackets from Juleslin and Loomstate are the things of dreams, and perfect to keep out the San Francisco breeze while you waltz around the city in your new duds. Engage my desire button! *SB*

Rag Co-Op

 541 Octavia St

 621.7718

www.ragsf.com

These are rags, not in the clean-up sense, but in the Residents Apparel Gallery sense, catch my drift? Environmentalist-cum-seamstress Blakey Bass picks and chooses from local designers and finds the cutest one-of-a-kind, handmade "rags" for this palace of local fashion. *SB*

 Carrots

 843 Montgomery St

 834.9040

www.sfcarrots.com

Sultry, fancy, finished, polished, beautiful—this is how I feel after a private shopping appointment at Carrots, where personal service is key. The hottest labels are here, so don't expect a bargain, but you get what you pay for, and you'll only walk out with things that fit perfectly and look great. I say skip the shopping routine and save up for one or two lasting outfits, many from eco-friendly designers, that'll be in style and keep their shape for years to come. These two sisters even dress men—yes, they dress men well. *SB*

 Heidi Says

 2426 Fillmore St

 749.0655

www.heidisays.com

Find a plethora of local designers at this local boutique, heavy on cool, casual clothes that'll make you wonder where your yacht is hiding. I got a sun hat from Heidi that I'll never go without when I'm in the sun! The purses here make me wish I was a purse person (instead I usually have a canvas tote in tow, unless a friend is kind enough to gift me with a nice bag, hint hint). *SB*

The Down Low on Shopping Bags in San Francisco

Yup! No plastic bags anymore! You have to pay extra if you forget your canvas tote—the mandatory accessory for any San Francisco resident and visitor. I have about one hundred of them at this point, and I've stashed them all over the place so I am never without one. Forget the plastic that takes centuries to break down, get with it and get canvas! *SB*

Ladita

827 Cortland Ave
648.4397
www.shopladita.com

Save your pennies and then come to Ladita, Cortland Avenue's greenest shop. Your house will be that much cuter, or that of your San Francisco hosts—in my opinion, there is no better place to get a cherished gift for a deserving friend. Find clothes in muted colors, accessories that aren't made in China, and plenty of other things to inspire you to grow your savings account for the occasion. *SB*

Lodge

Every place to rest your noggin

If you don't have a friend to stay with in San Francisco, there are a huge number of places where you can lay your head. Rooms in some of the finest hotels in the United States, or sweet B&B accommodations, are exciting but pricier options. For the low-budget traveler, motels, hostels, and camping opportunities will fit your needs. Pick a place to stay that is situated in an appealing area where you can dig in your heels and also walk to enticing destinations, so as to cut down on travel time and hit the streets of the city with the locals.

Bed and Breakfasts

Staying in a B&B in the middle of a major city like San Francisco is like staying in a local's home. Often owned and operated by longtime residents, these spots vary in price and amenities, but are all ideal when it comes to value and comfort. Plus, you don't have to worry about that morning meal! *SB*

Nob Hill Hotel

835 Hyde St
885.2987
www.nobhillhotel.com

The Inn San Francisco

943 S Van Ness Ave
237.0107
www.innsf.com

Artists Inn Bed and Breakfast

2231 Pine St
346.1919
www.artistsinn.com

White Swan Inn

845 Bush St
775.1755
www.jdvhotels.com/whiteswaninn

Washington Square Inn

1660 Stockton St
981.4220
www.wsisf.com

Annie's Cottage Bed and Breakfast

1225 Vallejo St
923.9990
www.anniescottage.com

Ocean Beach Bed and Breakfast

661 42nd Ave
668.0193
www.bbhost.com

Dolores Place

3842 25th St
824.8728
www.doloresplace.com

Petite Auberge

863 Bush St
928.6000
www.jdvhotels.com/petiteauberge

Edwardian II Bed and Breakfast Inn

3155 Scott St
922.3000
www.edwardii.com

Red Victorian B&B

1665 Haight St
864.1978
www.redvic.com

Noe's Nest

1257 Guerrero St
821.0751
www.noesnest.com

Top-End Hotels

The Orchard Hotel and Orchard Garden Hotel

665 Bush St; 362.8878
466 Bush St; 399.9807
www.theorchardhotel.com, www.theorchardgardenhotel.com

This luxury boutique hotel is serious about going green, meeting the highest standards in sustainable hospitality for a rather large hotel. Comfy and chic mix at this unpretentious palace, less showy than the other high-end spots and usually more affordable. Their new property, Orchard Garden Hotel, is the first LEED-certified hotel in San Francisco! *SB*

Fairmont Hotel

950 Mason St
772.5000
www.fairmonthotels.com/sanfrancisco

My favorite way to drop big bucks on a night of perfect luxury is the Fairmont. Even though it is a chain, it is the center of the universe as far as I'm concerned. There's some serious green policies in place too: hotelwide composting and grease recycling goes a long way; the soil of the many on-site plantings are enriched by the broken-down food scraps; and biodiesel fuels transit for the hotel. Retreat here and you'll have the experience of being royalty for a day. Period. *SB*

Clift Hotel

495 Geary St
775.4700
www.clifthotel.com

The Clift has recently been refurbished, and to my delight, it isn't at all over-done. Instead, each room is a white and cream dream that'll keep you put for an extra hour each morning, just floating in heavenly pleasure. It's hard to say which hotel is my favorite in the city, but certainly the Clift comes close. Try sitting in the turquoise lobby chair; it looks like a fancy prop left over from *Honey I Shrunk the Kids*. There are more affordable rooms here than many of the other high-end hotels on these pages. *SB*

Hotel Nikko

222 Mason St
394.1111
www.hotelnikkosf.com

This luxurious Union Square destination hotel is a place to seclude yourself amidst the busy city. Turn off for a moment and reminisce about the sights and sounds of your day in some of the most comfortable beds in the whole city. *SB*

More Luxury

Hotel Palomar

12 Fourth St
348.1111
www.hotelpalomar-sf.com

Palace Hotel

2 New Montgomery St
512.1111
www.starwoodhotels.com

Omni San Francisco

500 California St
677.9494
www.omnihotels.com

The Donatello

501 Post St
441.7100
www.shellhospitality.com

Hotel Metropolis

25 Mason St
775.4600
www.hotelmetropolis.com

Hotel Diva

440 Geary St
885.0260
www.hoteldiva.com

Cathedral Hill Hotel

1101 Van Ness Ave
674.4557
www.cathedralhillhotel.com

Sir Francis Drake Hotel

450 Powell St
392.7755
www.sirfrancisdrake.com

W San Francisco

181 Third St
777.5300
www.starwoodhotels.com

Handlery Union Square

351 Geary St
781.7800
www.handlery.com

Hotel Rex

562 Sutter St
433.4434
www.jdvhotels.com/hotels/rex

Airport Hotels

Inn at Oyster Point

425 Marina Blvd, South San Francisco
737.7633
www.innatoysterpoint.com

Located right next door to the calm bay waters, you can watch boats float by from your comfortable and reasonably priced bed. Transit is easy to and from the airport and the city itself. The nautical theme continues inside the rooms, populated mostly by genius geeks who come to conventions at the nearby biotech, nanotech, and regular tech conglomerates nearby. *SB*

There are few locally owned hotels near the airport, so if you are stuck down south, without the time and energy to trek on BART back into town, I would opt for the Inn at Oyster Point, which keeps its money local. Otherwise, here is information for some chains that will suit your needs if you've got an extremely early or extremely late flight.

Radisson Hotel

5000 Sierra Point Parkway at Marina Boulevard, Brisbane
467.4400
www.radisson.com

Residence Inn

13500 Veterans Blvd, South San Francisco
837.9000
www.marriott.com

Homewood Suites

2000 Shoreline Crt at Sierra Point Parkway, Brisbane
589.1600
www.hilton.com

Mid-Range Lodging

Chancellor Hotel

433 Powell St
352.2004
www.chancellorhotel.com

Built just after the 1906 earthquake, the Chancellor wishes to stay open long into the future, and to ensure that they've gone green—no chemical cleaners here! The classic simplicity here will give you the chance to rest easy, even just up the stairs from the Powell Street cable car. *SB*

Hotel des Arts

447 Bush St
800.956.4322
www.sfhoteldesarts.com

Stay inside the dreams of a local artist at this über-cool hotel. Midweek you can sometimes find rooms for $69, hard to believe when you consider this is surely the most inspiring stay to be had around town. Call directly to the hotel to book so you can pick your artist. *SB*

Hotel Triton

342 Grant Ave
394.0500
www.hoteltriton.com

Triton is the innovative and swanky hotel that has been a keystone in the hospitality industry's move to green. With reclaimed wood for floors, sophisticated recycling, nontoxic cleaning supplies, organic coffee, and recycled paper products, these stunning rooms with a view are the ultimate in ecocomfort. Stay in a celebrity suite for some extra flair, like the silk-smattered Jerry Garcia Suite or a stunning elegant room designed by Carlos Santana. *SB*

Hyatt Regency

5 Embarcadero Center
788.1234
http://sanfranciscoregnecy.hyatt.com

Yeah, I know it is a chain, but this beautiful hotel is also a San Francisco landmark. The famous lobby, a triangular interior space with a bar, restaurant, and towering chandelier and sculptures, plus a fun glass elevator, is somewhere I could hang for hours, guest or not. Hyatt hosts many local events and is always trying to move toward sustainability. In fact, the hotel hosted a Christmas light trade-in event for locals, where old sets were traded for free for eco-friendly LED lights. The impact of each of their moves in the green direction is wide-sweeping, because of the number of rooms and also the number of hotels worldwide. Chemical cleaners are on their way out, CFLs and employee healthcare are on their way in. *SB*

Renoir Hotel

45 McAllister St
626.5200
www.renoirhotel.com

Simple, affordable lodging right in the center of the action, Renoir Hotel is a historic building with motifs from days gone by, matched with a family-friendly vibe. *SB*

Miyako Hotel

1625 Post St
922.3200
www.jdvhotels.com

Joie de Vivre, San Francisco's most sought-after hotel company, has done it again. Miyako brings together the chic sophistication of Japanese style with San Francisco–style hospitality, creating a place that will please anyone with discerning taste.

Hotel Monaco

501 Geary St
292.0100
www.monaco-sf.com

One of the children of the Kimpton Group, one of the most eco-savvy hoteliers in the country, Hotel Monaco is a chain that cares. Art fills each public space, catching your eye when your face isn't buried in the fantastic flower arrangements. Set up shop in one of the deluxe suites and you'll be at home away from home, and for the same price as the high-end hotels charge for a regular queen bed.

Hotel Adagio

550 Geary St
775.5000
www.jdvhotels.com

Another Joie de Vivre masterpiece, Adagio is music to my ears. The inspiring design accents here will make you want to redecorate your own home—something about the deep charcoal and maroon colors even makes me fall asleep faster. Tasty treats from room service are worth the high price tag here—it seems JDV understands food almost as well as they understand hospitality.

Argonaut Hotel

495 Jefferson St
563.0800
www.argonauthotel.com

Kimpton-owned, I've included this chain because it is the best place to stay if you insist on residing wharf-side. For a truly San Francisco experience, it is hard to sort through the tourist traps on this famous strip, but Argonaut, complete with one of my favorite hotel restaurants, Café Pescatore (see page 151), sets itself apart from the mess of Fisherman's Wharf. Clean and basic, it is as comfortable and eco-friendly as this area of the city gets.

Grant Plaza Hotel

465 Grant Ave
434.3883
www.grantplaza.com

If your local friends bail out on you last minute, or you're not planning to dump big bucks into your accommodations, Grant Plaza will pick up the pieces and offer simple accommodations that are also comfortable.

Hayes Valley Inn

417 Gough St
431.9131
www.hayesvalleyinn.com

Hayes Valley is one of the best neighborhoods to stay in, and Hayes Valley Inn makes you feel like a local even if you've never set foot in San Francisco. Stroll around the streets directly under your nose—many of my favorite businesses are within a whisper!

Budget Hotels

Budget Choice Hotel

3201 Steiner St
866.656.8630

San Remo Hotel
2237 Mason St
776.8688
www.sanremohotel.com

Heritage Marina Hotel
2550 Van Ness Ave
776.7500
www.heritagemarinahotel.com

Taylor Hotel
615 Taylor St
775.0780
www.sanfrancisco-budgethotel.com

Marina Inn
3110 Octavia St
928.1000
www.marinainn.com

Hostels

With any of these hostels, you'll be paying the least for a roof, but you won't be getting the same kind of attention or service many European hostels offer. Try for the AYH Hostel in Fort Mason as a first choice, then peruse the others—each has an online booking system that makes it easy to find room availability. I bring my own sleeping bag and lock to keep everything safe and cozy, then head out to do more exploring (instead of indoor lazing) than I would in one of the high-end or midrange hotels. *SB*

AYH American Youth Hostel
312 Mason St
788.5604
www.hiayh.com

Elements Hotel
2516 Mission St
866.327.8407
www.elementshotel.com

Hostelling International City Center

685 Ellis St
474.5721
www.sfhostels.com

Adelaide Hostel

5 Isadora Duncan Ln
359.1915
www.adelaidehostel.com

European Guest House

761 Minna St
861.6634

USA Hostel

711 Post St
440.5600
www.usahostels.com

Pacific Tradewinds Hostel

680 Sacramento St
433.7970
www.sanfranciscohostel.org

Hostelling International Fisherman's Wharf

Fort Mason, Bay Street
771.7277
www.hiayh.org

Globe Trotters Inn

225 Ellis St
346.5786
www.globetrottersinn.com

555 Haight Guest House

555 Haight St
551.2555
www.555haight.net

Camping

There's not much in the way of camping in the San Francisco metropolis, but just outside the city there are a number of spots. Just be prepared to trek over hill and dale to get into the urban action. I like the idea of camping and taking a bike into the city—the dual nature of such a trip is inspiring.

Angel Island State Park

Ferries from San Francisco Ferry Building and Tiburon
www.angelisland.org/campsites.htm
(Mt. Livermore High Camp is the best)

Candlestick RV Park

650 Gilman Ave, across from Candlestick Park
822.2299
www.sanfranciscorvpark.com

Point Reyes National Seashore

Drakes Bay
www.nps.gov/pore/

Various camping spots in one of the most beautiful open spaces in the country, albeit far out there and inconvenient for most San Francisco travelers.

Chabot Family Campground

9999 Redwood Rd, Castro Valley
888.327.2757

This is the best place to camp in the East Bay, with quick access to all that Oakland has to offer, and also San Francisco. You can camp under oaks, fragrant eucalyptus, and redwoods.

Calendar

Really Really Free Market in Dolores Park

Last Saturday of every month
www.reallyreallyfree.org

Feria Urbana

Bimonthly fair, dates and locations vary,
see web site for details
www.feriaurbanasf.com

Illegal Soapbox Derby

Third Sunday of every month through
October
1–5p at Bernal Heights Park

Ballet Season

January to May
War Memorial Opera House, 301 Van
Ness Ave
865.2000
www.sfballet.org

January

Dine About Town

Usually January, sometimes extended into
February
Various locations
www.onlyinsanfrancisco.com/
dineabouttown

Golden Gate Kennel Club Dog Show

Last weekend in January
Cow Palace, 2600 Geneva Ave, Daly City
www.cowpalace.com

February

San Francisco Pillow Fight

Valentine's Day, 6p
Justin Herman Plaza, Embarcadero at
Market St

San Francisco Crab Festival

Throughout February
Fisherman's Wharf
www.sfvisitor.org/crab

March

ArtsFest

Events throughout the month of March
Various locations
www.artsfest.org

Pi Day

March 14 1–3p
Exploratorium, 3601 Lyon St
561.0399
www.exploratorium.edu/pi

San Francisco Flower Show

Second weekend in March
Cow Palace
www.gardenshow.com/sf

O'Reilly's Annual Beer and Oyster Festival

Spring, date varies
Fort Mason
www.oreillysoysterfestival.com

St. Patrick's Day

Second weekend in March
Between Embarcadero and Powell Street
on Market Street, and at most bars in
the city

The Bring Your Own Big Wheel Race

Easter Sunday, 4p
New location, check web site
www.jonbrumit.com/byobw.html

Asian American Film Festival

End of March, lasts 10 days
Various locations in SF and Berkeley
www.asianamericanfilmfestival.org

April

Cherry Blossom Festival

Two weekends in April
1759 Sutter St
563.2313
www.nccbf.org

Earth Day Clean-up Ocean Beach

Late in April
Ocean Beach at The Great Highway and
Fulton Street
www.oceanbeachfoundation.org

San Francisco International Film Festival

Late April to early May
Various locations
www.sffs.org

May

Dog Day on the Bay

First Sunday in May
Contact Hornblower Cruises for
reservations
www.hornblower.com

Cinco de Mayo

May 5
Dolores Park
www.sfcincodemayo.com

KFog Kaboom

Mid-May
Piers 30 and 32, off of Embarcadero
www.kfog.com/kaboom

Bay to Breakers

Third Sunday in May
www.baytobreakers.com

Carnaval

Last weekend in May
www.carnavalsf.com

Return of the Salmon Fest

Weekend late in May
Ferry Building
www.spawnusa.org

June

Another Hole in the Head Film Festival

First week in June
Roxie Theater
www.holehead.org

Union Street Festival

First Weekend in June
Union Street beginning
www.unionstreetfestival.com

Haight-Ashbury Street Fair

Second Sunday in June
www.haightashburystreetfair.org

Stern Grove

Mid-June through mid-August
Sundays, 2p
19th Avenue at Sloat Boulevard
www.sterngrove.org

San Francisco International LGBT Film Festival

Mid-June, lasts 10 days
Various locations
www.frameline.org

North Beach Festival

Third weekend in June
www.northbeachfestival.com
Centered at Columbus Avenue and Grant Street

Dyke, Trans, and Gay Pride Weekend

Last weekend in June
www.transgenderpride.org, www.
thedykemarch.org, www.sfpride.org

San Francisco Black Film Festival

June
Various locations
www.sfbff.org

Alice Summerthing

Sunday in June, week varies
Location varies

July

4th of July Waterfront Festival

4th of July
Pier 39, Fisherman's Wharf
705.5500
www.pier39.com

SF Labor Festival

Several weeks in July
Various locations and events
www.laborfest.net

Cable Car Bell Ringing Competition

Second Saturday in July, 12–1p
Union Square Plaza, Powell and Sutter streets
673.6864
www.sfmuni.com

Silent Film Festival

Second week in July
Castro Theater, Castro and Market streets
777.4908
www.silentfilm.org

Bastille Day

July 14
Belden Place off Bush St between Montgomery and Kearny streets

Midsummer Mozart Festival

Third week in July
Palace of Fine Arts and other locations
627.9141
www.midsummermozart.org

San Francisco Jewish Film Festival

July through August
Various locations
621.0556
www.sfjff.org

San Francisco Theater Festival

July 22
Yerba Buena Gardens, Center for the Arts and Zeum Theater, SoMa, 11a–5p
543.1718
www.sftheaterfestival.org

San Francisco Marathon

Late July or early August
Starting line on the Embarcadero at Mission Street
www.runsfm.com

North Beach Jazz Festival

Last week in July
Various North Beach locations
971.7577
www.nbjazzfest.com

August

Jerry Day

Early August
Jerry Garcia Amphitheater, 45 John F. Shelley Drive

San Francisco Playwrights Festival

August
Various locations
Main office: Playwrights Foundation, 131 10th St, third floor
626.0453
www.playwrightsfoundation.org

Afrosolo Summer Season

August through September
Various locations
771.2376
www.afrosolo.org

Aloha Festival

First weekend in August
Presidio
www.pica-org.org/AlohaFest

Positively 6th Street Fair

First Saturday in August
Sixth Street at Minna Alley
538.8100 ext 202
www.6thstreetfair.org

Nihonmachi Street Fair

Second weekend in August
Powell and Geary streets, Japantown
www.nihonmachistreetfair.org

ACC Craft Show

Second weekend in August
Fort Mason Center, Presidio
800.836.3470
www.craftcouncil.org

San Francisco Fashion Week

Last week in August
Various locations
www.fashionweek-sf.com

September

Opera Season

September through June
Orpheum Theater, 301 Van Ness Ave
864.3330
www.sfopera.org

Bernal Heights Outdoor Cinema

September
Various locations in Bernal Heights
neighborhood
www.bhoutdoorcine.org

Jewish Music Festival

September
Various locations
www.jewishmusicfestival.org

Viva Las Americanas

Mid-September
Pier 39, Fisherman's Wharf
705.5500
www.pier39.com

Up Your Alley Fair

Second weekend in September
Dore Alley between Folsom and Howard
streets
861.3247
www.folsomsstreetfair.com

Ghirardelli Square Chocolate Festival

Second weekend in September, 12–5p
Ghirardelli Square, 900 North Point St
www.ghirardellisq.com

Opera in the Park

Second weekend in September
Sharon Meadow, Golden Gate Park
864.3330
www.sfopera.com

San Francisco Fringe Festival

Various locations
673.3847
www.sffringe.org

Treasure Island Music Festival

Second week in September
Treasure Island Base
http://treasureislandfestival.com

San Francisco Gem and Mineral Show

Late September
San Francisco County Fair Building,
Ninth Avenue and Lincoln Way
564.4230
www.sfgems.org

Greek Food Festival

End of September
Annunciation Greek Orthodox Cathedral,
245 Valencia St
www.sfgreekfoodfestival.org

Folsom Street Fair

Last Sunday in September
Folsom Street corridor
www.folsomstreetfair.com

Autumn Moon Festival

Last weekend in September
Grant Avenue between California and
Broadway streets
www.moonfestival.org

San Francisco Blues Festival

Late September
Great Meadow, Fort Mason
979.5588
www.sfblues.com

West Coast Green

September
Bill Graham Theater, Opera Plaza
www.westcoastgreen.com

San Francisco International Dragon Boat Festival

Last weekend in September
Treasure Island
www.sfdragonboat.com

San Bruno Avenue Community Festival

Last weekend in September
San Bruno Avenue at Bacon Street
800.310.6563
www.sresproductions.com

Comedy Day

Last Sunday in September
Sharon Meadow, Golden Gate Park
820.1570
www.comedyday.com

San Francisco Shakespeare Festival

Early fall
Main Post Parade Ground Lawn in the
Presidio
www.sfshakes.org

October

Art Span's Open Studios

October through November
Various locations, weekends only
www.artspan.org

International Jazz Festival

October
Various locations
www.sfjazz.org

Fleet Week

Early October
http://fleetweek.us/fleetweek
Best view: Aquatic Park off Bay Street

Hardly Strictly Bluegrass Festival

First weekend in October
John F. Kennedy Boulevard in Golden
Gate Park
www.strictlybluegrass.com

Castro Street Fair

First Sunday in October
Castro Street corridor
www.castrostreetfair.org

LitQuake

Second week in October
www.litquake.org

Oktoberfest by the Bay

Second weekend in October
Festival Pavilion, Fort Mason Center
352.2678
www.oktoberfestbythebay.com

National Theatre Day

October 18
Various locations
430.1140
www.theatrebayarea.org

Fiesta on the Hill

Third Sunday in October
Cortland Avenue, Bernal Heights
www.fiestaonthehill.com

Exotic Erotic Ball

Last weekend in October
Cow Palace
404.4111
www.exoticeroticball.com

Pet Pride Day

Last Sunday in October 11a–3p
Sharon Meadow, Golden Gate Park

Halloween on Belvedere Street

Last weekend in October
Cole Street from Parnassus to 17th Street

Pumpkin Pandemonium

End of October
Pier 39, Fisherman's Wharf
705.5500
www.pier39.com

Bioneers

October
Marin Conference Center, off San Pedro Road, San Rafael
www.bioneers.org

The Heart of Cole Festival

October
Cole Street above Haight Street
heartofcolefestival@yahoo.com

November

FilmArts Festival of Independent Cinema

First week in November
Various independent movie houses
www.filmarts.org

San Francisco Green Festival

Mid-November
Concourse Exhibition Center, Brannan Street
www.greenfestivals.org

Run Wild

Thanksgiving
Golden Gate Park
759.2690
www.rhodyco.com

Holiday Ice Rink at Embarcadero Center

Early November through mid-January
Justin Herman Plaza, at the base of
Market Street
www.embarcaderocenter.com/ec/
Holidays/index.html

San Francisco Fall Antiques Show

November
Fort Mason Center
989.9019
www.ehss.org

Native American Film Festival

First weekend in November
Palace of Fine Arts
554.0525
www.aifisf.com

Hip Hop Dance Fest

Second week in November
Palace of Fine Arts
392.4400
www.sfhiphopdancefest.com

Animation Film Festival

Second week in November
Various locations
www.sffs.org

Latino Film Festival

November
Various locations
454.4039
www.latinofilmfestival.org

San Francisco International Auto Show

Last week in November
Moscone Center, SoMa
331.4406
www.sfautoshow.com

Celebration of Craftswomen

Last weekend of November and first
weekend of December
Herbst Pavilion, Fort Mason Center,
Presidio
431.1180
www.celebrationofcraftswomen.org

December

Parol Lantern Festival

Second weekend in December
Bayanihan Community Center, 1010
Mission St
348.8042
www.bayanihancc.org

New Year's Eve Festivities

December 31
Embarcadero Waterfront

Index

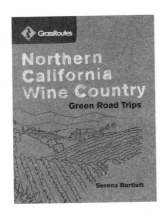